India-U.S. Relations and Asian Rebalancing

India-U.S. Relations and Asian Rebalancing

Edited by

Josukutty C.A.

Assistant Professor,
Department of Political Science,
University of Kerala, Thiruvananthapuram

New Century Publications
New Delhi, India

NEW CENTURY PUBLICATIONS
4800/24, Bharat Ram Road,
Ansari Road, Daryaganj,
New Delhi - 110 002 (India)

Tel.: 011-2324 7798, 4358 7398, 6539 6605
Fax: 011-4101 7798
E-mail: indiatax@vsnl.com • info@newcenturypublications.com
www.newcenturypublications.com

Editorial office:
LG–7, Aakarshan Bhawan,
4754-57/23, Ansari Road, Daryaganj,
New Delhi – 110 002

Tel.: 011-4356 0919

First Published: **July 2015**

ISBN: **978-81-7708-415-3**

Published by New Century Publications and printed at Salasar Imaging Systems, New Delhi.

Designs: Patch Creative Unit, New Delhi.

PRINTED IN INDIA

About the Book

The recent emergence of Asia as a formidable military and economic power constitutes the most significant development in the post-Cold War international politics. It incubates a new world order with apparent signals for a radical shift in international power equations. These developments in the Asia-Pacific and the growing camaraderie between India and the US have caught the attention of scholars across the world.

The aims and interests of the US, China, India and other regional/middle-level players, coupled with the strategic significance of South China Sea and East China Sea, makes the region a volatile one. The rise of China and its ambition to establish its hegemony in Asia directly challenges the primacy of the US. What role India will play in this ensuing power struggle is of strategic importance and interest. The so-called strategic convergence between India and US is the result of unprecedented rise of China and the schemes of the US to contain it.

This compendium contains 13 scholarly articles which survey various aspects of the emerging scenario in the Asia-Pacific. In the process, scholars draw valuable insights on the future trajectory of the bilateral and multilateral relations in Asia. This book includes contributions made by leading scholars who examine and analyse the meaning, dimensions and strategic significance of Asian rebalancing and its impact on India-US relations.

About the Editor

Dr. Josukutty C.A. is presently Assistant Professor, Department of Political Science, University of Kerala, Thiruvananthapuram. He obtained his M.A. and Ph.D. degrees from the University of Kerala. He has published 1 book and 20 articles in national and international journals of repute. He was Fellow of Salzburg Global Seminar (2007) and a Visiting Fellow at the United States Institute on Foreign Policy, University of Florida, US in 2010.

Dr. Josukutty was awarded a Major Research Project by the University Grants Commission (UGC), New Delhi in 2010. He also serves as Honorary Director, Survey Research Centre, University of Kerala and is currently General Secretary of the Association of Political Scientists, Kerala. His areas of teaching and research interest include India's foreign policy, human rights and cyber politics.

Contents

Contributors

Srikanth Kondapalli   Professor, Centre for East Asian Studies, Jawaharlal Nehru University (JNU), New Delhi.

Chintamani Mahapatra   Professor, School of International Studies, Jawaharlal Nehru University (JNU), New Delhi.

Monish Tourangbam   Assistant Professor, Department of Geopolitics and International Relations, University of Manipal, Manipal.

Anand V.   Research Scholar, Department of Geopolitics and International Relations, University of Manipal, Manipal.

Venkat Lokanathan   Assistant Professor, Department of Political Science, St. Joseph's College, Bangalore.

S.Y. Surendra Kumar   Assistant Professor, University of Bangalore, Bangalore.

Nanda Kishor   Assistant Professor, Department of Geopolitics and International Relations, Manipal University, Manipal.

B. Mohanan Pillai   Professor, Department of Politics and International Studies, Pondicherry University, Puducherry.

Shaijumon C.S.   Associate Professor, Indian Institute of Space Science and Technology, Thiruvanathapuram.

Anil Kumar P.   Assistant Professor, Department of Political Science, University College, Thiruvanathapuram.

Ninan Koshy   Political Commentator based in Trivandrum, Kerala, India, and formerly Visiting Fellow, Harvard Law School, Massachusetts.

Anu Unny   Assistant Professor, Department of Political Science, University of Kerala, Thiruvanathapuram.

Sandhaya S. Nair   Assistant Professor, Government Women's College, Thiruvanathapuram.

Sanjal Shastri   The London School of Economics and Political Science, London.

Introduction

By **Josukutty C.A.**

International relations and foreign policies tread on unknown and unpredictable tracks driven by the course of global developments and the vagaries of states' behavior. The emergence of Asia, spearheaded by the rise of China and India, is one such event with the potential to redraw the contours of international relations. The shift of global economic activity to Asia is only a prelude to the political and cultural shift on the anvil, the signals of which are visible across the world. Alignments and realignments are part and parcel of it. The entire scheme of Asian rebalancing is a natural and inevitable response of the existing superpower to the possible advent of a new occupant to that seat. Indo-US relations and the strategic significance attached to it has to be viewed and analyzed in the context of the ongoing geopolitical developments in the Asia-Pacific.

Asia is considered as the most important strategic site of the emerging world order. This region has been the cynosure of attention for several reasons: the confluence of the Pacific and the Indian Ocean with a number of significant littoral and hinterland countries, the regional and extra-regional interests of major powers like China, India, Australia, Japan and Korea; growing economic and technological hubs in the region; the strategic and political alignments and counter-forces and the diverse democratic experimentations taking place in the region. The game of power between the reigning superpower—the US and the emerging super power—China, has created new uncertainties in the region. Realizing the significance of the region, the US has been focusing its attention on Asia and India-Pacific, through what is variously described, as 'Asia Pivot' or 'Asian Rebalancing'. The US is remodeling its traditional 'hub and spoke' alliance system to the exigencies of the Asia-Pacific century. Many analysts interpret it as an attempt to contain China and consolidate US hegemony in the region. China is using its growing economic and political might to create its own spheres of influence in the Asia-Pacific. Other major and minor powers and regional organizations are increasingly becoming factors in the emerging contours of Asian rebalancing.

India is considered as an important geostrategic ally of the US in its Asian rebalancing and the increasing use of the term 'Indo-Pacific' symbolizes it. It is argued that there is a growing convergence of Indo-US interests as they are the stakeholders in the creation of an inclusive, participatory network of interdependence, cooperative trade, democracy promotion, economic development, security, peace and stability in Asia. This new found relationship is manifested in the growing bilateral and multilateral collaborations between India and the US. Bilateral treaties and agreements are being concluded in every conceivable sphere that ranges from defense to agriculture. At multilateral levels, the cooperation spans over democracy promotion to disaster management. Common positions on nuclear and strategic issues accord an extra mileage to the relationship. There has been a greater understanding between the two countries on economic, cultural and social spheres. The growing importance of the Indian Diaspora in the US provides an additional leverage for India. Many in India consider the current geopolitical scenario in Asia as a great opportunity for India to realize its ambition to become a world power. The growing US presence in the region has its share of opposition as well. The current politico-strategic alliance that India attempts to forge with the US has been critiqued as a compromise on its sovereignty and strategic autonomy.

The book is a collection of 13 scholarly articles that discuss and analyze various aspects and dimensions of Asian rebalancing and its impact on Indo-US relations. A few of the articles though do not fall directly within the general theme of the title, but are important additions to understand the contours of Asian rebalancing and the factors that are at play in Indo-US relations.

The basic reasons and issues of the conflictual relationship between China and the United States in South China Sea and East China that span over trade, investments, security and strategy are discussed by Srikanth Kondapalli in his paper, *China and U.S. in Asia-Pacific Rebalancing*. In the due course of the essay, he identifies and analyzes the nuanced diplomatic, strategic and military measures initiated by China to counter and reshape Asia-Pacific to its advantage including the forward momentum in its bilateral relationship with the US and looks into the possibility of the rivalry assuming global dimensions in the years to come. He concludes by saying that the US efforts to consolidate its hegemony and the Chinese revisionism portents more flux in the strategic environment in the region.

Chintamani Mahapatra and Monish Tourangbam examine the India component in the US strategy in their paper, *India-U.S. Rebalancing Strategy in Asia-Pacific*. The paper argues that one of the major goals of the US's Asia rebalancing strategy is to strengthen the country's relationship with new strategic partners and this is where emerging security cooperation between India and the United States becomes a relevant area of scrutiny. The paper also attempts to critically assess and analyze the rationale for the US rebalancing strategy, the emerging notions of this strategy and US motivations in assigning a role to India in its rebalancing strategy. In addition, the paper seeks to examine India's self-perceptions of its role in Asia-Pacific and its response to America's branding of India as 'a linchpin' of its rebalancing strategy and its implications for Indian national interests. The paper concludes by saying that a greater convergence between India and the US can only come from a more honest understanding and acceptance of differences, rather than harbouring of utopian ideas of commonalities.

Anand V. in his paper, *China's Responses to U.S. Rebalancing Strategy in Asia-Pacific*, argues that the past few decades have been witness to a strategic resurgence of the Asia-Pacific region, powered especially by the rise of China, acting both as a growth engine and a security concern for the regional countries. The US had retreated from the Asia-Pacific region in the 1970s and is now attempting a return to manage the geopolitical scenario through its rebalancing strategy that aims at containing China. This has given China an added impetus to intensify its historically rooted efforts to gain and sustain its foothold in the region. He examines at length China's response to Asian rebalancing that spans over a variety of measures from diplomatic persuasions to militarily offensive postures and probes China's strategic interests involved in the context. By linking China's strategic thinking to its behavioural tendencies in the region, the author draws the context for rationalizing China's moves to counter the rebalancing strategy of the US.

The article by Venkat Lokanathan, *U.S. Rebalance in Asia,* makes an attempt to critically analyze the US rebalance in Asia in the 21st century. Is the American pronouncements on Asian rebalancing symbolic or is it one of real intent? While answering this question, the chapter also traces the historical evolution of US geostrategic interests in the region. In the process, it is evidently substantiated that there is nothing new about Asian rebalancing as the US has always been a major player in the Asia-Pacific and friends and allies in Asia were seen as critical to the success of America's global strategy. While identifying key reasons for the growing American interests in the region, it attempts to debunk the notion that there is only one fundamental factor—that of containing China. Finally, the author briefly identifies four possibilities of the American rebalance for India and how New Delhi should respond.

S.Y. Surendra Kumar in his paper, *India-U.S. Strategic Convergence in South China Sea (SCS),* discusses the geostrategic importance of South China Sea (SCS) in the international arena and argues that the Indo-US relations can be further strengthened through maritime cooperation in SCS, as both the countries are important stakeholders in the region and their interest in the region are based on strategic, economic and maritime interests. The paper also examines the shared concerns of both the countries in SCS , such as China's assertive claim, countered by ASEAN countries; and limitation of regional groupings in resolving the dispute in SCS. Finally, the paper suggests feasible measures for the both the countries to achieve their strategic interest in SCS.

Nanda Kishor in his article, *U.S. and South Asia*, makes a departure from the dominant view of South Asia revolving around India towards US rebalancing strategy and attempts to take more opulent view from the other remaining nations in the region. The myth of associating anything in South Asia to India is the point of departure. The relevance of Indo-Pacific is extremely important at this juncture and South Asia has a vital role to play. The rebalancing has many push and pull factors that might not allow the US to realize its strategy without the help of South Asian countries. The attempt here is to make a reality check for the United States where it stands and what has been its presence in the region. The research throws up lot of stereotypes United States needs to move beyond and fix for its own betterment.

B. Mohanan Pillai's article, *U.S. Rebalancing Strategy in the Indo-Pacific Region*, is distinct, as it looks at Asian rebalancing in the political economy perspective. He argues that India's response to the US gestures is a result of general and calculated agreement on the political economy of the neo-liberal spectrum. The very basic ideological and moral precepts of India's foreign policy are compromised to accommodate larger interests of global capital. The convergence of Indo-US strategic interests is a reflection of this tacit understanding.

In the paper, *Indo-U.S. Economic Relations after Global Financial Crisis,* Shaijumon C.S. argues that the financial crisis experienced by the international system had serious geopolitical and economic implications. It has brought in new players like India and China, and it has exposed the domestic economic policy compulsions of the United States. However, the extent to which the challenges engendered by the crisis can be converted into opportunities by a country like India remains to be seen. The abundant global liquidity and financial integration that preceded the crisis has made many countries like India more vulnerable to financial contagion even where the core problems are home-grown. This study analyzes the trade and investment relations of India and US in the backdrop of global financial crisis.

Anil Kumar P. in his article, *Indo-Japanese Strategic Relationship,* analyses the role that middle powers are likely to play in the ensuing rivalry between China and the US in Asia-Pacific. After attempting a conceptual enquiry of middle level powers, he surveys the middle powers in Asia and looks at their responses to China and the US in the context of Asian rebalancing and finally focuses on Indo-Japanese strategic relationship. He concludes the chapters by stating that as the most important middle-level powers of the region, India and Japan have considerable leverage in shaping the geopolitics of the region by playing soft balancing with China and the US.

Ninan Koshy in his paper, *Indo-U.S. Defence Co-operation,* looks at Indo-US defence cooperation critically and argues that the Defense Framework Agreement is a plan to expand defence trade and rope in India as a junior partner of the US military schemes not only in the Asia-Pacific but also US-led military operations outside the purview of the authorization or permission of the United Nations. According to him, India-US strategic relationship is essentially a military relationship on American terms and primarily in American interests.

In the paper, *Politics of Climate Change,* Anu Unny assesses that inequality existing in the global climate change regime has brought the negotiations between the North and South to a standstill. Issues related to the sharing of emission reduction burden, question of per capita emission right, US non-ratification of the Kyoto Protocol, unilateral decision-making at the negotiation tables etc. have contributed to the prevailing policy paralysis. Inflexible stand of US and India which claim to represent the interests of North and South respectively on this issue area, is central to the stalemate in recent climate change negotiations. For breaking this deadlock, it is imperative that at first the US admits its 'historical responsibility' for the problem and commit itself to a binding emission reduction target before asking the developing countries including India to do so.

Sandhya S. Nair in her paper, *Indian Diaspora and Indo-U.S. Relations,* analyses the role of Indian Diaspora in Indo-US relations. Indians constitute one of the most successful immigrant communities in the United States. In terms of economic clout, political and bureaucratic representation and educational achievements, they constitute a critical mass. In addition to generating interest in South Asia and removing many anti-immigration laws, the community has played a vital role in creating a pro-India congressional lobby, in materializing the Indo-US Civilian Nuclear Deal, in bringing to light the duplicity of Pakistan in fighting terrorism and of course in generating the tremendous amount of goodwill that exists between the two countries.

Sanjal Shastri in the paper, *Some Realities of the 21st Century,* points out that the US's Asia rebalancing strategy comes at a time when South Asian states are experiencing rapid political changes as Pakistan, Nepal, Afghanistan, Bhutan, Bangladesh, Maldives and Sri Lanka are in very delicate phases. Though the ultimate responsibility for the democratic transition lies in the hands of the respective nations, India and the US could play the role of facilitators. This paper looks into the possibilities for India-US dialogue over the political changes in South Asia and the role they could play in aiding the process of political change.

I take this opportunity to place on record my deep sense of gratitude and appreciation to all the contributors for their scholarly papers and suggestions to this compendium. I am greatly obliged to the University of Kerala and Kerala State Higher Education Council for their financial and organizational support. I must also thank my colleagues, friends and students for their wholehearted cooperation and support. My thanks are also due to New Century Publications, New Delhi, for taking up the publication of this book.

Thiruvananthapuram   **Josukutty C.A.**

1

China and U.S. in Asia-Pacific Rebalancing

Srikanth Kondapalli

The United States under the Obama Administration introduced the concept of "rebalancing" in the Asia-Pacific region. [1] Previously termed as "pivot", the rebalancing strategy envisages reinforcing the US predominant position in the Asia-Pacific and reflects the reassessment in the post-Soviet global situation in which China rise, non-traditional security issues, etc. have become concerns. The rebalance is aimed at rationalizing US force structures in the trans-Atlantic and the Asia-Pacific to about 40:60 in favour of the Asia-Pacific, in addition to building ballistic missile defence (BMD) shield; "strengthening alliances" with Australia, Japan and South Korea, "deepening partnerships with emerging powers" like Singapore, Indonesia, Thailand, Vietnam and India; "building stable, productive and constructive relationship with China"; "empowering regional institutions" like the East Asian Summit; and "helping to build a regional economic architecture" in the form of Trans-Pacific Partnership (TPP) and others.

After the former US Secretary of State Clinton stated in July 2009 that the US is back in Asia (chongfan yadai), [2] a number of initiatives were undertaken by the US. As mentioned by Tom Donilon, the US National Security Advisor in March 2013, the rebalance include protection and sustaining of the order that the US had brought forth at the end of the World War II; thus, "The US government desires a stable security environment and a regional order rooted in economic openness, peaceful resolution of disputes, and respect for universal rights and freedoms". [3] In the light of the challenges to the liberal order—specifically to the global commons, viz. maritime, space and cyber—in the recent .

period and to the uncertainties of the rise of China and its responses to this order, the rebalance, TPP and BMD are supposed to reinforce the US-led order.

Hence, the rebalance includes mainly diplomatic, political, economic and military dimensions. It envisages half of US naval ships in Asia-Pacific; with the Pentagon's "afloat forward staging base" in the Pacific becoming a reality in future; 2,500 Marines at Darwin in April 2012 and possibly at Cocos Islands; BMD interceptors in Asia-Pacific; South China Sea—196th Infantry Brigade at Luzon, Philippines and the possibility of stationing troops at Subic Bay, in addition to surveillance planes; Singapore —plan to station combat ships at the naval facility; and the multinational exercise Rim of the Pacific (RIMPAC)—with 22 countries and 22,000 participants shaping the norms.

Although the US had "welcomed the rise of China" through "Most Favoured Nation" status, helping China to enter the World Trade Organization (WTO) and other measures that resulted in mutually beneficial trade and investment relations, China's efforts at global power transition and questioning the US leadership in the UNSC, UN, global commons, IMF/World Bank, at the regional level in Asia, etc.—is unnerving the latter. [4] China's conventional and nuclear build up, defence budget and challenges to the regional order and to the US allies in the region is another factor in this tussle with the US. [5] This was the context for President Obama's eight day trip to Asia in April 2014— postponed from October 2013. [6]

Triggers for the Rebalance

While the US rebalance policy is to re-assert US supremacy and expand further its interests in the Asia-Pacific region, two main areas/issues have become the triggers for the US renewed interest. These include South China Sea and the East China Sea— major areas for US trade, investments, security and strategy. Both these areas are crucial for the leadership position of the US since, in the recent period, a number of events have indicated to changes in the regional economic and security dynamics of the region—

often with a view that the US influence in these regions may be waning. China had been asserting itself, given its recent stature as the second largest economy in the world, displacing that of Japan in that position since 2010. Most of its exports and imports are currently passing through the East and South China Seas.

As a result of this new factor, the Chinese naval forces have initiated measures to protect the sea lanes of communications. There are also the factors related to sovereignty disputes, prospects for energy resources and domestically rising nationalisms in these regions. Japan had also indicated that its interests need to be protected and furthered. Likewise, South Korea, Vietnam and the Philippines have renewed their efforts to protect their interests in the region. These are some of the triggers for the US rebalance postures. While the rebalance is for the whole of the Asia-Pacific, the immediate triggers are related to the South and East China Seas.

South China Sea

The South China Sea region (SCS) had become vital for Asia-Pacific transit trade in goods and energy flows, national security (given the multiple claimants), resources availability (fisheries and energy), regional ambitions and international powers role. SCS, firstly, has in the recent period emerged as the third largest maritime global trade area, serving the US, China, Japan, South Korea and the Southeast Asian economies. SCS is composed of three areas, viz., Spratlys, Paracels and Zhongsha. The total area of the Spratlys is about 800,000 sq. km., covering about 200 islands, a majority of which are mostly submerged. Vital energy supplies pass through this area, originating from Africa and West Asia and transiting through the Straits of Malacca's and constitutes more than half of global energy flows. More than half of China's sea lanes (21 out of 39) pass through this region and account for an estimated 60 percent of China's trade.

An estimated US$ 6 trillion worth of global goods pass through this region. More than US$ 1 trillion of United States trade passes through this region and makes the US a key player.

More than half of Indian trade transits through the region and hence it insists on freedom of navigation. SCS is also rich in resources. It has abundant fisheries—with an estimated ten percent of global catch of sea food and providing nearly a quarter of protein for the 600 million people in the littorals. The Spratlys alone has an estimated collection of 7.5 tonnes of fish per sq. km. per annum. Since the 1990s, energy resources were also found, with US EIA estimating a potential output of 11 billion barrels of oil, while the China National Offshore Oil Company estimating in 2012 at more than 12 billion barrels of oil. However, this trade is challenged by either unilateral claims to the whole territory or by non-traditional security challenges. According to the International Maritime Organization estimates, between 1995 and 2004, the total number of piracy and armed robbery incidents in South China Sea accounted for 2,027 as against 497 in Malacca Straits and 939 in the Indian Ocean.

Secondly, SCS represents an acute security situation in the Asia-Pacific region due to clashing sovereignty claims. With a number of naval, maritime and fishing incidents increasing, affecting multiple actors, the SCS is poised to become an intractable and long-term conflict ridden region in the Asia-Pacific. China, along with Taiwan and Southeast Asian countries like Vietnam, Malaysia, Brunei and the Philippines, claim, wholly or in part, sovereignty over the SCS Islands. From the 1970s, China had shown interest in these islands (by occupying Xisha islands in 1974 and Mischief Reef in 1988) and by the 1990s, as potential energy resources were traced, China had advocated sovereignty over these islands with its "nine-dotted lines" based on historical rather than legal claims in the last few years. [7] China follows the median line principle in SCS while it argues for natural extension of continental shelf in the Yellow Sea.

China had been flexing its muscles in the region as reflected also in the March 2009 USS Impeccable and the December 2013 USS Cowpens incidents in which the Chinese naval vessels [8] trailed these vessels for its criticism of the US Secretary of State Clinton's July 2010 statement at Hanoi on support to "collaborative diplomatic process by all claimants". [9] China was also critical of the US President Obama and ASEAN members' joint declaration in September 2010 on "the importance of peaceful resolution of disputes, freedom of navigation, regional stability, and respect for international law, including in the South China Sea". China has termed these actions of the US as "internationalisation".

With China extending its "core interests" from Taiwan and Tibet to also include the disputed South China Sea and the United States clarifying at the meetings at Hanoi, Phnom Penh and Bali that free navigation in this area is a part of its national interests, last few years have witnessed acute diplomatic and military activity in the region. Further, when the US asked China to clarify the Chinese imposed nine-dashed line in the SCS in February 2014, Beijing was enraged.

In addition, China had expressed concerns on the US extending its military activities in the SCS region. These include in June 2010, the US-Japan joint naval exercises which were held in SCS code-named "Pacific Partnership 2010" with humanitarian aid as the focus. Later, in August 2010, the US conducted the first joint maritime exercise with Vietnam with the participation of USS George Washington and John McCain destroyer for a week in the SCS. After the April 2012 Scarborough Shoal Incident with Philippines, when the Chinese vessels were deployed to the region, the US decided to conduct joint exercises with the Filipino naval forces. In addition, the US surveillance and reconnaissance missions have been upgraded in the SCS.

China also made efforts to counter these moves and indicated to the contest with the US influence in the region. [10] Thus, in addition to imposing what is termed as anti-access and area denial strategy of not allowing other naval/air forces in the region, China had expanded its naval modernisation programme and begun large-scale naval exercises in the SCS, with some going beyond the region—such as the December 2012 naval exercise beyond Lombok Straits. This was to send a political message not only to the US but also to India, Australia and Japan, who in September

2007 conducted joint maritime exercises in the Bay of Bengal. China also installed radar in the Lombok Straits to counter the US radar in the Malaccas.

East China Sea

The East China Sea dispute between China and Japan is another hot spot with long-term consequences for regional security. It is related to sovereignty claims over the Senkaku Islands held by Japan but contested by China and Taiwan over energy resources, sea lanes of communications and rising and clashing nationalisms. On this issue, China appears to be testing the alliance between US and Japan.

The Senkaku islands are uninhabited [wuzhudi] islands located about 150 km. northeast of Taiwan and are claimed by China, Japan and Taiwan. [11] Known for their potential oil reserves according to the 1966 UN Committee report, and valuable for its rich fisheries and economic zone, these islands could be a flash point between China and Japan, as the late 2004 Japanese reports indicated. The dispute arose as a result of Japanese occupation of these islands from late nineteenth century and the subsequent events of withdrawal in the mid-1940s. China's claims on these islands—like that on the SCS—are based on historical reasons that that these islands came under its jurisdiction during the Ming Dynasty period in 1373 A.D. [12]

In February 1992, China passed the "Laws of Territorial Waters and Contiguous Zone" which incorporated Diaoyutai Islands along with Paracels and Spratly's Islands that were disputed territories with neighbouring countries for a long time. Article 8 of this law stated that China's navy "can order the eviction of foreign naval vessels" operating in these waters. On November 16, 1994, the United Nations Convention on the Law of Sea came into being. PRC ratified this convention in 1996. According to this law, the jurisdiction of the PRC over several million square kilometres of sea has been extended. [13] Japanese ratification of the International Convention on the Law of the Sea in 1996, its 1,000 nautical mile limit jurisdiction and so on, further complicated claims on the overlapping EEZs of the three in this region.

In September 2010, tensions between China and Japan came to the fore when the crew members of a Chinese vessel, approaching Senkaku Islands, were arrested by the Japanese coast guard. The issue was finally resolved at the two premiers meeting at Asia-Europe Meeting at Brussels in October. Anti-China protests broke out in Japan against the Chinese embassy and consulates, in the aftermath of the September 2010 Chinese trawler incident closer to Senkaku Islands. [14] Again in August 2011, Japan's Coast Guard shooed away a Chinese vessel near the Senkakus. China's drilling for energy resources in the disputed Chunxiao Islands is also leading to trouble in the region. Japan Self Defence Maritime Forces accuse China unleashing ships closer to the Japan's coast, while terming these as 'research activities'. On the other hand, the China Marine Surveillance (Haijian CMS) ships and aircraft drawn from the three sea fleets of viz. north, east and south, maintain round the clock surveillance over the disputed Chunxiao, Penghu and other islands and oil and field platforms in control of China.

In September 2012, Japanese government nationalised the three of the five island chain in the Senkakus. This was following the Tokyo Governor Ishihara's statement in the US for buying these islands which resulted in a dilemma for the Japanese government. Thus, fresh trouble brew up between Beijing and Tokyo after this and China sent surveillance ships and aircraft to the region resulting in the Japanese government taking military measures and invoking the US-Japan Treaty. In 2010, the US Secretary of State Clinton declared that the islands fall within the scope of the 1960 US-Japan Security Treaty. While the then US Defence Secretary Panetta went to Tokyo and Beijing to douse the feelings, the issue was kept alive with the anti-Japanese protests in China and responses in Japan.

Later, China on November 23, 2013 delineated an air defence identification zone (ADIZ) in the East China Sea. [15] Earlier the US had announced an ADIZ in 1950, and Japan took over in 1969 and expanded the ADIZ in 1972 and 2010. Some Chinese commentators stated that the purpose of this ADIZ was to break through the US-Japan efforts to blockade China at the first island chain. [16] The US Vice President Joe Biden said on December 3, 2013 that the US is "deeply concerned by the attempt to unilaterally change the status quo in the East China Sea. This action has raised regional tensions and increased the risk of accidents and miscalculations". [17]

Subsequently, Prime Minister Shinzo Abe visited the Yasukuni Shrine on December 26, 2013. Later, the US Secretary of State John Kerry during his visit to several capitals in Asia in February 2014 was critical of China changing the regional status quo and endorsing the US rebalances in the region. [18] More positive signals for Japan were forthcoming. The US President Obama on a visit to Japan in April stated "the Senkaku Islands are administered by Japan and therefore fall within the scope of Article 5 of the US-Japan Treaty of Mutual Cooperation and Security. And we oppose any unilateral attempts to undermine Japan's administration of these islands". [19]

China's Responses

In the background of the US rebalance, China had initiated a series of nuanced diplomatic, strategic and military measures including:

- Building "constructive, cooperative" and "new type" of relations with the US.
- Strengthening relations with major powers (US, Russia, EU).
- Reaching out to "emerging countries" (in the BRICS).
- Making comprehensive national strength as the primary goal —reflected in the "two centennials" project of building "well-off society" by 2020 and 100th anniversary of the People's Republic by 2049.
- Securing peripheries through the strategy of "erlang erdai" [two corridors, two belts] (referring to the south-western Bangladesh-China-India-Myanmar initiative and the western corridor through Pakistan on the one hand and the other to

include the two silk roads through Central Asia and maritime areas). [20]

- Military modernization. [21]

China's Efforts to Reshape the Asia-Pacific Order

In conjunction with the rise of China in the international system, thanks to the economic growth rates, the leadership in China made several overtures in the diplomatic, strategic, economic and military arenas to enhance their stature further at the global and regional levels.

While not being seen as threatening, the current US-led international order (of which China is a major beneficiary in terms of trade, technology and investments), China had been adopting a nuanced policy whereby its national interests are expanded further and with strategic sights on power transition at the global and regional levels in its favour.

Firstly, given the significance of the United States in the international system today, China and potential negative consequences if it opposes explicitly like the Soviet Union did, China began consolidating relations with the US in a number of ways. [22] Unlike the Soviet Union, China built mutually beneficial relations with the US which remained relatively stable for over four decades.

Secondly, China's leadership had approached the next tier of major powers, viz., Russia, European Union, Canada and others, specifically with a view to diversify trade and investments but also to secure its periphery. China is wary of the impact of the "coloured revolutions" on its domestic political situation and in Xinjiang and Tibet. It had expressed concerns on the spread of "Rose Revolution" in Georgia in 2003, Ukraine's 2004-2005 "Orange Revolution" and Kyrgyzstan's 2005 "Tulip Revolution". China and Russia countered the western-sponsored UN human rights criticism of the "Saffron Revolution" in Myanmar in January 2007. Working with Russia proved to be beneficial for China in military technologies, trade, coordination at the UN, space in Central Asia (through Shanghai Cooperation Organisation) and in its "pivot" to west through silk route to Europe.

Thirdly, China began active participation in the multilateral institutions as a cushion against any opposition from the US. Partly reflective of its ideological moorings and partly to enhance its bargaining position vis-à-vis the US and other western powers, China participated extensively in the recent multilateral initiatives, specifically with the emerging powers. The collective pressure of the emerging economies is reflected in the formation of the G-20, BRICS formation, participation in Asia-Pacific Economic Cooperation (APEC), proposed Trans-Pacific Partnership (TPP) and others. The G-20 mechanism represents an expansion in the G-7+1 framework with the rise of several countries such as Brazil, China, India, Indonesia, Turkey and others but also the diffusion of economic power in the world today. [23] G-20 also represents the view that multi-polarisation is at work as the established powers (the US) were unable to resolve global and regional security issues alone and that needed support and assistance from other powers in the international system. [24]

Issues related to North Korea, Iran, Syria and others have been raised at the summit meetings—often with acrimony. Eight summits of heads of governments took place till September 2013. The BRICS is an inter-governmental consultative, multilateral, trans-continental and emerging grouping that includes Brazil, Russia, India, China and South Africa. Five summit level meetings were held between these states (with South Africa invited from December 2010) at Yekaterinburg on June 16, 2009, Brasilia on April 15, 2010, Sanya on April 14, 2011, New Delhi on March 29, 2012 and Durban in early 2013.

These meetings discussed a host of issues including the international economic order in the light of the intensifying global financial and Euro Zone crisis, special drawing rights, reform of the Bretton Woods institutions, creation of a development bank as well as international security issues such as terrorism, climate change proposals, the Libyan and Syrian situations and the reorganization of the United Nations. For the proposed development bank—China's contribution will be 41 percent of the estimated US$ 100 billion corpus. [25] There is a suggestion for expanding further the BRICS to include other emerging countries such as Indonesia and Turkey. [26] Egypt recently had announced that its candidature in this grouping should be considered. [27] Thus, the BRICS is attempting to influence the "structural power" [rules, norms and the 'structure' of the relationship patterns within the international system] of the world, although such a project is still in its infancy.

Fourthly, to keep the regional initiative in its hands, China had been making concerted efforts to reshape the regional order. After taking over the reins of China in 2012, the new leadership under Xi Jinping and Li Keqiang, had made comprehensive blueprints for further consolidation of the rise of the country in the international system. The new leadership had proposed revising the old Silk Road both in the continental and maritime domains. President Xi Jinping, on a visit to Kazakhstan in September 2013, called for adopting an innovative cooperative model in building the new economic corridor connecting China with Central Asia and Europe. [28]

Subsequently, during his visit to Indonesia in October 2013, President Xi suggested to the idea of a maritime Silk Road connecting China with Southeast Asia, Indian Ocean and Africa. [29] Besides, two more thrust areas recently include the China-Pakistan Economic Belt and the Bangladesh-China-Myanmar-India (BCIM) initiative. [30] That these initiatives are of a long-term nature was indicated in May 2014, when at the 4th meeting of the 26-member Conference on Interaction and Confidence Building Measures in Asia at Shanghai, President Xi called for a new security cooperation architecture in Asia. [31] In order to overcome any US containment through the "rebalancing" strategy, China's new leadership proposed these two Silk Roads and two economic belts to wrest the strategic initiative in the Asian regional context.

Relations with the US

The test of the US rebalance will also be reflected in the

bilateral relations with China. Indeed, China and the US have evolved strategic relations gradually since the secret visit of Henry Kissinger to China in 1971 and after Nixon's visit of 1972 and Deng Xiaoping's visit in early 1979. In the last three decades, bilateral relations flowered to become one of the most important—if complicated—relationships in the world. Overall, relations changed from confrontation in the 1950s to "non-enemy, non-friend" by the 1970s. While the Bush Administration initially viewed China as a "strategic competitor", US wars on terrorism, Iraq and Afghanistan provided strategic space for China. By September 2009, the US was seeking from China "responsible stake-holder" position given the enormous increases in the latter's economic profile in the world. Soon, the US also suggested to "strategic reassurance" under the Obama Administration even as some like Brzezinski formulated G-2 (Group-2) with the US and China coordinating on regional and international issues. [32]

As a result of this forward momentum, today, the US and China have nearly US$ 600 billion in bilateral trade, with investments from the US to China (and vice versa). China had invested more than US$ 1 trillion in US Treasury Securities that cushions the bilateral relations. [33]

At the strategic level, both have evolved close relations unlike the US posture towards the then Soviet Union. Instead of an active containment policy that the US adopted towards the USSR, Washington normalised trade relations and extended Most Favoured Nation (MFN) treatment to Beijing in the 1990s. Later, it actively welcomed China in the World Trade Organization in 2001. Both thus are now intertwined in trade, investments, technology transfers, market exploration, etc. Indeed, as Obama stated, during his meeting with Hu Jintao on January 19, 2011, "We have an enormous stake in each other's success…The United States welcomes China's rise as a strong, prosperous and successful member of the community of nations".

At the security level, both are also engaged in strategic and economic dialogues since 2006—of which five such meetings by July 2013 brought forth an in-depth discussion and coordination on regional and international security issues. US Secretary Clinton stated at the May 3, 2012 dialogue, "we are working to build a relationship that allows both of our countries to flourish without unhealthy competition or conflict, while at the same time meeting our responsibilities to our people and to the international community". During this visit, she implied to re-writing the rule of power transition that does not consider zero-sum games between a rising country and a defending country. This meant an amenable nature of the US response towards China and sharply contrasts with the US position previously on the Soviet Union.

Bilateral relations were further cemented with three rounds of strategic security dialogues. Today, the discussions between the two encompass North Korean and Iranian nuclear issues to cyber security, from bilateral cooperation on climate change to military-to-military exchanges and maritime safety dialogues, from market access issues to intellectual property rights. 14 structured consultations between the two defence ministries were held in 2013 and China's military officers visited US naval ports and participated in the US-led exercises—including in the Gulf of Aden in August 2013, off the coast of Hawaii in September 2013 and in Cobra Gold exercises in Thailand in February 2013. [34]

Both actively cooperated in countering Soviet presence in Afghanistan in the 1980s with an in-depth military and intelligence exchanges, export of military equipment (stalled after the Tiananmen Square incident in 1989) and regional coordination with Pakistan. Despite differences on a number of issues, both characterise their relations as "comprehensive, cooperative, [and] mutually beneficial". Former foreign minister and State Councillor Yang Jiechi in his article of August 16, 2013 suggested that the meeting between Obama and Xi Jinping in Los Angeles in June 2013 resulted in building "a new model of major-country relationship based on mutual respect and win-win cooperation". Additionally Xi suggested to "non-conflict and non-confrontation"; mutual respect; and win-win cooperation with the US. These suggest to an upward swing in the US-China relations in the recent period and an effort by both the US and China to stabilise relations between the two.

However, there are differences between the two. These relate to arms supplies to Taiwan, US "hegemonic" role in East Asia and beyond, human rights and democracy spread, Tibet, currency and market economy status, proliferation of weapons of mass destruction, EP-3 incident in April 2001 and USS Impeccable incident in March 2009, China's anti-access and area denial strategies, December 2013 USS Cowpens incident, [35] etc. Both have also plans to counter each other at the political, diplomatic, strategic, and economic or even at the military levels. These include critic on "hegemony and power politics" versus authoritarianism, multilateral issues related to opposing US unilateralism on Iraq, Libya, Syria, etc. versus US alliances; and free trade and WTO/TPP mechanisms. Several Chinese military officials have also called for attacking the US with nuclear weapons, [36] even as some in the US advocate containment or even military action against China's interests. [37]

Conclusions

Overall, China's responses to the US rebalancing in the Asia-Pacific range from alarm to working with the US. China had shown an inclination to challenge the US at the regional level—Asian region—while gradually working with the US at the global level. To an extent, China had been the "revisionist" power at the regional but status quo at the global levels. As China's strength grows—from the current 2nd largest economy towards the largest in the world by the next decade—this rivalry between the US and China is expected to intensify—although both have created so many mutually beneficial stakes in each other. The US had approached the subject of China rise through cooperation, competition, hedging or even with elements of containment.

The US approach to the East China Sea and SCS in terms of rebalance is uneven, with more attention has been paid to the SCS rather than towards East China Sea. This is partly because, the US already has an alliance with Japan, while in the SCS region, it is searching for more reliable and enduring partners after the Subic

Bay that was vacated in the early 1990s at the Filipino behest. While this contest between the US and China has been a continuing phenomenon since more than a decade, many in Asia-Pacific region are concerned about the Chinese assertiveness in the region. China's close relations with North Korea, or its ability to stall consensus in the Southeast Asian groupings and massive display of coercive diplomacy in the region are posing concerns in the region. China has become the largest trading partner for many an Asia-Pacific countries and this economic aspect has its obvious political implications. These above factors have led to political divisions in the region with prospects for more flux in the strategic environment in the region.

Notes and References

1. See US President's speech, "Remarks by President Obama to the Australian Parliament", Canberra, November 17, 2011 accessed at: http://www.whitehouse.gov/the-press-office/2011/11/17/remarks-president-obama-australian-parliament. See also Kurt M. Campbell and Ely Ratner, "Why Washington Should Focus on Asia?", *Foreign Affairs*, May/June 2014 accessed at: http://www.foreignaffairs.com/articles/141241/kurt-m-campbell-and-ely-ratner/far-eastern-promises>; and Robert Sutter, "Sino-US Relations-1" ASAN Forum, January 27, 2014 accessed at: http://www.theasanforum.org/sino-us-relations-1/?dat=> and Hans Binnendijk, (ed.), 'A Transatlantic Pivot to Asia: Towards New Trilateral Partnerships', accessed at: http://transatlantic.sais-jhu.edu/publications/books/A%20Transatlantic%20Pivot%20to%20Asia.

2. In the context of Clinton's speech in this regard of "return to Asia", see the M.A. dissertation of Kong Guoliang, "*'Yadai zai pingheng' zhanlue xia Mei-Yue guanxi tanxi*", [Analysis of US-Vietnam Relations Under the 'Asia-Pacific Rebalancing' Strategy], *Foreign Affairs College*, Beijing, March 2013, pp. 5-6.

3. Remarks By Tom Donilon, National Security Advisor to the President, "The United States and the Asia-Pacific in 2013", *The Asia Society,* March 11, 2013 accessed at: http://www.whitehouse.gov/the-press-office/2013/03/11/remarks-tom-donilon-national-security-advisory-president-united-states-a>

and Amaani Lyle, "National Security Advisor Explains Asia-Pacific Pivot", March 11, 2013 accessed at: <http://www.defense.gov/News/newsarticle.aspx?ID=119505.

4. Some argue that the "Thucydides trap"—the increasing power of China vs. the established order of the US—will lead to a clash between the two. On the other hand, some argue that the US is entering into a structural—rather than cyclical—thinking of "isolationism" at the global and regional levels and making adjustments with Beijing. See "China-U.S. Relations: The Myth of the Thucydides Trap", *The Diplomat,* March 30, 2014, accessed at: http://thediplomat.com/2014/03/china-u-s-relations-the-myth-of-the-thucydides-trap/>; and Gideon Rachman, "Get Ready, The Indispensable Americans are Pulling Back", *Financial Times,* January 20, 2014 accessed at: http://www.ft.com/cms/s/0/a3b2a198-81c7-11e3-87d5-00144feab7de.html#axzz34V5rTbtf.

5. See on the challenges that China can pose at the Asian levels to the US predominance, Hugh White, "Sharing Power With China", *The New York Times,* March 19, 2014 accessed at: <http://www.nytimes.com/2014/03/20/opinion/sharing-power-with-china.html?_r=0> On the growing mutual mistrust between the two, see J.M. Norton, "Strategic Mistrust", *The Diplomat,* April 21, 2014 accessed at: http://thediplomat.com/2014/04/the-sources-of-us-china-strategic-mistrust.

6. Minxin Pei argued that despite several in the first Obama Administration have left—including the advocates of the rebalance such as Hillary Clinton, Tom Donilon, Robert Gates and Kurt Campbell—this Asia visit is aimed at conveying that the rebalance strategy is going to be a long-term plan of the US. See "America's Pivot Paradox: Ukraine, Syria, and Beyond", *National Interest,* April 24, 2014 accessed at: http://nationalinterest.org/feature/americas-pivot-paradox-ukraine-syria-beyond-10306. See also Timothy J.A. Adamson, Michael E. Brown, and Robert G. Sutter, "Rebooting the U.S. Rebalance to Asia", *Sigur centre for Asian Studies,* May 2014 accessed at: http://www.risingpowersinitiative.org/wp-content/uploads/RebootingRebalance_OnlineFinal.pdf.

7. Major events in the region include April 2012 when China's vessels first surrounded and then took control of Philippine held

Scarborough Shoal; November 2013 Hainan provincial congress directives requiring foreign fishing vessels (from January 1, 2014) to obtain approval to enter waters in the SCS under its jurisdiction; March 17, 2014 when China's Coast Guard ships prevented two Philippine-flagged ships from approaching Second Thomas Shoal; May 1, 2014 when China's drilling platform Haiyang 981 took control of Vietnam held areas.

8. There were more such incidents in the region including *Bowditch* in 2001 and 2002; *Bruce C. Heezen* in 2003; *Victorious* 2003 and 2004; *Effective* 2004; *John McDonnell* 2005; *Mary Sears* 2005; *Loyal* 2005. See Clarence J. Bouchat, *Dangerous Ground: The Spratly Islands and U.S. Interests and Approaches,* Carlisle Barracks, PA: US Army War College, Strategic Studies Institute, 2013, p. 19.

9. Marvin Ott, "Deep Danger: Competing Claims in the South China Sea", *Current History,* Volume 110, accessed at: http://www.currenthistory.com/pdf_org_files/110_737_236.pdf.

10. Robert Sutter termed this as "low-level perpetual contestation"—a "grey zone" between war and peace between the US and China. See Robert Sutter, "Sino-US Relations-3" *ASAN Forum,* March 21, 2014 accessed at: http://www.theasanforum.org/obamas-trip-to-asia-how-to-deal-with-china-in-the-gray-zone/?dat=. See also Paul Miller, "China, the United States, and Great Power Diplomacy", *Foreign Policy,* December 26, 2013 accessed at: http://shadow.foreignpolicy.com/posts/2013/12/26/china_the_united _states_and_great power_diplomacy.

11. According to a draft white paper on maritime policy of Taiwan's Cabinet-level Research, Development and Evaluation Committee in June 1999, Taiwan reiterated its jurisdiction over the Spratly's and Diaoyudao Islands. See for details, "White Paper Stresses Sovereignty over Two Sets of Disputed Isles", *Central News Agency,* Taipei, June 22, 1999, in SWB FE/3569 F/2 June 24, 1999.

12. These arguments are reflected in Ying Nan, "*Diaoyudao lishi yange ji zhanlue jiazhi*", History and the Evolution of the Strategic Value of Diaoyu Islands, *Xiandai Junshi* [*Contemporary Military*], Beijing, Volume 21, No. 3, Issue 242, March 1997, pp. 51-52.

13. See "Ocean Law Symposium Held", *China Daily,* Beijing, November 5, 1997.

14. According to Shimizu, China's military's pressure in the domestic

decision-making is one of the main reasons for the new-found China's assertiveness on the Senkaku islands issue. See Yoshikazu Shimizu, "China's Domestic Politics behind the Senkaku Incident", AJISS-Commentary No.107 accessed at:
http://www.jiia.or.jp/en_commentary/201012/16-1.html.

15. Emi Mifune argued that this measure by China is to isolate Japan and change the status quo in the region by force. See "Chinese Diplomacy in 2014: Hard Line against Japan, Accommodation toward U.S.", *Asahi Shimbun,* January 21, 2014, accessed at:
http://ajw.asahi.com/article/forum/security_and_territorial_issues/japan_china/AJ201401210064?f.

16. Kong Defang, "China's ADIZ Makes its Point", *People's Daily,* December 9, 2013, accessed at:
http://english.people.com.cn/90786/8479098.html.

17. "Remarks to the Press by Vice President Joe Biden and Prime Minister Shinzo Abe of Japan", accessed at:
http://www.whitehouse.gov/the-press-office/2013/12/03/remarks-press-vice-president-joe-biden-and-prime-minister-shinzo-abe-jap.

18. Robert Sutter, "Sino-US Relations-2", *ASAN Forum,* February 21, 2014, accessed at:
http://www.theasanforum.org/sino-us-relations-2/?dat.

19. "Obama: Senkakus 'Within Scope' of U.S.-Japan Treaty", *Japan News,* April 23, 2014, accessed at:
http://the-japan-news.com/news/article/0001227627.

20. Wang Yuzhu, *"Erlang erdai' gouzhu zhoubian hezuo xin geju"*, ["Two Corridors, Two Belts' to Build a New Pattern of Cooperation in the Neighbourhood"], *Zhongguo Baodao* [*China Report*], January 2014, Issue 119, pp. 32-33.

21. For a recent assessment, see the US Department of Defense, China Report 2014, accessed at:
http://www.defense.gov/pubs/2014_DoD_China_Report.pdf.

22. On the argument that China will not be able to confront the US, due to domestic agenda of the Chinese leadership, see Robert Sutter, "Why China Avoids Confronting the U.S. in Asia", March 19, 2014, accessed at:
http://www.chinausfocus.com/foreign-policy/why-china-avoids-confronting-the-u-s-in-asia-2.

23. For the view that China should closely associate with the G-8 as G-8+1, see Chen Chuanwei, *"Ba guo jituan yu Zhongguo"* [G-8 and China], M.A. dissertation submitted to Xiangtan University, April

2004.

24. Xu Xiaochun argued that as the comprehensive national strength of China is increasing in the recent period, China should emphasise on multi-polarity in order to expand its influence among the major powers and deal with the peripheries. See *"Guoji gequ yu Zhongguo duojihua waijiao zhanlue de jiangou"* [International Pattern and Building of China's Multi-polar Diplomatic Strategy], *Xin Shiye* [New Horizons], May 2003, pp. 8-10. Another author Hao Jian argued that China should not compromise on the human rights issue or democracy or other "fundamental interests" but should work through these institutions for change in the power structure. See Hao Jian, *"Guoji tixi yu Zhongguo daguo waijiao zhanlue celue xuanze"* [International System and China's Choice of Great Power Diplomatic Strategy], *Zhonggong Guizhou shengwei dangxiao* [China's Communist Party Guizhou Provincial Party School Journal], No. 99, May 2005, pp. 62-63.

25. Scott Rose, "China Agrees to Give 41 percent of $100 Billion BRICS Reserve Pool", *Bloomberg,* September 6, 2013, accessed at: http://www.bloomberg.com/news/2013-09-05/china-agrees-to-give-lion-s-share-of-100-billion-brics-pool-1-.html.

26. Sara Schonhardta, "BRIC ambitions for Indonesia", *Asia Times,* September 2, 2010, accessed at: http://www.atimes.com/atimes/South_Asia/LI02Df05.html>and John Fraser, "Building Brics: Will group grow to include Turkey, Indonesia?" December 1, 2012, accessed at: http://www.theeastafrican.co.ke/news/Will-group-grow-to-include-Turkey-Indonesia/-/2558/1634442/-/wbut48z/-/index.html.

27. "Egypt Looks for BRICS Entry", March 19, 2013, accessed at: http://indrus.in/news/2013/03/19/egypt_looks_for_brics_entry_2303 7.html.

28. *"Xi Jinping fabiao zhongyao yanjiang xu gongjian 'sichou zhilu jingjidai"*, [Xi Jinping delivers an important speech calling for the construction of "Silk Road economic zone"], *Xinhua,* September 7, 2013, accessed at: http://news.xinhuanet.com/world/2013-09/07/c_117272280.htm.

29. See Wu Jiao, "Xi in Call for Building of New Maritime Silk Road", *China Daily,* October 4, 2013, accessed at: http://usa.chinadaily.com.cn/china/2013-10/04/content_17008940.htm; Lan Xinzhen, "Silk Road Resurrection: New Economic Belt Brings a Wealth of Opportunity

for China, Central Asia and Europe", *Beijing Review,* November 7, 2013 and "*Xinsilu xin mengxiang' tegao: Shijie ruhe gongying? Zhongguo zhengzai poti*", *Xinhua,* May 8, 2014, accessed at: http://news.xinhuanet.com/world/2014-05/08/c_1110604423.htm.

30. In May 2013, during the maiden overseas visit of Premier Li Keqiang to New Delhi, India and China in the Joint Statement suggested ways to further this BCIM initiative.

31. "CICA Shanghai Summit Sets Milestone", *China Daily,* May 22, 2014, accessed at:
 http://www.chinadaily.com.cn/china/2014-05/22/content_17534782.htm.

32. James Jay Carafano, "Why a U.S.-China 'G-2' Won't Work", *National Interest,* January 6, 2014, accessed at: http://nationalinterest.org/commentary/why-us-chinese-g-2-wont-work-9653.

33. US$1.2 trillion in the US Treasury Securities account for nearly 9 percent and hence constitutes US largest creditor. Tseng Fu-sheng argued that despite China's rise in its power and such investments in the US, in several indicators, it is far below in the power matrix with the US. See "Big But Not Strong: China Still Can't Compete with the US", March 20, 2014, accessed at: http://bambooinnovator.com/2014/03/29/big-but-not-strong-china-still-cant-compete-with-the-us. Further, according to Teng, there are restrictions on the conversion of the Chinese currency in the international market with a mere 1 percent in the foreign exchange reserves of central banks worldwide, compared with 60 percent in the US dollar and 25 percent in the euro.

34. Wu Zurong, "Can Hagel Promote US Constructive Role in Asia?", April 7, 2014, accessed at: http://www.chinausfocus.com/foreign-policy/can-hagel-promote-us-constructive-role-in-asia.

35. See Kurt Campbell, "How China and American Can Keep a Pacific Peace", *Financial Times,* January 2, 2014, accessed at: http://blogs.ft.com/the-a-list/2014/01/02/how-china-and-american-can-keep-a-pacific-peace/>; and Pu Zhendong and Zhang fan, "Better Dialogue Urged After Naval Incident", *People's Daily,* December 16, 2013, accessed at: http://english.peopledaily.com.cn/90786/8485595.html.

36. Lieutenant General Xiong Guangkai, deputy Chief of General Staff, reportedly told Chas Freeman in March 1996 that "you [Americans]

are not going to threaten us again because, in the end, you care a lot more about Los Angeles than Taipei". See Greg May, "China's Opposition to TMD is More about Politics than Missiles", *Foresight,* Tokyo, February 2000, accessed at: http://www.nyu.edu/globalbeat/usdefense/May0200.html.   Later Major General Zhu Chenghu made a similar remark at a briefing in July 2005.

37. In the light of the Chinese establishment of the ADIZ in East China Sea, it was reported that Colonel TX Hammes of the US Marine Corps in 2012 suggested an "offshore control" strategy wherein US Navy blockades China's harbours and naval bases through attack submarines and aircraft and attacks China's sea lanes of communications to reduce China's power projection capabilities. See "Potential US Blockade of China Suggested by Japanese Monthly", March 5, 2014, accessed at: http://www.wantchinatimes.com/news-subclass-cnt.aspx?id=20140305000036&cid=1101. Another observer, Evan N. Resnick suggested that US and China could engage in military skirmishes on five reasons, viz., rising military budget of China; US rebalance, US alliances, nations in the region seeking support from the US and also due to the absence of any security arrangement/understanding between the US and China. See "Five Reasons for China and US to Go to War", *New Strait Times,* January 14, 2014, accessed at: http://www.wantchinatimes.com/news-subclass-cnt.aspx?id=20140114000089&cid=1101. See also Sean Mirsky, "Stranglehold: The Context, Conduct and Consequences of an American Naval Blockade of China", *Journal of Strategic Studies,* February 12, 2013, accessed at: http://carnegieendowment.org/2013/02/12/stranglehold-context-conduct-and-consequences-of-american-naval-blockade-of-china/fowj. "Navy Official: China Training for 'Short Sharp War' with Japan", February 18, 2014, accessed at: http://news.usni.org/2014/02/18/navy-official-china-training-short-sharp-war-japan.

2

India-U.S. Rebalancing Strategy in Asia-Pacific

Chintamani Mahapatra and Monish Tourangbam

The US rebalancing strategy towards Asia-Pacific has spawned debates and deliberations in strategic communities around the world. Academics and policy analysts, since the inception of this policy, have tried explaining its rationale and implications for the Asia-Pacific region and the global arena. The China factor has been ubiquitous in this policy, and many quarters in China have undoubtedly seen it as a "China Containment' policy. Though the centrality of India's expected role in the rebalancing strategy and India's approach towards the policy as such has drawn the attention of the strategic community in India, there is no vibrant debate in India yet about the role the country should play. Even the Government of India's response is muted. It is, thus, imperative to examine the India component in the US strategy and its strategic significance and implications for Indian national interests. One of the major goals of the US Asia rebalancing strategy is to strengthen the country's relationship with new strategic partners and this is where the emerging security cooperation between India and the United States becomes a relevant area for scrutiny.

Following India's unprecedented economic rise in recent years, there is a visible and vigorous attempt by New Delhi to project India's intentions and capabilities to play a role in areas beyond the country's immediate vicinity. Conversely, India's rising profile in both economic and strategic spheres has been noted around the world—both by major powers and others. And as debates abound on new emerging powers and the relative decline of the United States, the paradigm shift seen in

Indo-US relations has impacted deliberations on the future of Asia-Pacific. Most notably, strategic commonalities between India's Look East Policy and the US rebalancing strategy are expected to make India a vital link in the US pivot.

But, given the chequered history of Indo-US relationship, there is still a lingering sense of mistrust between the American and India leaderships, with India often being seen as a reluctant partner by the former and the US as an unreliable power by the latter. Moreover, India, given its sensitivities to regional geopolitical complexities and its traditional strategic orientation is understandably found to be more cautious and ambivalent in its approach to balance of power games in Asia-Pacific. Hence, the paper attempts to critically assess the rationale for the US rebalancing strategy and the emerging notions of this strategy. Based on this understanding, the paper seeks to analyze US motivations in assigning a role to India in its rebalancing strategy. In addition, the paper seeks to examine India's self-perceptions of its role in Asia-Pacific and its response to America's branding of India as 'a linchpin' of its rebalancing strategy.

US Rebalancing Strategy

In contemporary international relations, it is not hard to discern the centrality that Asia-Pacific has come to occupy, and more than any other factor, the rise of China has fundamentally altered the geopolitical significance of this region. Various permutations and combinations are being made to decipher the evolving balance of power politics in the region, with the management of rising China being the fulcrum of deliberations. Howsoever Washington might try to shift the debate regarding its rebalancing strategy from the China angle, America's reinvigorated attention to the Asia-Pacific is essentially dictated by the country's predominant strategy to sustain its primacy, and its efforts towards precluding the rise of a peer competitor.

In recent times, in response to repeated Chinese criticism

that the rebalancing strategy was primarily aimed towards containing China, US officials including successive Secretaries of Defense have tried to emphasize the non-military aspect of the strategy. First and foremost, the United States has been trying to highlight the point that America was neither an outsider nor it ever went away from the Asia-Pacific region. In other words, the Pacific theatre was and has always remained an elemental part of the US strategy, and that the United States geographically was as much a Pacific country as it was an Atlantic country. As the US Secretary of Defense Chuck Hagel contended, "America has been a Pacific power for more than two centuries. Our ties to this region—economic, cultural and security—are unbreakable and broadly supported by Americans of both political parties".

America's foreign policy since the end of World War II and its rise as an undisputed global power has always been guided by the goal to sustain US primacy in world affairs. The US strategic thinkers and planners singularly strategized to prevent the rise of a rival power. During the Cold War, it was the threat of Communism and Soviet expansionism that chiefly determined American national security policy. The containment doctrine followed by successive US administrations accounted for founding and strengthening of the North Atlantic Treaty Organization (NATO), Central Treaty Organization (CENTO), Australia, New Zealand, United States (ANZUS) Security Treaty and Southeast Asia Treaty Organization (SEATO) and a number of bilateral alliances across the globe. The end of the Cold War removed the Soviet threat and made America the unchallenged sole superpower of the globe. But the unprecedented growth of the Chinese economic and military power has begun to cause worry in Washington's policy-making circles in recent years.

The uncontested American Hegemony in the Asia Pacific, backed by the presence of thousands of American troops in Japan and South Korea and a host of US military bases in Japan, South Korea, Australia and a few Southeast Asian countries, began to face new challenges when China's influence in the region began to expand and American allies found in China, huge economic opportunities. Consequently, sustaining US primacy in the region became the guiding principle of the Asia rebalance strategy. Unilateral moves and muscle flexing by China in cases of maritime disputes in the South China Sea and the East China Sea have induced America's allies as well as new partners in Southeast Asia to express their intentions for an increased US engagement in the Asian continent, specifically through Association of Southeast Asian Nations (ASEAN) mechanisms like the Treaty of Amity and Cooperation and the ASEAN Defence Ministers Meeting (ADDM) Plus, or the East Asia Summit. In the mean time, the need for the United States to stay engaged in the economic dynamism of the Asia-Pacific region and amplify the shared interests for the United States and countries in the region has found bipartisan support in the American political spectrum.

Despite differences over the conduct of US foreign policy and questions raised by the opposition over effectiveness of US policies in the Asia-Pacific, there seems to be no dissensions regarding the centrality of this region for US national interests.

Besides lending voice to the now-usual rhetorical flair that the rebalancing strategy was not targeted towards any single country, former Presidential aspirant and noted Republican leader John McCain contended, "the idea that we must rebalance US foreign policy with an increasing emphasis on the Asia-Pacific region is undoubtedly correct...we face immediate decisions that will determine the vector of American power in the Asia-Pacific region— diplomatically, economically, and militarily—for decades to come...if we fail, we'll drift off the course and fall behind. However, if we get these big decisions right, we can create the enduring conditions to expand the supply of American power, to strengthen American leadership, and to secure America's national interests across the Pacific".

Many US officials in recent years have tried to add to how

the rebalancing strategy is understood in the outside world, including the popular Foreign Policy article '*America's Pacific Century*' written by former Secretary of State Hillary Clinton, one of the primary advocates of the strategy. Successive US Defense Secretaries have frequently used the Shangrila-Dialogue forum to enunciate to the world what the United States intends to achieve with its rebalancing strategy, emphasizing on the diplomatic, economic and cultural elements of the strategy. But at the same time, US Defense Secretaries from Robert Gates to Chuck Hagel have constantly pointed out the central role that the US Department of Defense would play in US foreign policy orientation towards Asia-Pacific, and that fiscal challenges in the United States would not deter the American involvement in the region.

A clear acknowledgement has emerged from the US government that it would continue to be involved in the region "with appropriate forces, posture, and presence" as a "21st century Asia-Pacific nation (Gates; Donilon)". The US policy planners consider the Asia-Pacific region as centre of both opportunities and challenges. In terms of economic vitality of the region, the US envisions the region as the centre of gravity for the 21st century, explaining all forms of bilateral and multilateral initiatives in the region that could benefit the US economy at large. Economic interdependence between the US and China is something fairly recognized by Washington and reflected in the importance accorded to US-China relations.

However, the rise of China is apparently not seen as "peaceful" by many countries in the region, and sustaining US primacy is something intricately connected to the safety and security of US alliance partners and other emerging partners in the region. China's declaration of an Air Defence Identification Zone (ADIZ) in the East China Sea and the prompt US response of flying B-52 bombers over the Senkaku/Diaoyu Islands defying China, exposed the vulnerabilities and potential conflict points between the pre-eminent global power and a rising China, the latter largely seen as harbouring ambitions to attain strategic primacy at least in the Eastern hemisphere a la America's Monroe Doctrine in the western hemisphere (Rapp-Hooper; Keck).

Beijing's announcement of the ADIZ is essentially consonant with its escalating assertive behaviour in the region and the ambitious Area Denial/Anti-Access strategy being developed by the PLA which are indicative of Beijing's desire to outline its sphere of influence. The US Strategic Guidance paper '*Sustaining U.S. Global Leadership: Priorities for 21st Century Defense*' released in January 2012 has unmistakably explained the American understanding of the Chinese intentions. According to this paper, China would "continue to pursue asymmetric means to counter" America's "power projection capabilities". The paper then declares that the US military would "invest as required to ensure its ability to operate effectively in anti-access and area denial (A2/AD) environments (Department of Defense 4-5)". Subsequently, US Defense Secretary Chuck Hagel came out with an official response seeking to assure the allies that such actions by China would not change how the United States conducted "military operations in the region". Hagel emphasized America's responsibility in times of potential threat to provide security to its allies in the region.

The essence of the rebalancing strategy thus could be attributed, among other things, to the evolving geopolitical significance of the Asia-Pacific region requiring the US government to ensure the endurance of its alliances and partnerships in the region. An Asia that is home to some of the fastest growing economies of the world is also home to the countries with mounting defence expenditures. The acute security dilemma and bourgeoning strategic uncertainties in the region have contributed to American decision to rebalance its strategy.

Even as the US government emphasizes that the strategy did not mean that the US military was retrenching from its role as "a global force for security and stability", it did not also deny that that the military would "of necessary rebalance towards the Asia-Pacific region" and that Washington had chosen to make Asia-Pacific a priority (Panetta). Of some of the important partners that the United States looks forward to include in its strategy, India figures prominently.

India in US Rebalancing Strategy

Though the rise of China has managed to capture debates and deliberations around the world, the emergence of India as a global power and expectations from India has also become a pertinent theme of strategic discussion. The new paradigm in Indo-US relations is expected to impact the future of the regional order in Asia-Pacific and the global order at large. Even as India-US relationship hogged limelight in recent times for all the wrong reasons, most prominently being the diplomatic row over the arrest of the Indian diplomat Devyani Khobragade, the larger strategic rationale that brought the two countries together remain unaltered. And the strategic imperatives of the relationship that led both New Delhi and Washington affirm to the undoubtable significance of the relationship can be most notably found in convergence of interests in America's rebalancing strategy and India's Look East Policy.

Like the rebalancing strategy of the US, India's Look East Policy is a broad-based policy that aims to promote and protect India's national interests through a more stable and secure Asia with interdependent economies built on the principle of mutualism. But, at the same time, both the policies also aim towards precluding the rise of an uncertain Asia with an aggressive power free to resort to unilateral moves in the region.

The string of relationships that the United States has woven with Southeast Asian countries is in unison with the kinds of relationships that India has been building with its Southeast Asian partners. Both Washington and India are well aware that the elephant in the room is the management of China's rise, a task made more complex by the enormous economic cooperation with China. Significantly, economic ties have failed to translate into adequate trust between the US and China or India and China. In other words, despite the economic opportunities offered by China's economic dynamism and its growing military and economic strength has not resulted in the conviction that China's rise would necessarily remain peaceful.

This eminently explains the open US position that the rise of a powerful and democratic India is in the interest of the United States. Many Indian analysts also appear persuaded that the sustenance of American power and influence in Asia is in the interest of India (Council on Foreign Relations and Aspen Institute India).

The then Secretary of Defense Leon Panetta made it quite apparent during his India visit in mid-2012 that the Obama Administration saw great prospect for India-US strategic cooperation as the arc of convergence widened between the two countries. Emphasizing the need to further augment the emerging defence cooperation between the two countries, he said, "…America is at a turning point. After a decade of war, we are developing a new defence strategy—a central feature of which is a "rebalancing" toward the Asia-Pacific region. In particular, we will expand our military partnerships and our presence in the arc extending from the Western Pacific and East Asia into the Indian Ocean region and South Asia. *Defense cooperation with India is a linchpin in this strategy.*"

Similarly, the Pentagon's Strategic Guidance Paper of 2012 asserted that "US economic and security interests are inextricably linked to developments in the arc extending from the Western Pacific and East Asia into the Indian Ocean region and South Asia" and that cementing the US alliances in the region and building new partnerships was at the heart of the new US strategy. The document singularly points out that the United States is also *investing in a long-term strategic partnership with India to support its ability to serve as a regional economic anchor and provider of security in the broader Indian Ocean region* (Department of Defense)".

No doubt, an effective policy convergence between the two countries is vital but the road ahead, especially so between two large and functioning democracies, cannot be all roses and no thorns. And the centrality that the China factor is accorded in this strategy creates both opportunities and challenges for India-US bilateral relationship, and can largely be attributed for the varying responses that the rebalancing strategy and the role that it envisions for India has got from the Indian strategic community.

India's Response to the US Rebalancing Strategy

While the US has given enough indications to co-opt India into its Asia rebalancing strategy, the Ministry of External Affairs or the Ministry of Defense has not responded officially to the US strategy. The strategic community in India, however, has been engaged in a debate on this issue and various viewpoints have come to the fore.

For example, Brahma Chellaney contends that the US rebalancing strategy is "…all about China, with the US bolstering alliances and friendships with countries around China's periphery, including India, Japan, the Philippines, Vietnam, Indonesia and South Korea" even if the Obama Administration was "reluctant to say or do anything publicly that might raise China's hackles". Actually, the Obama Administration has said many things that have "raised China's hackles", but Washington refrains from making the rebalancing strategy appear as a brand new "containment of China strategy". The prompt flying of B-52 bombers to defy China's declaration of an Air Defense Identification Zone, reiteration of the significance of US-Japan alliance treaty and US-Philippines mutual defence treaty, American opposition to China's nine-dash-line territorial claim in South China Sea and Obama's meeting with Dalai Lama are but a few instances of "raising China's hackles".

Moreover, given America's complex interdependence with

China, the US government has understandably been on a mission mode to de-emphasize the military component of the strategy and emphasize that the rebalancing strategy does not translate into an effort to contain China. However, the Strategic Guidance Paper that is seen as the Holy Grail guiding the new US strategy in Asia-Pacific clearly pictures the uncertainty in the nature of China's rise and its probable implications for regional and global stability. The document says, "the maintenance of peace, stability, the free flow of commerce, and of US influence in this dynamic region will depend in part on an underlying balance of military capability and presence.

Over the long-term, China's emergence as a regional power will have the potential to affect the US economy and our security in a variety of ways. Our two countries have a strong stake in peace and stability in East Asia and an interest in building a cooperative bilateral relationship. However, the growth of China's military power must be accompanied by greater clarity of its strategic intentions in order to avoid causing friction in the region. The United States will continue to make the necessary investments to ensure that we maintain regional access and the ability to operate freely in keeping with our treaty obligations and with international law (Department of Defense)".

America's complex tango with the Chinese has created anxiety in India over the prospects of a world jointly managed by a power in relative decline and a power undergoing fastest rise. Despite the new paradigm of India's equations with the United States, Washington and New Delhi continue to have different perceptions of how they should manoeuvre their strategic sails in the future. If the American officials find India a reluctant partner, many in the Indian policymaking circles and the wider strategic community see the US as an unreliable power that could leave India in the lurch, if it did not serve its strategic interests. Indians remember how the American government during the Cold War, in regular fashion, offered rhetorical flourishes on how India could serve as a democratic counterweight to the communist Chinese model, and constantly stated how the Americans had discernible stakes in the success of India.

However, the same US later on courted the Chinese through rapprochement, giving a red carpet for 'red China' to the UN Security Council. So, now, when the Americans concerned with the rise of a possible peer competitor in the eastern hemisphere, try to court India as a possible counterweight, New Delhi has reasons to be vigilant, even as it struggles to deal with the rise of an economic and a potential military behemoth across its eastern borders.

C. Rajamohan argues that "the Obama administration's rebalancing towards Asia has compelled New Delhi to think more clearly about the costs and benefits of a tight embrace with the United States". Many in India's strategic community do recognize the geopolitical significance of America's rebalancing strategy, and affirm that the policy could possibly "…compel Beijing to be more reasonable towards India", since "…the greater the US pressure in the Pacific, the more likely that China would want to keep its south-western frontiers tranquil (Ibid)". Moreover, many concur that India could not depend on mere internal balancing to match China, and hence signifying the need for the United States and other Asian partners in India's external balancing. However, many considerations besides economic interdependence tempered "Indian enthusiasm for US rebalancing towards Asia (Ibid)".

Significantly, the argument that China would like to see a tranquil south-western border at the time of rising pressure in the Pacific may not be true all the time. In fact, China has picked up quarrel with Japan, the Philippines, Vietnam and India all around the same time in recent months. Apart from discretion demanded by the geopolitical consequences of provoking China's hostility, domestic opposition to overt alliance with the United States and the salience that is accorded to India's need to maintain its strategic autonomy also inform Indian strategic calculations. It is noteworthy that when US Vice President Joe Biden, during his India visit in 2013, remarked that there was "...no contradiction between strategic autonomy and a strategic partnership", New Delhi refused to buy this argument lock, stock and barrel. The Indian government sent strategic signals to point out that it did not want to be seen as allying with the US against China and that it wanted to retain its freedom of decisions and actions while facing the geopolitical consequences of China's rise and US response to the same.

Certainly, India and the United States share a larger strategic vision that encompasses maintenance of security and stability in the Asian region, and preventing China from unilaterally undermining it. The two countries aspire to jointly become a stabilizing force in the emerging Asian balance of power and to ensure that no unilateral force emerges in the region whose influence writ large, would be detrimental to their interests.

However, history does not disappear soon, and as such, there are still lingering concerns and a persisting mistrust between India and the US, reminiscent of the mutual mistrust of the Cold War period. And, inadequate mutual faith between the two countries is something that spills over and impedes both sides from going ahead full-steam on issues spreading across the political, economic, security and strategic realms. India is often afflicted with apprehensions that China's growing strength vis-à-vis the United States could lead to mutual Sino-US accommodation of interests, to the detriment of India's interests in Asia-Pacific.

The logic of self-help in an anarchical world order then makes India aspire for a robust defence capability that could close the critical gap vis-à-vis the Chinese military modernization. It is worthwhile recalling how in 2009 at the start of his presidential career, President Barack Obama sent a harshly criticized strategic signal to India by suggesting a more active Chinese role in South Asia, thus only fuelling concerns regarding the possibility of a US-China power condominium in the region (Rajamohan; Chellaney).

Recent attempt by Indian strategic and foreign policy analysts to reassess and readapt the policy and practice of Non-Alignment to the changing milieu of world affairs, titled '*Non-Alignment 2.0*' has also emphasized that maintaining strategic autonomy is germane to India's foreign policy. It calls attention to the attempt by many Asian powers "to hedge their bets against excessive dependence on a major power". The much debated India's strategic document points out:

"The core objective of a strategic approach should be to give India maximum options in its relations with the outside world—that is, to enhance India's strategic space and capacity for independent agency—which in turn will give it maximum options for its own internal development (Khilnani, et al.)".

India has indeed emerged in many ways. Its economy has come off age from a poor and industrially backward country to one that commands an economy that is fairly consequential for the health of the global economy. India's service sector, particularly the information technology sector, has made India an IT superpower.

By dint of its demographic and territorial size, large human resources, enormous natural resources and articulate political elite, India since its Independence has had the potential of being a major power in the regional and international system. During the Cold War, newly independent India under the leadership of its internationally popular leader Prime Minister Jawaharlal Nehru was often found punching above its weight. India, with its leadership and the emphasis on Non-alignment was seen charting its own course, away from the strategic competition ensuing between the two superpowers then. India has often been seen as the leader of the normative kind, which despite all its attributes did not have much of a role in international agenda-sitting. However, the opening of the Indian economy provided Indian businesses the avenues to be a part of the rapidly emerging globalization, and helped put it at the centre of the story, along with faster growing neighbour China.

For instance, its economic prowess, attractive soft power and military hard power, along with a vibrant middle class, have elevated India's status regionally and globally. For long, India has been seen as a leader and cheerleader in the developing world and a voice for the least developed countries at the global arena. But, India is undergoing a phase of transition, as it shows signs of graduating from a mere developing country, to an emerging global player, and whose voice would not only be heard but listened to at the highest table of agenda-setting in global affairs. The direction of global affairs has largely been determined by a handful of powers that have the capabilities and also the willingness to shape the course of international affairs. China's rise has often loomed larger than that of India in the sheer scale of growth and implications in regional and global affairs. Nevertheless, India despite its current limitations and the much talked-about lack of political will has drawn world attention to its potential role as an important international leader.

Many western commentators have criticized India as a 'naysayer' when it comes to taking up international responsibilities and burden-sharing (Narlikar; Hoffman Paper). India, traditionally has maintained taboos when it comes to international engagements, especially so with great powers, and a not so exemplary history of 'Indo-US relationship' has not helped matters (Ollapally). But, it is also true that as India's economic achievements and military power grow, and the horizons of its national interest extends beyond the inner circle of South Asia, it will gradually develop the intention and willingness to get into the shoes of a 'great power'. And as the US tries to preserve its pre-eminence in Asia despite debates over its relative decline, and as India's foreign policy becomes more commensurate with its capabilities, the two countries are on a convergent path. The joint statement from the Singh-Obama summit in September 2013, rightly pointed out, "...the two countries have crossed a threshold in their relations where both recognize that successes at home and abroad are further advanced by their cooperation (Ministry of External Affairs)".

If for India, the US is important as a global power that could substantially help push up India's influence globally, as it did with the signing of the civilian nuclear agreement and helping India gain the Nuclear Suppliers Group (NSG) waiver, India is equally important for the furtherance of US foreign policy objectives in the Asia-Pacific region. India could be what some call the "bridge state" in the changing global order. The document *Non-Alignment 2.0* has pointed out:

"The structures of competition in the global system will present India with a range of partnership choices. For a start, India will be sought after in great power competition. This presents a great historical opportunity for India. This diverse identity and the multiple interests that it underpins are actually our greatest strategic assets at the global level. For it means that India can be a unique bridge between different worlds. Indeed, India's bridging potential is one we must leverage and turn to our active benefit (Khilnani, et al.)".

However, reflecting the complexities and ambiguities attached to India's relationship with a global power that faces challenges to its hegemonic order and a probable superpower rising along its border, the same document contends, "the US can be too demanding in its friendship and resentful of other attachments India might pursue. The historical record of the United States bears out that powers that form formal alliances with it have tended to see an erosion of their strategic autonomy...China remains suspicious of India's partnerships, and in particular sees improved Indian ties with America and Japan in simple zero-sum terms. It follows that over the long-run, the triangular relationship between India, China and America will need very careful management...The prospect that India is a potential partner can give it leverage, both with the country courting it and with potential rivals. India must leverage to the full extent possible this dual diplomatic potential (Ibid; Mahapatra)".

Conclusion

The US, India and most Southeast Asian countries clearly have major strategic divergences with a rising China and share a common interest in managing their mutual relationships to ensure a stable and peaceful Asia. Peaceful rise of China is acceptable to all, but ensuring its sustenance is equally desirable for all. After all, India, America and other Asian countries have developed complex economic interdependence with China and hope it would prevent armed conflict with China. When it comes to hedging China, responses from all these countries are understandably subtle and their attention appears geared towards: 'how to manage rising China without provoking any major untoward incident having regional and global ramifications'. Both Washington and New Delhi look for ways to control Beijing's aggression, simultaneously making various diplomatic cushions so as to prevent any crash landing of their ties with China.

Hence, in the pursuit of a pragmatic and clear-headed 'strategic partnership', a more nuanced understanding and clearer view is required of why India and the US need each other, what the US expects India to do, and what India is willing to do, what India wants the US to do, and what the US is willing to do. A greater convergence can only come from a more honest understanding and acceptance of differences, rather than harbouring utopian ideas of commonalities. In building on its now ubiquitous policy of rebalancing strategy towards Asia-Pacific, Washington perhaps needs to follow a more integrative approach taking into consideration the views of allies and partners rather than merely giving policy prescriptions.

References

Biden, Joe (2013), "Remarks by Vice President Joe Biden on the U.S.-India Partnership at the Bombay Stock Exchange", The White House, Office of the Vice President, July 24, available at:

http://www.whitehouse.gov/the-press-office/2013/07/24/remarks-vice-president-joe-biden-us-india-partnership-bombay-stock-excha.

Chellaney, Brahma (2012), "Report: U.S. Strategy in the Asia-Pacific", Al-Jazeera Center for Studies, February 15, available at: http://studies.aljazeera.net/ResourceGallery/media/Documents/2012/2/15/2012215105384657334U.S.%20Strategy%20in%20the%20Asia-Pacific.pdf.

——"Whatever One Calls It, The US Asia Policy is All about China", *Taipei Times,* November 20, 2012, available at: http://www.taipeitimes.com/News/editorials/archives/2012/11/20/2003548131/2.

Clinton, Hillary (2011), "America's Pacific Century", *Foreign Policy,* October 11, available at: http://www.foreignpolicy.com/articles/2011/10/11/americas_pacific_century.

Council on Foreign Relations and Aspen Institute India (2011), "The United States and India: A Shared Strategic Future", Joint Study Group Report, September, available at: file:///C:/Users/Acer/Downloads/USIndia_jointstudygroup_IIGG.pdf.

Donilon, Tom (2011), "America is back in the Pacific and will uphold the Rules", *Financial Times,* November 27, available at: http://www.ft.com/intl/cms/s/0/4f3febac-1761-11e1-b00e-00144feabdc0.html#axzz2uLFVd9AT.

Gates, Robert M. (2011), "Secretary of Defense Speech", Speech at the Shangri-La Dialogue, Singapore, June 4, available at: http://www.defense.gov/speeches/speech.aspx?speechid=1578.

Hagel, Chuck (2013), "Statement by Secretary of Defense Chuck Hagel on the East China Sea Air Defense Identification Zone", US Department of Defense, November 23, available at: http://www.defense.gov/releases/release.aspx?releaseid=16392>

——"The US Approach to Regional Security", Speech at the Shangri-La Dialogue, Singapore, June 1, 2013, available at: http://www.iiss.org/en/events/shangri%20la%20dialogue/archive/shangri-la-dialogue-2013-c890/first-plenary-session-ee9e/chuck-hagel-862d.

Hoffman, Steven A. (2010), "Change in India-US Diplomatic Practices: An Interim Report", IDSA Occasional Paper No. 10,

available at:
http://www.idsa.in/system/files/OP_India-USDiplomaticPractices.pdf.

Keck, Zachary (2013), "US Bombers Challenge China's Air Defense Identification Zone", *The Diplomat,* November 27, available at: http://thediplomat.com/2013/11/us-bombers-challenge-chinas-air-defense-identification-zone.

Khilnani, Sunil et al. (2012), "Non-Alignment 2.0: A Foreign and Strategic Policy for India in the Twenty First Century", available at: http://www.cprindia.org/sites/default/files/NonAlignment%202.0_1.pdf.

Mahapatra, Chintamani (2011), "Complex Cold Warriors: US-China Relations and Implications for India", *Journal of Defence Studies,* 5(3), July, pp. 25-31.

McCain, John (2012), "Why Asia Wants America", *The Diplomat,* May 22, available at: http://thediplomat.com/2012/05/why-asia-wants-america/?allpages=yes.

Ministry of External Affairs (2013), "Joint Statement on Prime Minister's Summit Meeting with President Barack Obama in Washington D.C.", September 27, available at: http://www.mea.gov.in/in-focus-article.htm?22265/Joint+Statement+on+Prime+Ministers+Summit+Meeting+with+President+Barack+Obama+in+Washington I DC+September+27+2013.

Narlikar, Amrita (2013), "India Rising: Responsible to Whom", *International Affairs,* 89(3), pp. 595-614.

Ollapally, Deepa (2011), "India: The Ambivalent Power in Asia", *International Studies,* 48(3 and 4), pp. 201-222.

Panetta, Leon E. (2012), "Partners in the 21st Century", Speech at the Institute of Defence Studies Analyses, New Delhi, June 6, available at: http://www.idsa.in/keyspeeches/LeonEPanettaonPartnersinthe21stcentury.

——"Speech of the Defense Secretary", Shangri-La Dialogue, Singapore, June 2, available at: http://www.defense.gov/speeches/speech.aspx?speechid=1681.

Rajamohan, C. (2013), "India: Between Strategic Autonomy and Geopolitical Opportunity", Roundtable: Regional Perspectives

on U.S. Strategic Rebalancing, *Asia Policy,* No. 15, January, pp. 20-25, available at:
http://www.nbr.org/publications/asia_policy/free/AP15/AP15_B_Asia_balanceRt.pdf.

Rapp-Hooper, Mira (2013), "East China Sea ADIZ: A Turning Point in US-China Relations?", *The Diplomat,* December 20, available at:
http://thediplomat.com/2013/12/east-china-sea-adiz-a-turning-point-in-us-china-relations.

US Department of Defense (2012), "Sustaining U.S. Global Leadership: Priorities for 21st Century Defense", January, available at:
http://www.defense.gov/news/defense_strategic_guidance.pdf.

3

China's Responses to U.S. Rebalancing Strategy in Asia-Pacific

Anand V.

Introduction

The geostrategic region of the Asia-Pacific has been growing in significance, fuelled by the growth of its resident powers and their increasing interactions among each other and with the major powers of the world. China had a historically central role in the region, which receded during the emergence of Western colonial powers into the region. However, since the past few decades, the Asia-Pacific region has been witnessing a resurgence of China's role and stature. China has been increasing its power projection capabilities in the region, and has created a significant degree of clout. However, the strategic environment which China inhabits is far from fully supportive of its strategic ambitions. China's Asia-Pacific neighbourhood, in particular, is becoming increasingly hostile due to the threat perceptions of regional states arising from China's assertive behavioural trend.

The rebalancing strategy of the US in the Asia-Pacific region, which was articulated at the beginning of the second decade of the twenty-first century, certainly indicates an intensification of this emerging geopolitical dynamics in the region. China has certainly taken this move by the US into consideration in its geostrategic calculus and has been formulating measured responses. In this context, it becomes imperative to analyze the responses of China to the US' rebalancing strategy in the Asia-Pacific.

This paper would focus on the assessment of these specific

reactions, as well as its rationale, for which China's strategic interests in the Asia-Pacific need to be probed. By assessing the various facets of America's rebalancing strategy, its effects on China's ambitions in the Asia-Pacific can be inferred. Linking China's strategic thinking to its behavioural tendencies in the region would provide a meaningful context for understanding China's rationale and moves to counter the rebalancing strategy of the US.

Strategic Realm of the Asia-Pacific

The geopolitical region of Asia-Pacific does not have a fixed and commonly accepted definition with respect to the span of area it encompasses, as it has been kept largely ambiguous by the users. The origins of this rather loosely defined strategic construct dates back to the 1960s and 1970s, when powers like US, Japan and Australia tried to link the East Asian security environment with that of the Pacific. The US, not being an Asian power, has therefore been using the term to legitimize its involvement in Asia, utilizing the 'Pacific' part of its identity (McDougall).

The broadest definition of Asia-Pacific would cover regions including the Pacific littorals of Northeast Asia, Southeast Asia, Oceania, North America and Latin America, conforming to that of the Asia-Pacific Economic Co-operation [APEC] (Hu). However, this paper operationalizes the Asia-Pacific to the area of responsibility under the US Department of State's Bureau of East Asian and Pacific Affairs for the purpose of delimitation, and also to differentiate it from the emerging geopolitical construct of the bigger and more inclusive Indo-Pacific region.

This delimitation is preferred since the subject of analysis, China's geopolitical behaviour, is with reference to the US rebalancing as strategized by the US Department of State (East Asian and Pacific Affairs). According to this demarcation, the Asia-Pacific region covers entire East Asia [consisting of Northeast and Southeast Asia] and Oceania, stretching from

China to French Polynesia and from Mongolia into New Zealand, and comprises of 38 nations and dependent territories.

The region is strategically significant because of its potential as well as its scale of impact on the world stage. On the political front, the region is home to several established and rising powers of international politics. Among these players, China is an acknowledged nuclear weapon power and a permanent member of the United Nations Security Council [UNSC], the momentous growth of which is treated with both admiration and apprehension globally. North Korea is the other nuclear weapon power in the region which has been treated as an international pariah. Japan, South Korea and Australia are the other major powers in the region which have significant role in both the regional and global affairs on their own, as well as based on their alliance with the US. Indonesia has a dominant clout in Southeast Asia and has emerged as a key driver of consensus building in the region.

The Association of Southeast Asian Nations (ASEAN) has emerged as the principal binding force in the Asia-Pacific, acting as a base for regional integration efforts in the Asia-Pacific. The region is also significant due to the ongoing 'power transition'—the power shift from the West to the East, and the corresponding 'recovery of Asia' (Nye). This is especially significant at a time when the Global Financial Crisis of 2007-08 has led to a relative decline in the global clout of the West, with respect to the Asia-Pacific economies. The region is also currently contributing to a quarter of the global defence spending (IHS Jane's).

On the economic front, the Asia-Pacific has emerged as the engine of the global economy, and is currently contributing to 40 percent of the world's economic growth (East Asia Pacific Economic Update). The region is home to economic giants like China and Japan which are the third and fourth largest economies, economic powerhouses like South Korea, Australia and Singapore, as well as emerging economies like

Indonesia, Thailand, Malaysia, Philippines and Vietnam (GDP ranking, PPP based). The region is home to one-third of the world's population and over one-quarter of the GDP (US Department of State). About a third of the global exports come from this region, and it also holds two-thirds of the global foreign exchange reserves (Cossa, Glosserman and McDevitt).

Being a geostrategic derivative of the geographic Western Pacific Basin, the region evidently has a dominantly maritime character. As a result, maritime security considerations weigh decisively in understanding the region's geopolitical significance. The region is home to one of the world's six most important chokepoints—the Strait of Malacca. [1] The Strait carries 40 percent of the global trade (Reuters) and 35 percent of global oil flow. With more than 50,000 merchant ships sailing through the strait, which at its narrowest part is only 2.7 km. wide, this perilous Strait undoubtedly has a bottleneck effect on maritime commerce (World Oil Transit Chokepoints). As the attention of the world shifts to the Asia-Pacific in context of the power transition, so does the need to secure the maritime interests of its growing stakeholders.

US Rebalancing Strategy in the Asia-Pacific

In the wake of World War II, the eminent American geo-strategist Nicholas Spykman identified the 'Rimland' region encompassing the Eurasian rim as having utmost importance in the practice of American geostrategy (Sempa). During the Cold War, this was heavily manifested in terms of the US efforts to contain the Soviet Union from Germany to the Korean peninsula. However, the US defeat in Vietnam led to its gradual strategic retreat from the Asia-Pacific region. In the first two decades of the post-Cold War era, the US efforts were dominantly utilized in dealing with the challenges emanating from the Western half of this Rimland, reflected in its military interventionism in the Balkans, Afghanistan and the Persian Gulf. However, the emerging significance of the Asia-Pacific has forced a shift in the American geostrategic calculus towards focussing on the relatively neglected eastern section of the Rimland.

An era of American interventionism characterized by the Presidency of George W. Bush during the first decade of the twenty-first century had led to the US being transfixed in its 'Global War on Terror' with the taxing military interventions in Afghanistan and Iraq. Whereas, rising global powers like China utilized this period of American distraction to establish its clout in the Asia-Pacific. [2] In order to shift its attention back to the increasingly significant Asia-Pacific and reasserting America's Pacific identity, the Presidency of Barack Obama decided to adopt a strategy of 'pivoting' to the region, after initiating a withdrawal from both the theatres (The White House).

The US decided to rebalance to the Asia-Pacific due to its recognition of certain key trends. The ongoing global power shift to the region means that the Asia-Pacific is turning into a dominant source of prospective threats and opportunities which would have critical implications for the US interests. The rapid emergence of China as a potential competitor to the US has meant that the latter would have to limit such a development by maintaining a strong strategic presence in China's backyard, which also coincides to be the Asia-Pacific. Moreover, the allies of the US like Japan directly experience the security dilemma arising from China's rise, a concern which needs to be reassured through strengthening the US alliance system. Evidently, the US does not want to surrender its global leadership role to any other power in the region. Moreover, as the Asia-Pacific is becoming a hub of the global economic activity, it becomes essential for the US to maintain and expand its economic interests in the region. As the US is trying to emerge from its economic downturn amidst debates on the relative decline of its global supremacy, it has become inevitable from its part to renew its engagement with this region.

The US has been implementing its rebalancing strategy

through various means. Primarily, the strategy demands a 'forward deployed' diplomacy (Clinton). [3] The US has been attempting to reinvigorate its existing alliance system in the Asia-Pacific and has also been forging renewed partnerships with countries outside its alliance system [4] like Indonesia, Malaysia, Vietnam and Singapore. The US has also been enhancing and widely dispersing its military deployments in the region as part of its 'pivot' policy. As part of this policy, the US has declared that it will redistribute its naval forces in such a way that the existing 50:50 percent split between the Pacific and the Atlantic will be transformed into a 60:40 split in favour of the Pacific by 2020 (US Department of State). [5] The US has also been actively engaging those regional countries who are uneasy with China's growing military might through basing, naval exercises, troop rotation and arms sales.

One of the first major steps in this regard was to begin rotation of US marines through Darwin, as announced by Obama during his historic visit to Australia (The White House). The US has been working on the 'Air-Sea Battle' concept since 2009 as one of its key military initiatives to project and sustain power in the global commons, in general, and to deter a rising China from challenging the US military might in the Asia-Pacific region, in particular. This concept seeks to counter China's efforts to deny the US access to the Western Pacific by striking the radar and long range precision missile facilities on the Chinese mainland using stealthy bombers and submarines (Air Sea Battle Office). [6]

The US has also been seeking to push forward its economic diplomacy in the region as part of its rebalancing strategy. One of the key initiatives in this respect has been the Trans-Pacific Partnership [TPP] regional free trade agreement. Negotiations on TPP have been ongoing among 12 nations in the Pacific Rim, out of which Australia, New Zealand, Brunei, Japan, Malaysia, Singapore and Vietnam are from the Asia-Pacific region (Office of the United States Trade Representative). This can be seen as a major attempt by the US to ensure its role in setting the economic compass of the region; a role which it fears might be taken over by China, who is absent from this grouping.

The use of 'pivot' has given way to 'rebalancing' during the second term of Obama's Presidency, when John Kerry became his Secretary of State, as the US has been trying to reassure Europe and the Middle East against the concern of neglect and China from the threat of containment (Liu). However, the strategy has been subjected to much criticism due to perceived ineffectiveness and lack of follow-up, as US is becoming further enmeshed in the Western rimland. The Syrian and Ukrainian crisis have majorly contributed to this distraction, as well as America's own polarized domestic politics and budget cuts which have been affecting its strategic plans. However, allegations about any apparent 'retreat' of the rebalancing strategy have been rejected by the US administration (Keck). There have also been official views which suggest that the US is broadening the region to Indo-Asia-Pacific, considering India's pivotal role (US Department of Defence). [7] Nevertheless, it can be inferred that the US rebalance strategy is in specific, intended to reconsolidate America's primacy in the world order, and in specific, to check China's challenge to this status quo.

China's Regional Stakes and Strategic Thinking on the Asia-Pacific

China has increasing stakes in the Asia-Pacific. The rebalance of the US to the Asia-Pacific has been fundamentally impacting the regional ambitions of China. The threat perceptions to China's regional stakes can be viewed through three prisms—core national interests, maritime shift and regional power status.

China's core national interests, [8] as articulated by the Chinese government in its White Paper on China's Peaceful Development, includes upholding state sovereignty, national security, territorial integrity and national reunification, China's political system established by the Constitution and overall social stability, and the basic safeguards for ensuring sustainable economic and social development (Information Office of the State Council, PRC). These are interests, which according to China, it will never compromise at any cost. Therefore, these can be seen as the red lines which set the limits of China's commitment to 'peaceful development'. When it comes to state sovereignty, national security, territorial integrity and national reunification, the Taiwan factor plays a dominant role. The Republic of China [ROC] or Taiwan, which exists as an entity separate from the PRC, is considered by China as a renegade province awaiting reunification.

The UN recognized the ROC as the sole representative of the Chinese nation until 1972, when this status and membership was switched to PRC. This international recognition of the PRC and the 'One-China principle' has still not resolved the bilateral/domestic issues across the Taiwan straits. In addition, China also remains suspicious of the US which has been following an ambiguous policy with respect to Taiwan. This has been due to the US keeping open the option of arms sales to the island, despite its formal recognition of the PRC and normalization of bilateral ties through the three communiqués in 1972, 1979 and 1982. [9] Any move by Taiwan to declare its independence will have a domino effect, whereby the separatist tendencies of other regions like Tibet, Xinjiang and Inner Mongolia may also be intensified. The latest inclusions to the core interests of China in the Asia-Pacific region have been the externally contested maritime territories over which it has made historically, yet non-legally backed claims. They include the South China Sea along with the Spratley and Paracel islands, which China has claimed under its 'nine-dotted lines', and parts of the East China Sea which has been disputed with Japan (The Times of India).

China's rise on the world stage has been triggered by the economic reforms unleashed by Deng Xiaoping in the late

1970s. This has led to the evolution of market economy system in China, the growth of which is dependent heavily on external trade. The bulk of this trade has been carried out through Pacific coast of China. Since a major chunk of China's exports are finished goods, the raw materials as well as the energy resources also use this maritime pathway to fuel China's export-led growth. This flow of raw materials, products and energy therefore is heavily reliant on the Sea Lanes of Communication [SLOCs] of the Asia-Pacific region. As a result, it is essential for China to protect and sustain the maritime shift which has shaped its present rising stature. China's interests are not only restricted to the trade routes, but also on the resources in the Asia-Pacific.

The maritime territories over which China has disputes with its neighbours have rich reserves of fossil fuels which could be useful to China due to the proximity of these territories. [10] China has already surpassed the US as the world's largest net importer of oil, driven by its economic scale and growth demands (Financial Times). China also has a growing demand for natural gas so as to offset its environmentally detrimental coal consumption. Even though the Asia-Pacific region contributes directly only 2 percent of China's oil imports and 53 percent of its natural gas imports, the sea lanes of the Pacific Ocean is the transit route for almost 90 percent and 95 percent of all its oil and natural gas imports, respectively (US Energy Information Administration). Similarly, all of China's seaborne trade is carried out through the Pacific Ocean, and the Asia-Pacific region contributes to a significant portion of its overall trade volume, housing a majority of its customer base. Hence, the maritime Asia-Pacific is the most vital region for ensuring China's economic rise.

China's historically dominant stature in the Asia-Pacific is one another important aspect which has been driving China's strategy in the region. China had sustained a tribute system in Asia through the centuries until the Western colonial system made inroads into the continent. In the Asia-Pacific, this system spanned from Japan to Indonesia. This tribute system, even though hierarchical based on the acceptance of China's primacy in the region, was not exploitative or violent, and was hence sustained for centuries (Kang). [11]

Geopolitically, this system ensured sufficient protection for China's Han heartland by keeping its neighbours in check in the region until the Western colonial powers altered this status quo. China would therefore like to re-establish its lost stature in the Asia-Pacific region, as it is intrinsically linked to its national identity. China's ongoing maritime shift in itself is reminiscent of its maritime propensities during the Ming dynasty when its treasure fleet under Admiral Zheng He ventured on historically unparalleled expeditions of maritime diplomacy (Yoshihara and Holmes). China's claim on the South China Sea and East China Sea has been based primarily on ancient historical claims, mirroring the level of importance China has been giving on its historical status. China's President Xi Jinping has projected the concept called the 'Chinese dream' of national rejuvenation (Xinhua News Agency) [12], which also reflects this aspiration to regain its lost geopolitical clout in the region. These historically rooted considerations, together with the present day strategic requirements are therefore strengthening the Chinese ambitions of re-establishing a Sino-centric, unipolar Asia (Ahn).

These considerations feed into the Chinese strategic thinking and thus affect the way China views and reacts to the US rebalancing strategy. These factors, therefore serve as conditioning agents which determine China's responses to the changes in its strategic environment in the Asia-Pacific. As a result, it is clear that the renewed interest of the US in the region will be seen by China to be as a highly potent geopolitical challenge, which needs to be surmounted in order to achieve not only its strategic ambitions, but also to ensure its national security.

China's Measured Responses

With an increased focus of the US towards the Asia-Pacific, its activities have been found to impact China's national security and interests in the region. As a result, China has articulated its response to the growing US presence in the Asia-Pacific region through various means using its growing military, diplomatic and economic resources.

Progressive Control of the Maritime Realm through Active Defence and A2/AD Strategies: Firstly, China is pursuing a strategy of steady and progressive control of the maritime realm. Ever since Admiral Liu Huaqing initiated the projection of the nation's naval forces in the 1980s, China has been attempting to gain command over the waters of the Western Pacific in a phased manner, based on two important geo-strategic constructs—the three seas and the two island chains.

China attempts to progressively take control over the near seas, the mid-far/middle seas, and finally the far seas. The first and second island chains stand as the barriers separating the three seas (Yoshihara and Holmes). The island chains simultaneously provide protection as well as act as constraints to the entry of foreign navy and the outward march of the Chinese navy, respectively. As a result, the three seas and the two island chains remain central to Chinese naval strategy in the Western Pacific, and therefore its military capability requirements. The American re-emphasis on the Asia-Pacific provides China with an increased necessity to push forward its naval strategy with more zeal.

China's responses with respect to its naval capabilities have been based on the concept of 'active defence' whereby offensive means have been utilized for defensive ends. The 'Anti-Access/Area-Denial (A2/AD)' strategy is the manifestation of this strategy in the Western Pacific. By this means, China has been trying to deny the US carrier fleet access to the Western Pacific, so as to ultimately keep it out of bounds of the second island chain, thereby securing the near and middle seas. China's naval vessels spearhead the offensive element in this game plan as a sword, while the missile forces secure the defences across the island chains as a shield. The aircraft carriers and stealth based airpower serve to neutralize the forward deployed bases of the US in the Western Pacific, while the conventional as well as nuclear submarine forces penetrate the island chains.

China currently has only one aircraft carrier in operation, the refurbished Soviet/Ukrainian 'Varyag', which was renamed as the 'Liaoning' and commissioned in 2012. China is also working on its second aircraft carrier and two more are supposed to follow in the near future (Reuters). In addition, China is supposedly building the world's largest submarine base at the Yalong Bay in China's Hainan Island (Want China Times).

This is especially important since China's Jin class ballistic missile nuclear submarines are reportedly capable of carrying the JL-2 Inter-Continental Ballistic Missile, which has a range of 7,400 km. Three Jin class submarines have already been delivered to the People's Liberation Army Navy and two more are under construction, and the JL-2 has apparently attained initial operational capability. The Anti-Ship Ballistic Missile of China, the DF-21D, is supposed to have a range exceeding 1,500 km., and therefore serves to secure the area up to the second island chain by keeping it out of bounds for the US Carrier Strike Groups. To offset the Ballistic Missile Defence systems of the US in the region, China has also been developing the required countermeasures (Office of the Secretary of Defense, US).

China uses not only its naval and missile forces, but also its space and cyber prowess to neutralize any American-led offensive action in the near and middle seas against it. China has deployed a constellation of ocean monitoring satellites as well as other high resolution reconnaissance satellites with capabilities such as Synthetic Aperture Radar for keeping an eye on the Western Pacific. The Yaogan series of reconnaissance satellites have been assumed to be of dedicated military use, as their orbital configurations and payloads have been speculated to be directly contributing towards the A2/AD strategy (Chandrashekar, Ganesh and Raghunath).

China is expected to further increase the fleet of such satellites in the near future, so as to ensure its surveillance capabilities in the region. Apart from these, increasing number of communication transponders and the indigenous satellite navigation systems, the Beidou series, which went operational across the Asia-Pacific in 2013 has bolstered China's strategic independence and capabilities in the region (South China Morning Post). China's developments in the field of anti-satellite technology, as demonstrated by its test in 2007 also add to China's regional deterrence posture with respect to the US (Office of the Secretary of Defense, US).

The discovery of the existence of a highly organized cyber-espionage unit in 2013 [13] has confirmed the growing focus of China in cyber-warfare (New York Times). The threat of strategic communication being compromised in crisis situations through cyber attacks also presents a grave challenge to the American strategy in the region. Thus, through a combined use of offensive and defensive deployments, China strategizes to keep itself secure from the US advances in the Western Pacific as part of its rebalancing strategy in the Asia-Pacific.

Diplomatic Posturing towards Regional Players: Along with military deployments, China has also been posturing diplomatically with respect to the US as well as other regional players. China's new leadership, under Xi, has proposed a "new model of major country relationship" with the US, based on the principles of non-confrontation, mutual respect and win-win cooperation. This seems to be a move towards normalization of the ties between the two powers, which have been much disturbed after the US initiated its rebalance strategy. This change in bilateral relations came up due to the geopolitical necessities faced by both the nations, as well as a change in leadership in Beijing.

On the one hand, China has become extremely wary of the perception that it is being subject to a US-led strategy of containment, through the latter's allies and partners in the Asia-Pacific region. Therefore, as the security atmosphere becomes more tense, a major part of China's response necessitates keeping lines of communication open with the US, and re-emphasising the red lines in the Asia-Pacific. On the other hand, the US had economically been under strain since 2008, and has also been militarily stretched due to its prolonged engagement with the centre of the rimland, including Afghanistan, Iraq, Libya and Syria. This had made it relatively less capable of keeping up with the expectations of its allies and partners in the East. As an outcome of this renewed bilateral diplomatic engagement, the US invited China to join the TPP negotiations from which it had so far been excluded, as well as the Rim of the Pacific [RIMPAC] naval exercise for the first time (Zongze).

China's primary trepidation about the rebalancing strategy of the US comes from the fact that it involves the strengthening of alliances and partnerships of its neighbours with America. China is involved in bitter maritime territorial disputes with Japan, the Philippines and Vietnam, and the increased profile of the US in this picture shifts the power balance against China's favour. Perceiving this shift of balance, China has augmented its military coercion and diplomatic attraction in a two-pronged approach. China has heightened the aggressiveness on its stand on the South and East China Sea. On the East China Sea, it has established an Air Defence Identification Zone (ADIZ) [14] over the disputed waters and islands with Japan.

Even though the US and its allies—Japan and South Korea initially attempted at testing China's resolve on the ADIZ, they seem to have toed China's line later, as the US asked its airlines to comply with the ADIZ (The Hindu). China has also been utilizing its historical victimization under Japanese aggression as a tool against a nationalistic renewal in Japan led by Prime Minister Shinzo Abe. Events like Abe's visit of the Yasukuni shrine has been much publicized by China in the international scene as an act of defiance against the post-War (World War II) status quo. China has been utilizing this to mobilize international public opinion against Japan, especially keeping in mind the US, which has been the leading stakeholder of the post-War order. China has also been mindful in wooing the fellow victim of Imperial Japanese aggression, South Korea, with this act. China also maintains its control as well as its role as a point of contact between North Korea as a strategic advantage that it has in North East Asia.

In the South China Sea, China has extended its administration over the island territories as well as the fisheries zone. In 2012, China raised the administrative status of the South China Sea islands from county level to prefectural level (Global Times). Later, in 2014, China stepped up its control over the South China Sea waters by requiring foreign fishing vessels to obtain approval from the Hainan provincial government before operating in the area (Kardon). China thus seems to have taken valuable lessons from the Japanese strategy over the disputed Diaoyu islands and implemented them in the South China Sea to gain legitimacy over the territory. Japan has offset its weak historical claim with strong administrative claims, which China appears to cultivate in the South China Sea, supplementing its long standing historical claims. China has also been stepping up its use of force in clashes with both Vietnam and Philippines over the disputed areas.

Simultaneously, China has also shown a readiness to break from its adamant stand on bilateralism and against multilateralism in the resolution of the maritime territorial disputes in the South China Sea. China has suggested in 2013 that it will work with the Association of South East Asian Nations (ASEAN) countries to come up with a Code of Conduct (CoC) in the South China Sea (Ministry of Foreign

Affairs, PRC). However, efforts are yet to match up to words, and as a result, the offer stands only at the realm of rhetoric without translating into reality. China's strategy behind this may be to buy sufficient time for effectively strengthening its hold over its infamous 'nine-dashed line' claim over the South China Sea, through a policy of legitimacy through sustained occupation.

China has also initiated a mechanism whereby the economies of the Asia-Pacific can be linked with its reminiscent of the Sino-centric era in the region's history. The ancient maritime Silk Road, which was the main maritime artery for trade, commerce and cultural exchanges in the region has been reintroduced in the contemporary era by China under the initiative, the "21st Century Maritime Silk Road". [15] With this initiative, China appears to seek the reclamation of its centuries' old clout in the region, as well as deal with the rebalance strategy of the US by wooing the countries of the region towards its economic bandwagon.

Conclusion

The US had retreated from the Asia-Pacific region after facilitating China's rise in the region, and is now attempting a return to the region to keep a check on what it helped evolve. The US retreated from the region in the late 1970s with an understanding struck with China on preventing any efforts for regional hegemony from either side. America has, however, come to realize that China's rise has far exceeded its expectations to the point where it can challenge the US efforts to dominate the Asia-Pacific, which is fast becoming the key holder for global pre-eminence. Therefore, the rebalancing strategy of the US and the responses from China is situated in the context of a geopolitical game or a struggle for supremacy in the Asia-Pacific.

As a result of the US act of rebalance towards the Asia-Pacific, a major trend which can be observed is the intensification of China's efforts to gain and sustain its foothold in the region. The US rebalance strategy has definitely emboldened countries like Japan, Vietnam and the Philippines to strengthen their stand against China's regional assertion. As a result, it can be argued to have helped China to pursue its strategic ambitions with more vigour, as seen by its emerging two pronged policy of enhanced military assertion and diplomatic engagement. China's shift from a strategic culture which emphasized hiding strength and biding time has become all the more visible in the past few years, one which has become a necessity with the evolving US rebalancing strategy. At the same time, it has also been seen that the geopolitical and geo-economic constraints of China and the US have been forcing them to seek out compromises and coexistence in the Asia-Pacific region.

Endnotes

1. The others five important chokepoints are the Panama Canal, Danish Straits, Turkish Straits, Suez Canal, Bab el-Mandab and Strait of Hormuz. For more details, see,
   http://in.reuters.com/article/2010/03/04/idINIndia-46652220100304.

2. The US troop deployment in the Asia-Pacific region peaked at 800,000 during the Vietnam War, after which it gradually dropped until it touched a nadir of under 100,000 during the Presidency of George W. Bush. For more details, see,
   http://www.atimes.com/atimes/World/WOR-01-300114.html.

3. The former US Secretary of State, Hilary Clinton, who served during the first term of the Obama administration, has identified six key lines of action for the rebalancing strategy in her famous 2011 article, *America's Pacific Century,* in the Foreign Policy Magazine: strengthening bilateral security alliances; deepening working relationships with emerging powers, including with China; engaging with regional multilateral institutions; expanding trade and investment; forging a broad-based military presence; and advancing democracy and human rights. For more details, see,
   http://www.foreignpolicy.com/articles/2011/10/11/americas_pacific_century.

4. The US allies in the Asia-Pacific include Japan, South Korea,

Australia, Thailand and the Philippines.

5. This additional 10 percent naval deployment of the US to the Pacific will lead to the positioning of a total of six aircraft carriers, a majority of its cruisers, destroyers, Littoral Combat Ships, and submarines in the Asia-Pacific. The declaration was made by Leon Panetta, the Former US Secretary of Defence during the Shangri-La Security Dialogue at Singapore on June 2, 2012. For more details, see,
http://www.defense.gov/speeches/speech.aspx?speechid=1681

6. The Air-Sea Battle concept envisions *disrupting* the C4ISR networks of the adversary using cross-domain (air, sea, land, space and cyberspace) operations to gain decision advantage, destroying the enemy capabilities using air, land and naval operations to regain freedom of action, and defeating the adversary's weapons using force projection through denied zones to sustain offensive operations. For more details, see,
http://www.defense.gov/pubs/ASB-ConceptImplementation-Summary-May-2013.pdf.

7. The term 'Indo-Asia-Pacific' was first used by Samuel J. Locklear, the Commander of the US Pacific Command in an address to the U.S. Indonesia Society in Jakarta on February 8, 2013. For more details, see,
http://www.defense.gov/news/newsarticle.aspx?id=119243.

8. The first mention of China's core interests was in July 2009 by the then Chinese State Councillor Dai Bingguo during the first round of the China-U.S. Strategic and Economic Dialogue. For more details, see,
http://www.china.org.cn/world/2013-08/26/content_29824049.htm.

9. The Taiwan Relations Act of 1979 which promised to provide Taiwan with arms of a defensive character and the 'six assurances' listed below which the US gave to Taiwan in 1982, have been the basis of this ambiguity:

- The United States would not set a date for termination of arms sales to Taiwan.

- The United States would not alter the terms of the Taiwan Relations Act.

- The United States would not consult with China in advance before making decisions about U.S. arms sales to Taiwan.

- The United States would not mediate between Taiwan and

China.

- The United States would not alter its position about the sovereignty of Taiwan which was, that the question was one to be decided peacefully by the Chinese themselves, and would not pressure Taiwan to enter into negotiations with China.
- The United States would not formally recognize Chinese sovereignty over Taiwan.
  The US has also not sold advanced fighter jets to Taiwan since the past two decades. For more details, see,
  http://thediplomat.com/2014/01/why-the-us-will-not-sell-advanced-fighters-to-taiwan.

10. The US Energy Information Agency (EIA) estimates that the East China Sea has between 60 and 100 million barrels of oil (mmbbl) in proven and probable reserves and between 1 and 2 trillion cubic feet (Tcf) in proven and probable natural gas reserves. For more details, see,
    http://www.eia.gov/countries/regions-topics.cfm?fips=ecs.
    The EIA also estimates that the South China Sea contains approximately 11 billion barrels of oil and 190 trillion cubic feet of natural gas in proved and probable reserves. For more details, see, http://www.eia.gov/countries/regions-topics.cfm?fips=scs.

11. This hegemonic system was constructed through the propagation of Chinese cultural superiority and the attractive powers of Confucian ideas and materialistic benefits and not through coercive force. The relative hierarchical status of the tributary states depended on the similarity of these tributary states to China and not on relative power considerations. For more, see, David C. Kang's 2010 article on "Hierarchy and Legitimacy in International Systems: The Tribute System in Early Modern East Asia", available at:
    http://www.tandfonline.com/doi/abs/10.1080/09636412.2010.52
    4079#.U0VFXHQndZM.

12. Xi Jinping, after taking charge as the General Secretary of the Communist Party of China, has spearheaded the notion of the 'Chinese dream'. The concept was introduced by him during his visit to an exhibition at the National Museum of China in Beijing, where he pledged to realize the "great renewal of the Chinese nation". For more details, see,
    http://news.xinhuanet.com/english/china/2012-
    11/29/c_132008231.htm.

13. In 2013, Mandiant, an American computer security firm exposed the existence of P.L.A. Unit 61398, which has been conducting cyber-espionage on American corporations, organizations and government agencies, through a report. For more details, see, http://www.mandiant.com/apt1.

14. An ADIZ is a publicly defined area extending beyond national territory in which unidentified aircraft are liable to be interrogated and, if necessary, intercepted for identification before they cross into sovereign airspace. Apart from China, countries like include India, Japan, Norway, Pakistan, South Korea, Taiwan, and the United Kingdom have established their ADIZs. For more details, see,
http://www.foreignaffairs.com/articles/140367/david-a-welch/whats-an-adiz.

15. The development of a 21st century maritime Silk Road was proposed by Xi Jinping in his speech to the Indonesian parliament at Jakarta in October 2013. The proposal involves resurrection of the historic trade route in the 21st century which would bolster China's economic and cultural ties with the maritime nations of South and Southeast Asia. For more details, see,
http://www.chinadaily.com.cn/china/2013xiapec/2013-10/04/content_17008913.htm.

References

Ahn, Byung-joon (2012), "China's Search for Grand Strategy after the Cold War", *The Korean Social Science Journal.*

Air Sea Battle Office (2013), "Air-Sea Battle", May, available at: http://www.defense.gov/pubs/ASB-ConceptImplementation-Summary-May-2013.pdf.

Chandrashekar, S., et al. (2011), "China's Anti-Ship Ballistic Missile: Game Changer in the Asia-Pacific", Bangalore: National Institute of Advances Studies.

Clinton, Hilary (2011), "America's Pacific Century", October 11, *Foreign Policy,* available at: http://www.foreignpolicy.com/articles/2011/10/11/americas_pac ific_century.

Cossa, Ralph A., et al. (2009), "The United States and the Asia-Pacific Region: Security Strategy for the Obama Administration", Washington, D.C.: Center for a New American

Security, available at:
http://csis.org/files/media/csis/pubs/issuesinsights_v09n01.pdf.
"East Asia Pacific Economic Update" (2013), October, World Bank, available at:
http://www.worldbank.org/en/news/press-release/2013/10/07/developing-east-asia-slows-but-continues-to-lead-global-growth-7-1-percent-2013.
"East Asian and Pacific Affairs", n.d., US Department of State, available at:
http://www.state.gov/p/eap/ci/index.htm.
Financial Times (2013), "China Tops US as Leading Net Oil Importer", October 8, available at:
http://www.ft.com/intl/cms/s/0/4aef8e74-3062-11e3-9eec-00144feab7de.html#axzz2yYX1OHRz.
"GDP Ranking 2012" (2013), December 8, World Bank, available at:
http://data.worldbank.org/data-catalog/GDP-ranking-table.
"GDP Ranking, PPP-based" (2013), December 18, World Bank, available at:
http://data.worldbank.org/data-catalog/GDP-PPP-based-table.
Global Times (2012), "China Raises Administrative Status of South China Sea Islands", June 21, available at:
http://www.globaltimes.cn/content/716392.shtml.
Hu, Richard Weixing (2009), "Building Asia-Pacific Security Architecture: The Challenge of Hybrid Regionalism", Washington, D.C.: The Brookings Institution, available at:
http://www.brookings.edu/research/papers/2009/07/asia-pacific-hu.
IHS Jane's (2014), "Global Defence Budgets Overall to Rise for First Time in Five Years", February 4, available at:
http://press.ihs.com/press-release/aerospace-defense-terrorism/global-defence-budgets-overall-rise-first-time-five-years.
Information Office of the State Council, PRC (2011), "White Paper on China's Peaceful Development", available at:
http://english.gov.cn/official/2011-09/06/content_1941354.htm.
Kang, David C. (2010), "Hierarchy and Legitimacy in International Systems: The Tribute System in Early Modern East Asia", *Security Studies*.
Kardon, Isaac (2014), "Hainan Revises Fishing Regulations in South China Sea: New Language, Old Ambiguities", *China Brief,*

14(2), available at:
http://www.jamestown.org/programs/chinabrief/single/?tx_ttnew
s%5Btt_news%5D=41836&tx_ttnews%5BbackPid%5D=25&c
Hash=92ea9a23748ea174f7a3d452a9c44770#.UuXMHNIVHc.

Keck, Zachary (2014), "US Swears Asia Pivot Isn't Dead", April 2, available at:
http://thediplomat.com/2014/04/us-swears-asia-pivot-isnt-dead.

Liu, Wen (2013), "From Pivot to Rebalance: The Weight of Words in US Asia Policy", March 22, available at:
http://contextchina.com/2013/03/from-pivot-to-rebalance-the-weight-of-words-in-u-s-asia-policy.

McDougall, Derek (2007), "Asia-Pacific in World Politics", Boulder: Lynne Reinner Publishers.

Ministry of Foreign Affairs, PRC (2013), "Foreign Minister Wang Yi On Process of Code of Conduct in the South China Sea", August 5, available at:
http://www.fmprc.gov.cn/mfa_eng/wjb_663304/wjbz_663308/a
ctivities_663312/t1064869.shtml.

New York Times (2013), "Chinese Army Unit is Seen as Tied to Hacking Against U.S.", February 18, available at:
http://www.nytimes.com/2013/02/19/technology/chinas-army-is-seen-as-tied-to-hacking-against-us.html?pagewanted=all.

Nye, Jr., Joseph S., "Understanding 21st Century Power Shifts", n.d., available at:
http://www.worldfinancialreview.com/?p=1128.

Office of the Secretary of Defense, USA (2014), "Annual Report: Military and Security Developments Involving the People's Republic of China 2014", available at:
http://www.defense.gov/pubs/2014_DoD_China_Report.pdf.

Office of the United States Trade Representative, "Trans-Pacific Partnership (TPP)", n.d., available at:
http://www.ustr.gov/tpp.

Osawa, Jun (2013), "China's ADIZ over the East China Sea: A Great Wall in the Sky?", December 17, available at:
http://www.brookings.edu/research/opinions/2013/12/17-china-air-defense-identification-zone-osawa.

Reuters (2014), "China Building Second Aircraft Carrier: Reports", January 18, available at:
http://www.reuters.com/article/2014/01/19/us-china-carrier-idUSBREA0I02C20140119.

—"Factbox: Malacca Strait is a Strategic Chokepoint" (2010), April 4, available at:
http://in.reuters.com/article/2010/03/04/idININdia-46652220100304.

Sempa, Francis P. (2006), "Spykman's World", April, *American Diplomacy,* available at:
http://www.unc.edu/depts/diplomat/item/2006/0406/semp/sempa_spykman.html.

South China Morning Post (2013), "China's Beidou Navigation System Ccompletely Open for Asian Neighbours, official says", Hong Kong, December 27, available at:
http://www.scmp.com/lifestyle/technology/article/1390989/chinas-beidou-navigation-system-completely-open-asian.

The Hindu (2013), "U.S. Rejects China ADIZ, But Asks Airlines to Comply", November 30, available at:
http://www.thehindu.com/news/international/world/us-rejects-china-adiz-but-asks-airlines-to-comply/article5407816.ece.

The Times of India (2013), "China's Expanding Core Interests", May 11, available at:
http://timesofindia.indiatimes.com/home/opinion/edit-page/Chinas-expanding-core-interests/articleshow/19992246.cms.

The White House (2013), "Remarks by President Obama and President Xi Jinping of the People's Republic of China Before Bilateral Meeting", June 7, available at:
http://www.whitehouse.gov/the-press-office/2013/06/07/remarks-president-obama-and-president-xi-jinping-peoples-republic-china-.

—"Remarks by President Obama and Prime Minister Gillard of Australia in Joint Press Conference" (2011), November 16, available at:
http://www.whitehouse.gov/the-press-office/2011/11/16/remarks-president-obama-and-prime-minister-gillard-australia-joint-press.

—"Remarks By President Obama to the Australian Parliament" (2011), November 17, available at:
http://www.whitehouse.gov/the-press-office/2011/11/17/remarks-president-obama-australian-parliament.

US Department of Defence (2009), "Locklear Calls for Indo-Asia-

Pacific Cooperation", February 8, available at:
http://www.defense.gov/news/newsarticle.aspx?id=119243.

US Department of State (2012), "Secretary of Defence Speech: Shangri La Security Dialogue", June 2, available at:
http://www.defense.gov/speeches/speech.aspx?speechid=1681.

—"The East Asia-Pacific Rebalance: Expanding U.S. Engagement" (2013), December 16, available at:
http://www.state.gov/r/pa/pl/2013/218776.htm.

US Energy Information Administration (2014), "China", February 4, available at:
http://www.eia.gov/countries/cab.cfm?fips=ch.

Want China Times (2014), "Hainan's Yalong Bay: China's New Nuclear Submarine Base", February 18, available at:
http://www.wantchinatimes.com/news-subclass-cnt.aspx?id=20140218000017&cid=1101.

"World Oil Transit Chokepoints" (2012), August 22, US Energy Information Administration, available at:
http://www.eia.gov/countries/regions-topics.cfm?fips=wotc&trk=p3.

Xinhua News Agency (2012), "Xi Pledges Great Renewal of Chinese Nation", November 29, available at:
http://news.xinhuanet.com/english/china/2012-11/29/c_132008231.htm.

Yoshihara, Toshi and James R. Holmes (2010), "Red Star over The Pacific", Annapolis: Naval Institute Press.

Zongze, Ruan (2013), "A New Model of Major-Country Relations: The New Driving Force Behind China-US Relations", December 24, available at:
http://www.chinausfocus.com/foreign-policy/a-new-model-of-major-country-relations-the-new-driving-force-behind-china-us-relations.

4

U.S. Rebalance in Asia

Venkat Lokanathan

The Obama Administration's renewed emphasis on the Asia-Pacific region was officially pronounced when he addressed the Australian Parliament on November 17, 2011. President Obama for the first time announced his "deliberate and strategic decision" to designate the Asia-Pacific region as "a top priority" and the US would play "a larger and long-term role" in shaping the Asia-Pacific region. Earlier in the same month, Secretary of State Clinton in her article in *Foreign Policy* titled 'America's Pacific Century', called for America's foreign policy to "pivot" to the Asia-Pacific. She stated that the "future of politics will be decided in Asia, not Afghanistan or Iraq and the US will be right at the centre of the action". She detailed on US plans to strengthen its military presence in the region. She succinctly observed that it is the US which "maintains peace and security, defends freedom of navigation and ensures transparency".

Secretary Clinton emphasised the importance of the Asia-Pacific's economic development, trade routes, resources and investment opportunities for the US. The Asia-Pacific's "remarkable economic growth and potential for continued growth", she wrote, "depends on the security and stability that has long been guaranteed by the US military" whose presence has to be further strengthened. Likewise, most of the strategic documents crafted by the Department of Defense resonate by positing that the US defense policy and prioritization will "of necessity rebalance towards the Asia-Pacific".

Strategic Importance of the Asia-Pacific

The announcement of the US rebalance in Asia-Pacific has

revolved around three important fundamentals, namely: (a) An emerging Asia-Pacific as the playground of the great game; (b) Transitioning of the American strategic lenses from Europe to Asia-Pacific; and (c) The rise of China and its attendant implications. In this context, India, through its Look East policy has emerged as an important player in the region. Recent developments in the region throw up important questions that need to be studied and analysed in a detailed manner.

Is the Obama pivot to Asia the first pronouncement of intent by the United States to increase its strategic influence in the region? No. The United States is integrated with the Asia-Pacific region at multiple levels. No other developed country, with the possible exception of Canada, has such strong societal connections with the Asia-Pacific region.

Thus, Obama's rebalance to Asia is not a story of US disengagement and then re-engagement in Asia. Instead, it seems more like a matter of emphasis and priority that the US holds towards Asia. Thus, a close look on the past relations between US and Asia helps in understanding that Obama administration has built on an elaborate foundation of already existing US-Asia relations.

From its earliest days, the United States has been deeply involved in Asia. In 1784, the Empress of China left New York harbour, sailing east to China and arriving in Macau. It returned to the United States carrying a consignment of Chinese goods that generated a profit of US$ 30,000. In 1835, 13 years before the United States even had a 'west coast', the US Navy East India Squadron was established which marked the beginning of continued US military presence in the Western Pacific. In 1844, China granted the United States trading rights through the Treaty of Wanghia. After making an unsuccessful attempt to negotiate a trade agreement with Japan in 1846, Commodore Matthew C. Perry concluded the Treaty of Kanagawa, which opened Japanese markets to the US goods and provided protection for shipwrecked American sailors a decade later (Cossa, et al., 2009). It also included provisions for a coaling station for US steam ships sailing the great circle route from San Francisco to China's Pearl River delta, which later became America's first Asian base. In 1898, Guam and the Philippines were ceded to the United States after the Spanish-American War.

Over the course of its relations with East Asia, the United States has adopted multiple approaches to protect and advance its interests. The Open Door Policy (1899-1900) was a US initiative for the protection of equal privileges among countries trading with China and in support of Chinese territorial and administrative integrity. President Theodore Roosevelt worked to balance imperial Russia's efforts to develop an exclusive sphere of influence in Northern China by aligning the United States with Japan during the Russo-Japanese war. At the Washington Conference of 1920, the United States supported multilateral efforts to preserve the post-War status quo in the Asia-Pacific region and ensure the territorial integrity of China through great power cooperation. Multilateralism failed in this instance, since the agreements had no provisions for action other than to consult.

Asia-Pacific in the American Cold War Calculus

Since the Pearl Harbour attack on America by Japanese forces in December, 1941, maintaining a balance in the Asia-Pacific has been a part of US foreign and defence policy. Dr. Brahma Chellaney has pertinently observed that, after the Pearl Harbour attack, "United States clearly signalled that American security begins not off the coast of California but at the western rim of the Pacific Ocean and beyond". The United States signed a security treaty with Japan and South Korea after the Second World War and established close ties with Taiwan. From here onwards, the United States felt it was essential to remain strategically engaged in Asia-Pacific affairs. Following the Second World War and throughout the Cold War, the United States relied on a series of bilateral alliances with Japan, the Republic of Korea, Australia, New Zealand, the Philippines, Thailand and the Republic of China to help secure its interests in the Asia-Pacific region.

Although New Zealand was kept out of the Australia-New Zealand-United States Security Treaty (ANZUS) since the mid-1980s, the rest of this alliance structure has essentially remained in place and continues to serve as the foundation for US security strategy in Asia. There is no doubt that Europe, being the immediate neighbourhood of the Soviet Union, occupied a bigger priority during the Cold War as witnessed through the Marshall Plan.

However, the US had been deeply engaged in the Asia-Pacific region for more than two centuries to pursue their enduring national interests. Its alliance with Japan; intervention on behalf of South Korea in the Korean war; signing the SEATO agreement; its active support for Taiwan; the involvement in the Vietnam War; its attempt at rapprochement with China; the tacit understanding with China to disintegrate the Soviet Union; and their subsequent cooperation against the Soviet occupation in Afghanistan clearly established that Asia was also an active playground for the US. Asian friends and allies were seen as critical to the success of America's global strategy in many respects. Therefore, US sought the cooperation with these allies as necessary to deter potential threats, counter regional aggression, ensure regional peace, monitor attempts at proliferation of weapons of mass destruction, and help protect sea lanes of communication both within the region and from the region to the Indian Ocean and Persian Gulf. Thus, the US has a long standing history of constructive engagement in the Asia-Pacific region.

Asia-Pacific Post-Cold War

The Asia-Pacific region continued to assume importance in the American strategic calculus post-Cold War. The centrality of the alliances and the broader strategy aimed at sustaining and enhancing them was outlined by the United

States in the immediate post-Cold War era by a series of East Asia strategy reports. The first report in 1990 made the case for a continued US commitment to the Asia-Pacific region and a continued military presence, even though reduced, as it witnessed the slow collapse of the Soviet Union. It explained the need for burden sharing and laid out a phased reduction in overseas deployment levels—a similar but much more substantial redeployment was being implemented in Europe as the demise of the Soviet threat in 1990-91 made it a lesser priority for the US. The second report, in 1992, assessed the progress to date in the readjustment of the US presence and explained how those changes matched the post-Cold War security environment.

While the 1990-1992 reports were released by the White House, the two Clinton-era reports were issued by the Department of Defense. The third report, in 1995, was designed to reassure friends and allies in the region that the US commitment to Asia remained solid. Its key message was that the United States would maintain the presence of 100,000 military service personnel in the region. Another notable feature was the recognition of the potential significance of new multilateral security initiatives in the region with the Clinton administration announcing a "New Pacific Community Initiative", in 1993, thus elevating the importance of the Asia-Pacific Economic Cooperation (APEC), a forum for promoting trade and good economic relations in the region. In 1995, President Clinton announced the normalization of relations with Vietnam and promised to welcome China's president to Washington and to energize negotiations leading to China's accession to the World Trade Organization (WTO).

The fourth report, in 1998, aimed to serve as a document of transparency at a time when there were fears of increasing militarization of the region. Therefore, the US intended to set an example and make its intentions and objectives crystal clear. The document reaffirmed the 1995 commitment to maintain 100,000 troops in the region. Like the 1992 report, it assessed the progress made in implementing the policies of its predecessor and explained how those adjustments fit the evolving security environment. The 1998 strategy report not only focused on the US presence, but also underscored US readiness to engage Asian nations across a range of security concerns. The United States tried to engage closely with China with the Chinese President visiting Washington in 1998 and subsequently China joining the WTO in 2001.

The United States endorsed the new Association of Southeast Asian Nations (ASEAN), Regional Forum (ARF) and other security dialogues, and made the case for security engagement on both bilateral and multilateral levels. More recently, Asia's vast oceans with immense potential for exploiting natural resources have also led to increasing maritime competition. Additionally, China, India and the US are making serious efforts to secure the sea lanes of communication with the presence of important straits including Malacca, Lombok and Sunda, in and around the region. Most of the world trade passes under the sea lanes of these straits. These are also vital sea lines of communication for the United States and its allies, partners, and friends. The world's six largest ports, both container and cargo, are in Asia. According to the official estimates about 60 percent of the US exports are to feed the hungry growing economies of Asia-Pacific. Asia is also seen as a battleground for ideological hegemony with the battle for democracy likely to continue in the future with a wider range of successful development models jostling for supremacy.

The US felt the need to have such comprehensive policies because by 1996 the East Asian region, propelled by dynamic economic growth, had become the centre of world power. It was growing faster than any other region of the world, expanding at 7.5 percent per annum between 1974 and 1993. As a result, East Asia became a primary source of new global output. It led the world in rates of savings and investment, and trade expanded enormously. The region's economic performance had been so robust that many observers, including the World Bank used adjectives such as 'path breaking' and 'miraculous' to describe the economic transformation.

Subsequently, this region, post-Cold War, has been the productive motor of the global economy, whether it was the Asian Tiger economies in the early 1990s or India and China over the last decade. 61 percent of the world's total population resides in the Asia-Pacific region. In this regard, India's former Ambassador to the United States, Nirupama Rao, in a speech, observed that, "according to the IMF, over the last three decades, Asia's share of global GDP grew from 10 percent to 30 percent, its standard of living rose six times, and half a billion people were brought out of poverty. In the last decade alone, emerging Asia has grown by an average annual rate of over 7 percent".

Asian governments and government controlled institutions hold about two-thirds of the world's US$ 6 trillion-plus foreign exchange reserves. Simultaneously, the American economy has been on a slump for the better part since the turn of the century. The global recession of 2008-2009 also did not majorly affect the Asian countries. The recession saw the world's major economies experiencing a slowdown in their economy, while many Asian countries still managed to have a double digit growth. The United States sees the economic potential in Asia as a wonderful opportunity to revitalise its own economy. This also fits perfectly into the capitalist mode of decision-making in the US.

Over the past four decades, the interest in multilateral cooperation and cooperative security has flourished in the Asia-Pacific. This trend has been led by the 10 Southeast Asian nations that comprise ASEAN, which was formed in 1967. South Asia has the eight-nation South Asian Association for Regional Cooperation (SAARC), the Pacific Islands have their 16-nation Pacific Island Forum (PIF), and most Central Asian nations along with China and Russia are members of the

Shanghai Cooperation Organization (SCO). Hence, this region is acting as a foundation for a range of new institutional innovations taking root.

Crucially, China has joined these associations and since then such multilateral forums have become a major diplomatic tool in Beijing's relations with its Asian neighbours. Although, the US has been playing a leading role in ASEAN initiatives, APEC Leaders' Meeting and other institutional initiatives like the Asian Regional Forum, ASEAN plus Three, and the East Asia Summit, it does not wish to be left out of the region's economic activities. Therefore, US's economic interests and its willingness to be a part of this emerging web of prosperity has pushed the Americans to strengthen the regional architecture and build relations with ASEAN. In the near future, much of the competition for influence will be played out on the terrain of access and who gets membership in which institutions.

American interests in the region were mutually-reinforcing: security is necessary for economic growth; security and growth make it more likely that human rights will be honoured and democracy will emerge; and democratization makes international conflict less likely because democracies are unlikely to fight one another. The United States in its 'National Security Strategy of Engagement and Enlargement' published in July 1994 emphasized on enlarging the community of market democracies while deterring and containing a range of threats to their nation, their allies and their interests. Focusing on new threats and new opportunities, its central goals were: to enhance security by maintaining a strong defense capability and promoting cooperative security measures; to open foreign markets for global economic growth; and to promote democracy abroad.

In accordance with the National Security Strategy, this document explains US defense policy toward furthering these goals in the Asia-Pacific region. The Strategy emphasized on maintaining a strong defense capability to enhance US security and to provide a foundation for regional stability through mutually beneficial security partnerships. The regional security strategy emphasized upon strengthening bilateral alliances which were at the heart of US strategy towards Asia for many decades. The United States expressed its commitment to contribute to regional security through active participation in new multilateral forums like the ASEAN Regional Forum. Through such multilateral mechanisms the countries of the region sought to develop new cooperative approaches to achieve greater stability and security.

The US continued to build on the already existing objectives in the Asia-Pacific region. It further strengthened its alliance with Japan through the April 1996 Joint Security Declaration and subsequently revised the Guidelines for US-Japan Defense Cooperation in September 1997. Further, it reaffirmed its security alliance with Australia through the 1996 Joint Security Declaration (Sydney Statement) pledging mutual cooperation on regional and global security concerns.

The United States is also apprehensive about four potential nuclear conflicts in Asia between Israel and Iran; India and Pakistan; India and China and North and South Korea. Additionally, any conflict between China and its neighbours in the Southeast and East Asia could quickly assume serious proportions. The US believed that there was an urgent necessity to achieve 'deterrence stability' to ensure that any low intensity conflicts between these countries would not threaten to assume nuclear proportions. It is in this context that one must also view American attempts at rapprochement with India in the early post-Cold War years.

Additionally, the United States is also, in recent times, increasingly concerned about nuclear terrorism by violent non-state actors in the region. The security of nuclear weapons in Pakistan, North Korea and even India has forced the United States to actively monitor and engage with the region. Neither diplomatic initiatives like the Six Party Talks nor the pressure of sanctions imposed by the UN Security Council Resolutions have succeeded in pressuring North Korea to abandon its nuclear programme. It is also worth noting that the threat of nuclear proliferation in Asia does not come only from North Korea but also from Pakistan where possibility of jihadi extremists getting access to, and even acquiring control of nuclear weapons or material cannot be ruled out. India, China and Pakistan are expanding, upgrading arsenals and enhancing the ranges and efficiencies of their delivery systems.

Where does China figure in the American rebalance? After overtaking Japan, the Chinese economy has been on course to overtake the US economy to emerge as the world's largest economy. According to the latest assessment by the Organisation for Economic Cooperation and Development (OECD), this will take place by 2016 (The Guardian, 2013). The Economist (London) had predicted in December 2011 that China would overtake the US economy in 2018, and hit the $20 trillion mark, while the Chinese sources have indicated that China would overtake the US economy in 2019. China's rise however is not only an economic rise. China's claims that its rise is, and will remain peaceful, are increasingly being questioned and debated.

This is mainly due to the faster pace of its military modernisation fuelled by its economic rise leading to a rapidly growing defense budget and its political ambitions. Within the past decade, China has made phenomenal strides in acquiring impressive military capabilities in the realms of cyber security and space and by acquiring submarines and aircraft carriers for its navy. These capabilities have startled its neighbours, and put other world powers, including the US on alert. China seems to be developing A2AD (Anti-Access and Area Denial) capabilities to deter-even-US naval missions in the Asia-Pacific region. On December 2013, China announced the creation of an Air Defence identification Zone (ADIZ) over the Senkaku/Diaoyu islands in East China Sea.

China's military modernisation has become a matter of controversy and debate. It is because of its unusually fast pace and, even more because of its unexpected, assertiveness and aggressive behaviour. China's assertion of territorial claims in the South China Sea, particularly vis-à-vis Vietnam and the Philippines has taken many in the region by surprise. These claims have been projected by China as a part of its 'core national interests'. [1] Such assertions are not confined only to South China Sea, but have also been visible in the East Asia Sea vis-à-vis Japan over the disputed Senkaku Island which has aroused emotive nationalism and public protests. China has stepped up its naval movements in the disputed area. The equally robust Japanese response has generated sharp tensions between the two neighbours. China's territorial claims have also been evident in the Himalayan region in its unresolved border dispute with India.

Besides, China is also seen to be increasing its access and strategic presence in a number of Indian Ocean countries. Its support for building and upgrading ports in Pakistan (Gwadar), Sri Lanka (Hambantota), Bangladesh (Chittagong) and Myanmar (Sittwe) has been noted by a number of strategic analysts in the region. These ports are apparently commercial facilities for facilitating China's growing energy imports and trade but the possibility of their strategic use in any future eventuality cannot be ruled out.

Time and again, as US senior administration officials have explained, that US is aware of China's emergence as a new geopolitical power. It realises that China's rise is enduring since the liberalisation of its economy in 1978 and not a flash in the pan. A China that is an antithesis with its history of communism and penchant for maintaining secrecy; unreliability of its political structure; rapid economic growth; ability to engage in cyber warfare, ambitious military, naval, space and air modernisation programmes and aggressive forays into South, East, Central Asia, Africa makes Beijing a threat to Washington's hegemony and has hence clearly unnerved the US.

The US also does not like the idea of a regional hegemon as it threatens to decouple US from old alliance partners who, it believes, are getting agitated with China's rise. Thus, this challenge presented the United States with two options: (a) either walk away, or (b) get more active. The rebalance essentially is an announcement by the US of choosing the second option from the above. So, the rebalancing is essentially a refreshing of its old partner alliances (Japan, South Korea and Australia) and building new partner alliances (Myanmar, Indonesia, India etc.) through preferential Free Trade Agreements through the Trans Pacific Partnerships.

The US is repackaging the conventional containment theory as rebalancing and how it is important for its allies in the region. Although various American officials have publicly denounced the possibility of a containment strategy, the point to be noted here is that the US realises that it is tied too closely, economically to China to engage in the conventional containment strategy that was adopted against the Soviet Union. Ironically, growing economic ties, largely characterised by a negative balance of trade has actually created complications for the US, unlike the Cold War, where the confrontation with the Soviet Union could be blatantly aggressive and was seen as a simple "Zero Sum" game.

Hence, rebalancing, for the US, is about walking the tight rope between balancing 'congagement' i.e. containment through engagement with China and through developing TPPs with regional allies. The US has also realised the importance of a narrow military strategy, a shift of only 3 percent (57 percent to 60 percent presence) of its forces to protect any denial in power projections when required. This is essentially an attempt by the US at evolving a response to China's strategy of anti-access area-denial. Critically, the rebalance is a symbolic announcement of American intent of maintaining force as an option but stopping others from using force.

Since the pronouncement of the policy made in 2011-2012, the US rebalancing policy has undergone two major phases. Initially, much of the emphasis of the policy was placed on the military initiatives in the region. China seemed too sceptical of America's actions. Beijing took steps to demonstrate its power in maritime territorial disputes with US allies—the Philippines and Japan. Chinese commentators claimed that the disputes with the Philippines and Japan were caused in part by stronger US support for these allies under the new US policy. Senior US officials, notably Director of National Intelligence, James Clapper, saw the strong Chinese actions in the disputes with the Philippines and Japan as being motivated in part as a response to the new US emphasis on the Asia-Pacific region (Sutter et al., 2013). Against this background, the Obama administration adjusted its approach in late 2012, by decreasing the military initiatives. Thus, Obama emphasised more on economic and diplomatic efforts, and even called for closer engagement with China. This helped to reduce a source of tension in US-China relations.

Keeping these developments in mind, what does the US want from India? There are four possibilities: (a) A formal relationship/partnership with India in the region as part of its rebalancing; (b) If option 'a' is not achievable, then at least a strategic cooperation in regional and global areas of converging interests; (c) If option 'a' and 'b' are unachievable then a self-equipped India to act as a balancer to China; and (d) if none of the above options work, put in place measures to deter an India bandwagoning with China.

So how should India react? It is clear that the Indo-US relations have exited the "honeymoon" period and differences have emerged significantly in the recent past. While, the US wants the strategic relationship to address common regional and global challenges, India has always emphasised on the bilateral relationship. It is widely acknowledged that this relationship cannot develop into an 'all weather' alliance. India needs to engage cautiously and cannot ill afford putting all its eggs in one basket. Growing Indo-US camaraderie can create the danger for it to get tied down by China's own containment policy vis-à-vis Pakistan. India must develop its policy in the region at its own pace and not be dictated by the agenda that the US sets. The success of the Indo-US strategic relationship will depend upon how the slower, more prolonged and often frustrating decision-making process in India will compliment the capitalist mode of decision-making in the US. Ultimately, the consequences of the rebalancing strategy could have significant implications for India in the larger context of the strategic partnership between both countries.

India needs to continue to strategically engage with China on areas of convergences. Additionally, it needs to invest in stronger relations with key regional countries including Japan, Korea, Australia, Indonesia, Singapore and Vietnam. This will provide a strong deterrence to any aggressive Chinese ambitions. This could also force China to engage with India. An India that has strong engagements with the United States and China could act as a 'strategic balancer' in US-Sino relations. In this regard, there is a certain discomfort at the rapid re-emergence of the term "Indo-Pacific, especially in the last two years. The term symbolically thrusts India in the forefront as a natural stakeholder in a region that overlaps with China's increasing assertiveness and territorial claims.

Endnote
1. The concept of 'core interests' implies that if need be, force can and will be used for the protection of these interests, as in the case of Taiwan and Tibet.

References
"A National Security Strategy of Engagement and Enlargement", July 1, 1994, available at: http://nssarchive.us/NSSR/1994.pdf. Accessed February 20, 2014.

"America's 'Pacific President? Obama Opens First Post-election Trip with Visit to Thailand", *NBC News*, November 18, 2012.

"Asia Trip to Refocus on the Most Rapidly Growing Region: U.S.", *The Hindu*, November 10, 2012.

Banerjee, Dipankar (1999), "Security in South Asia: Comprehensive and Cooperative", New Delhi: Manas Publications, pp. 1-38; 189-216.

Brock, Williams R. (2013), "Trans-Pacific Partnership (TPP) Countries: Comparative Trade and Economic Analysis", Congressional Research Service, June 10, available at: https://www.fas.org/sgp/crs/row/R42344.pdf.

Campbell, Kurt (2011), "Public Lecture on US Engagement in Asia", Department of State, October 10, available at: http://www.state.gov/p/eap/rls/rm/2011/10/175241.htm, Accessed on August 18, 2012.

Carter, Ashton (2013), "The U.S. Defense Rebalance to Asia", Speech at the Centre for Strategic and International Studies, Washington, D.C.

Chellaney, Brahma (2012), "Report: U.S. Strategy in the Asia-Pacific", *Al Jazeera Centre for Studies*, February 15, available at:
http://studies.aljazeera.net/ResourceGallery/media/Documents/2012/2/15/201221510538465734U.S.%20Strategy%20in%20the%20Asia-Pacific.pdf.

Chellaney, Brahma (2013), Talk on "China, the US and India in the Indo-Pacific: Congruence and Conflict of Interests", *Asia Centre*, Bangalore, December 28.

Chellany, Brahma (2012), "America's Unhinged Pivot", *Project Syndicate*, November 12, available at:
http://www.project-syndicate.org/commentary/america-s-unhinged--pivot-by-brahma-chellaney.

Clinton, Hilary (2011), "Secretary Clinton on India: A Vision for 21st Century", Address at the Anna Centenary Library on July 20, available at:
http://iipdigital.usembassy.gov/st/english/texttrans/2011/07/20110720165044su0.7134014.html#axzz2tS4tGcc2.
Accessed February 16, 2014.

Clinton, Hillary (2011), "America's Pacific Century", *Foreign Policy*, November, available at:
http://www.foreignpolicy.com/articles/2011/10/11/americas_pacific_century?page=full, Accessed August 29, 2012.

Cossa, Ralph Aa, Brad Glosserman, Michael A. McDevitt, Nirav Patel, James Przystup and Brad Roberts (2009), "The United States and the Asia-Pacific Region: Security Strategy for the Obama Administration", February, available at:
http://csis.org/files/media/csis/pubs/issuesinsights_v09n01.pdf.
Accessed February 13, 2014.

Cossa, Ralph and Brad Glosserman (2012), "Regional Overview: US Rebalances As Others Squabble", *Comparative Connections*, Volume 14, No. 2, September, p. 2.

CRS Report for Congress (2001), 'China-U.S. Aircraft Collision Incident of April 2001: Assessments and Policy Implications", October 10, available at:
http://www.fas.org/sgp/crs/row/RL30946.pdf.
Accessed February 20, 2014.

Curtis, L. Gerald (1994), "The United States, Japan, and Asia: Challenges for U.S Policy", New York: W.W. Norton- and Company, pp. 122-139, 229-238, 261-269.

Department of Defense (2012), 'Sustaining US Global Leadership: Priorities for 21st Century Defense", Washington D.C: Department of Defense, available at:
http://www.defense.gov/news/defense_strategic_guidance.

Department of Defense (2013), "Remarks by Secretary Hagel at the IISS Asia Security Summit, Shangri-La Hotel, Singapore", Washington D.C., June 1, available at:
http://www.defense.gov/transcripts/transcript.aspx?transcriptid=5251. Accessed February 20, 2014.

Department of Defense (1998), "The United States Security Strategy for the East Asia-Pacific Region", November 25, available at:
http://www.fas.org/man/docs/easr98.html. Accessed February 12, 2014.

Department of Foreign Affairs (1998), "Australia-United States Ministerial Consultations: 1998 Sydney Statement Joint Security Declaration", Australian Government and Trade, available at:
http://www.dfat.gov.au/geo/us/ausmin/sydney_statement.html. Accessed February 13, 2014.

Department of State (2013), "The East Asia-Pacific Rebalance: Expanding U.S. Engagement", *Fact Sheet Bureau of Public Affairs*, Washington D.C., December 16, available at:
http://www.state.gov/r/pa/pl/2013/218776.htm.

Department of State, "Milestones: 1899-1913, Secretary of State John Hay and the Open Door in China, 1899-1900", Office of the Historian: Washington D.C., available at:
http://history.state.gov/milestones/1899-1913/hay-and-china.

Green, Michael (2012), "US Turns Its Gaze to the Pacific", *The World Today,* February-March.

Greenert, Jonathan and Mark Welsh (2013), "Breaking the Kill

Chain: How to Keep America in the Game When Our Enemies Are Trying to Shut Us Out", *Foreign Policy Journal,* May 16, available at:
http://www.foreignpolicy.com/articles/2013/05/16/breaking_the _kill_chain_air_sea_battle. Accessed February 20, 2014.

Hathaway, Robert M. (2012), "India and the US Pivot to Asia", February 24, available at:
http://yaleglobal.yale.edu/print/7638.
Accessed February 19 2014.

Hiebert, Murray and Liam Hanlon (2012), "ASEAN and Partners Launch Regional Comprehensive Economic Partnership", Centre for Strategic and International Studies, December 7, available at:
https://csis.org/publication/asean-and-partners-launch-regional-comprehensive-economic-partnership.

Inderfurth, Karl F. and Ted Osius (2013), "India's 'Look East' and America's 'Asia Pivot': Converging Interests", *Centre for Strategic and International Studies,* Volume 3, Issue 3 March.

"India and US Hold Defence Talks Asia-Pacific Countries Should Settle Bilateral Disputes as per International Law: Antony", Press Information Bureau (PIB), Release ID: 84715, June 6, 2012.

Johnson, Chalmers and E.B. Keehn (1995), "East Asian Security: The Pentagon's Ossified Strategy", July-August, available at:
http://www.foreignaffairs.com/articles/51212/chalmers-johnson-and-e-b-keehn/east-asian-security-the-pentagons-ossified-strategy. Accessed February 12, 2014.

Karnad, Bharat (2013), "The Kerry-Hagel Duo", *The New Indian Express*, March 8, available at:
http://www.newindianexpress.com/opinion/article1492458.ece.

Kousar, Azam, J. (1996), "Discourse in Trust: US-South Asia Relations", New Delhi: South Asian Publishers, pp. 53-57, 184-185, 231-236, 322-325.

Manyin, E. Mark, Stephen Daggett, Ben Dolven, Susan V. Lawrence, Michael F. Martin, Ronald O'Rourke, and Bruce Vaughn (2012), "Pivot to the Pacific? The Obama Administration's 'Rebalancing' Toward Asia", *Congressional Research Service*, available at:
http://www.fas.org/sgp/crs/natsec/R42448.pdf.

Mehta, Pratap Bhanu et al. (2012), "Non-alignment 2.0: A Foreign and Security policy for India in the Twenty First Century", Centre for Policy Research, available at: http://www.cprindia.org/workingpapers/3844-nonalignment-20-foreign-and-strategic-policy-india-twenty-first-century. Accessed February 16, 2014.

Metzger, Robert S. (2012), "US-India Defence Cooperation towards an Enduring Relationship", *Indian Defence Review*, Volume 27, No. 2, April-June.

Mohan, C. Raja (2013), "China's Rise, America's Pivot and India's Asian Ambiguity", *Seminar,* Volume 641, January, available at: http://www.india-seminar.com/2013/641.htm.

Mukherjee, Pranab (2006), "Text of the Speech", June 3, available at: http://www.iiss.org/en/events/shangri%20la%20dialogue/archive /shangri-la-dialogue-2006-f1a5/second-plenary-session-636b/pranab-mukherjee-ba2f. Accessed February 16, 2014.

Muni, S.D. (2010), "President Obama's India Visit: Substance in Symbolism", ISAS Brief No. 176, November 16.

Muni, S.D. (2011), "India's 'Look East' Policy: The Strategic Dimension", ISAS Working Paper No. 121, February 1.

Muni, S.D. (2012), "Hillary Clinton Visits India: Understanding the Unstated", ISAS Insights No. 164, May 15.

Muni, S.D. (2012), "Trilateral Consultations: US for 'Constructive Ties with India and China", *The Tribune,* Chandigarh, May 19.

"Obama Calls Himself 'America's First Pacific President' and Hails Expanded US Engagement in Asia", *Daily News*, November 14, 2009.

Ollapally, Deepa M. (2013), "Indian Debates on America's Rebalance to Asia", Sigur Centre for Asian Studies, July, available at: http://www.risingpowersinitiative.org/wpcontent/uploads/Policy Brief_Jul2013_India3.pdf. Accessed February 16, 2014.

Ollapally, Deepa M. and Rajesh Rajagopalan (2011), "The Pragmatist Challenge to Indian Foreign Policy", *The Washington Quarterly*, Volume 34, No. 2.

Overholt, William (2008), "Asia, America, and the Transformation of Geopolitics", Cambridge University Press: New York.

Panetta, Leone (2012), "Text of Secretary Panetta's Speech at the IDSA", June 6, available at: http://www.idsa.in/video/AddressbyLeonEPanettaDefenceSecret ary. Accessed February 16, 2014.

Perry, William J. (1995), "United States Security Strategy for the East Asia-Pacific Region", Department of Defense, February, pp. 1297-1313, available at: http://www.ioc.utokyo.ac.jp/~worldjpn/documents/texts/JPUS/19950227.O1E.html. Accessed February 12, 2014.

Raghavan, Srinath and Mahesh Rangrajan (2010), "Engagement Sans Entanglement", *Seminar*, Volume 605, available at: http://www.indiaseminar.com/2010/605/605_srinath_and_mahesh.html. Accessed February 16, 2014.

"Rebalancing America's Ties to Asia: An Assessment of the Obama Initiative", available at: http://carnegieendowment.org/files/120611_transcript_RebalancingAsiaTies.pdf. Accessed October 10, 2012.

Rustow, A. Dankwart (1967), "Asia and United States Policy: America's Role in World Affairs", New Jersey: Prentice-Hall, pp. 10-23, 84-108.

"Strategic Guidance Document", US Department of Defense, January 3, 2012.

Sutter, Robert G. et al. (2013), "Balancing Acts: The U.S. Rebalance and Asia-Pacific Stability", August, Elliott School of International Affairs, available at: http://www2.gwu.edu/~sigur/assets/docs/BalancingActs_Compiled1.pdf. Accessed February 20, 2014.

Tow, T. William and William R. Feeney (1982), "U.S. Foreign Policy and the Asian Security: A Transregional Approach", Colorado: Westview Press.

Twining, Daniel (2012), "Were the India-U.S. relations Over Sold?: Part II", *Foreign Policy*, June 12, available at: http://shadow.foreignpolicy.com/posts/2012/06/12/were_us_india_relations_oversold_part_2.

Vandenbosch, Amry and Richard Butwell (1966), "The Changing Face of Southeast Asia", Lexington: University of Kentucky Press, pp. 360-369, 401-409.

Weitz, Richard (2012), "Pivot Out, Rebalance In", *The Diplomat*, May 3, available at: http://thediplomat.com/2012/05/03/pivot-out-rebalance-in/?all=true. Accessed September 6, 2012.

Wilder, Dennis C. (2009), "Why Would a G-2 Hurt?", *Washington Post*, April.

Yahuda, Michael (1996), "The International Politics of the Asia-

Pacific", London: Routledge.
Yebai, Zhang (1993), "Isolationism and U.S. Intervention in Asia", in 'The United States and the Asia Pacific Region in the Twentieth Century', The Chinese Association for American Studies and the Institute of American Studies, New Delhi: Modern Press.

5

India-U.S. Strategic Convergence in South China Sea (SCS)

S.Y. Surendra Kumar

India supports freedom of navigation in international waters including in SCS, and that rite of passage in accordance with accepted principles of international law.

—S.M. Krishna, India's former Foreign Minister

US has national interest is mainly for freedom of navigation, open access to Asia's maritime commons, and respect for international law in SCS…and it supports a collaborative diplomatic process by all claimants for resolving territorial disputes without coercion.

—Hillary Clinton, US's Former Secretary of State

India's relationship with US is growing rapidly since the end of the Cold War, precisely due to the strong political, nuclear and economic factors. Subsequently, the relationship is also shaped by the shared strategic interest on global commons and China's rise. However, in the recent times, the South China Sea (SCS) also constitute a key issue in shaping the bilateral ties and there is possible scope for strategic convergence between the two countries. In this regard, the vital reasons for India-US strategic convergence are as follows.

Geostrategic Importance of SCS

Since decades, the SCS is drawing considerable international attention due to variety of reasons, and one such reason is its geostrategic significance. The SCS is a semi-enclosed sea of around 3.5 million sq. km., extending from eastern end of Singapore Strait to Taiwan Strait and bordered by China, Taiwan and all Association for Southeast Asian Nation (ASEAN) members, excluding Laos and Myanmar.

Moreover, it is an crucial transit connecting the Indian Ocean and Western Pacific with vital sea lanes of communication that ensure the flow of international trade and transport of resources and energy for many regions. In comparison to Suez Canal, three times more oil and liquefied natural gas (LNG) is transported through the SCS and 15 times more than the Panama Canal. [1] As a result, it is regarded as one of the world's busiest international sea lane, as half of world's super tanker traffic and world's merchant fleet sail and pass through the region's waters. Thus, the SCS acts as a critical commercial and strategic passageway.

In addition, the region is also rich in natural resources, i.e., the region is rich in fish stocks, as 10 percent of world's fish are caught in this region, and many regard that desire to access fisheries have to certain extent intensified the conflict. [2] Interestingly, SCS is regarded as the richest sea in the world in terms of marine flora and fauna, coral reefs, mangroves, sea grass beds, fish and plants. Moreover, minerals and metals are found on a large scale, which are worth billions of dollars in annual income and most of these metals and minerals are found specifically in exclusive economic zone (EEZs) which are also contested areas.

Subsequently, it has unexplored oil and natural gas. According to a Russian survey an estimated (1995), six billion barrels of oil might be located in Spratly Islands of which 70 percent would be natural gas. [3] However, the Chinese estimate the region to contain 150 billion barrel of oil and natural gas and refer this as 'Second Persian Gulf'. Apparently, the exploration of deep sea petroleum and natural gas has increased the contribution of marine economy in national gross domestic product (GDP) of country in terms of wealth and employment. For instance, Vietnam intends to increase the share of maritime economy contribution to its

GDP from 48 percent in 2005 to 55 percent by 2020. [4] Overall, due to the availability and accessibility to sea's oil, gas reserve, fishing and ocean resources it has complicated the conflict and the region has turned into a battle field of increasing claims and counter claims by the regional actors. Thus, the geostrategic location of SCS is not just attractive to China and ASEAN nations, but also to India and the US.

Shared Strategic Interest

Apart from the SCS strategic location and availability of vast natural resources, both India and the US have similar strategic interests in SCS, which acts as a basis for the formation of strategic convergence.

India's Strategic Interests: India continues to have a legitimate aspiration in emerging as a regional hegemony in South Asia and also as a maritime power not just in the Indian Ocean, but beyond this region. This was elaborated by PM Manmohan Singh, that Indian Ocean is India's 'strategic footprint', [5] connecting the Southeast Asia, Far East and beyond, which would strengthen India's successful rise, achieve security ambitions and become the predominant maritime security provider in the region stretching from the Red Sea to Singapore. Thus, India's maritime ambition goes beyond Indian Ocean that includes SCS. This aspect is clearly articulated in the India's Maritime Military Strategy (2007), where it emphasised SCS and Pacific Ocean as among secondary areas of endeavour for the Indian sea services. S.D. Muni argues, "South China Sea may look far off from the Indian mainland but it is not really so when India's territorial footprints in the western Indian Ocean, in the form of Andaman and Nicobar Islands, are kept in view". [6]

India regards the SCS as an integral part of its development, as 55 percent of its trade passes through this region and the security of international ships is vital in order to protect its imports and exports. Thus, protecting the SLCOs constitute a vital interest for India. Besides this, India is also concerned about the conflicting claims of countries in SCS, leading to regional instability which in a way affects India's engagement with Southeast Asian countries. This concern was articulated by Sanjay Singh, India's Secretary (East), Ministry of External Affairs, that, "SCS was witnessing competing claims and common objective was to see that seas and oceans become regions of co-operation instead of competition particularly as our energy security and trade depends on them". [7]

India in order to meet its energy requirements, has undertaken many collaborative projects with the SCS nations, particularly with Vietnam, which has been opposed by China. For instance, in 2009, when India's Oil and Natural Gas Corporation (ONGC) Videsh Ltd. was surveying in areas of Vietnam, the Chinese government warned and protested. Nevertheless, India continued with its work as it had got assurances from Vietnam to complete its work. In another incident, in July 2011, the Indian naval vessel INS Airavat was moving towards Nha Trang in Southern Vietnam, the Chinese government warned India, through the radio message asking India to keep out of Chinese waters.

The Vietnamese President Truong Tan Sang visited India in October 2011, and concluded the three year agreement to expand and promote oil exploration in SCS and has now reconfirmed its decision to carry on despite the Chinese challenge to the legality of Indian presence. [8] China evidently did not receive these developments well. Jiang Yu, a spokesperson for the Chinese Foreign Ministry was quoted as stating, "...as for oil and gas exploration...we are opposed to any country engaged in the waters under China's jurisdiction. We hope foreign countries do not get involved in the South China Sea dispute". [9]

In response to the growing India-Vietnam energy cooperation, China issued a demarche to New Delhi in November 2011, underlining that Beijing's permission should be sought for exploration in Blocks 127 and 128— without it, OVL's activities would be considered illegal.

However, Vietnam, underlined the 1982 UNCLOS to claim its sovereign rights over the two blocks being explored, and requested India not to bow down to China's pressure. [10] Despite the Vietnam assurance, India is moving cautiously, as it does not want to antagonise China, like in May 2012, India decided to return Block 128 to Vietnam on the basis that exploration was not commercially viable, and not necessarily due to China's pressure. However, in July 2012, when Vietnam gave OVL more incentives in terms of a longer period to prove commercial viability, India decided to continue the joint exploration. Subsequently, Vietnam decided to extend the OVL contract for hydrocarbon exploration in Block 128, reiterating that it valued India's presence in the SCS for regional strategic balance. [11]

Despite stiff opposition by China, the Indian government have always defended its contracts with Vietnam on the basis that: (a) it falls under the Vietnam's EEZ and continental shelf, which is well within the norms of international law, (b) India is involved in drilling for gas in SCS since 1988, however, China began to raise objections only since 2003, when the first joint venture for offshore oil and natural gas exploration in Vietnam's Lan Tay field along with Petro Vietnam and BP became functional in 2003, (c) India's half of the trade passes through this region, thus it has the right to access. This was emphasised by India's former Foreign Minister S.M. Krishna in response to China's opposition that "India supports freedom of navigation in international waters including in SCS, and that rite of passage in accordance with accepted principles of international law", [12] and (d) there is also perception that when China can involve in India's backyard—Indian Ocean and South Asia—India also can do it. [13]

Subsequently, while China opposes India's entry into the SCS, it continues on building strategic projects in Pakistan Occupied Kashmir (POK) and on deploying troops there. Thus, India's strategic interest and growing relations with Vietnam in oil and natural gas exploration constitutes a major concern for China. In this regard, India in November 2012, declared that the country is ready to deploy naval vessels in the SCS to protect its oil exploration interests as tensions climb.

Overall, India's stand on SCS has been consistent and insists on peaceful resolution of the dispute. This was also retreated during the 2010 ASEAN Region Forum (ARF) meeting, where India along with 11 of the 27 participating countries backed the US multilateral approach, instead of China's "bilateral approach" for resolution of the SCS disputes. Subsequently, India joined other countries to openly declare that the SCS should remain open for international navigation. The Indian position on the security situation in the SCS was made clear by the Former Indian Foreign Secretary Nirupama Rao (July 2011), where she reiterated that the region's [SCS] importance as an important shipping route and India's support for freedom of navigation in sea lanes. [14]

US Strategic Interest: Unlike India, the US is partially dependent on the SCS; however its policy is mainly guided by: (a) annual trade worth US$ 5.3 trillion passes through the SCS, in which US trade accounts for US$ 1.2 trillion. [15] As a result, if a crisis occurs, the diversion of cargo ships to other routes would harm regional economies due to the increase in insurance rates and longer transits, (b) maintaining the US-led order at sea, including the international law of the sea, pursuant to US interpretation; especially the freedom of navigation which includes the activities of US military ships, (c) protecting the interests of allies, especially the strategic maritime routes for Japan, South Korea, Taiwan and the Philippines, (d) managing China's (naval) outreach to ensure that its rise will not upset the present US-dominated system, and (e) safeguarding the interests of US oil and gas corporations in the region. These interests are fundamental and permanent; it is difficult for the US to bargain with China because most of these interests are inextricably tied to the leadership position that the US wants to sustain in the existing global system. [16]

Overall, US strategic interest in the region was emphasised

by US Secretary of State, Hillary Clinton at the July 2010 ASEAN Regional Forum (ARF) meeting, "US has national interest in mainly for freedom of navigation, open access to Asia's maritime commons, and respect for international law in SCS…and it supports a collaborative diplomatic process by all claimants for resolving territorial disputes without coercion". [17] Moreover, it also insists on right to carry military activities in SCS, including within coastal states for stability in the region". [18] Thus, in order to safeguard its own and the interest of its allies, US has justified its military presence for promoting the freedom of navigation and legally in tune with the provisions of UNCLOS, although it has not yet ratified UNCLOS, but honours the provisions of UNCLOS as customary international law.

Apparently, the Chinese aggressive posture on SCS, has also compelled many SEA nations to move closer to US to counter China and meet its economic and energy interest, which the US is ready to reciprocate. With regard to resolution of the dispute, US have consistently maintained that it wants a peaceful resolution acceptable to all the claimants. This was also emphasised by President Obama by vocally backing the ASEAN claimant's right on territorial claims, even saying that freedom of navigation and resolution of claims accepted by all nations is in US national interest. [19] Overall, the US policy has been to support ASEAN-led DOC; raise the dispute at regional security forums; provide capacity building support to its allies and partners; and rebalance forces in Asia; and emphasise that the territorial disputes should be resolved peacefully, without coercion, intimidation, threats, or the use of force. Interestingly, US strategic interest converges with interests of India. In this regard, many have being emphasising on the strengthening of India-US bilateral cooperation in SCS.

Shared Concerns
In addition to its strategic interest, both India and the US have shared concerns that have impact on their interests and

peace and security in the ASEAN region.

China's Claims: The region consists of more than 200 islands; however the dispute is confined mainly to four Islands like the Paracel Island, Spratly, the Pratas, and Macclesfield Banks. Among these, highly disputed are the Spratly and Paracels, which is claimed by China and many Southeast Asian nations. Generally, the dispute gained momentum in 1982, with United Nation Convention on the Law of the Sea (UNCLOS), elaborating on what constitutes as the territorial sea (12 nautical miles), exclusive economic zone (200 nautical miles), continental shelf (can extend beyond 200 nautical miles), contiguous zone (24 nautical miles) and free for all high seas. [20] As a result, this paved way for each country staking contradictory claims over the SCS.

Apparently, China's claims are the broadest and cover all of the Spratly and Paracel islands and most of the SCS. China lays claim over large portions of these waters and China's official media at regular intervals asserts that at least three million sq. kms. of the SCS is Chinese maritime territory. [21] The basis for Chinese claims is the 2000 years old history, as they continue to believe that it was their ancestors like Ming and Han dynasties who discovered and occupied the territories of SCS. Subsequently, from time to time, the Chinese government have attempted to legitimise their claims. For instance, in 1947, through the production of location map of SCS, in which most of the island was shown belonging to China. In August 1951, the Chinese premier Zhuo Enlai issued a statement during the Allied Peace Treaty Negotiations with Japan, asserting China's territorial claims. [22]

Subsequently, in September 1958, it reaffirmed its claim to these islands when it asserted the rights to territorial waters during the Jinment crisis. In addition to this, China's National People's Congress (NPC) in February 1992, passed the law of territorial waters and contiguous zone that claims complete control over the land features in SCS and their adjacent waters and asserts that it has power to exercise jurisdiction over its territories. [23] Subsequently, in 1998, the NPC again passed a law related to EEZ and continental shelf of the PRC, in which it claimed additional maritime rights beyond those contained in the 1992 law. [24] In a landmark step in December 2007, the NPC passed a law creating a county-level city in Hainan province called Sansha to administer China's claims in the SCS, including the Paracel and Spratly Islands.

In response to these developments, both Malaysia and Vietnam in May 2009, made a joint submission to the United Nations (UN) regarding the proposed outer limits for their continental shelves beyond 200 nautical miles. In reaction, China also attached a diplomatic note to the UN Secretary-General emphasising its claim over the territory and also attached a map with the contested nine-dashed line, which they call it the traditional maritime boundary line or *chuantong haijiang xian*. [25]

Interestingly, in March 2010, China listed SCS claims among its 'core interest' along with previous claims of Taiwan, Tibet and Xinjiang. It affirmed this interpretation again in April 2011, in a note verbal to the UN Commission on the limits of the continental shelf by stating that the Spratly islands were fully entitled to territorial waters, EEZ and a continental shelf. [26] In mid-2012, the Chinese government issued a new electronic passport for its citizens with the map of the U-shaped line claiming most of the SCS.

In November 2012, Hainan provincial government announced new regulations allowing law enforcement vessels to board, inspect, detain, expel or confiscate foreign ships conducting "illegal" activities within the Chinese waters. [27] As a result of its strong claims, it raised objections and condemned any attempts made by other claimant countries on engaging in SCS in the form of oil and minerals exploration. Obviously, this act of China has been consistently opposed by Vietnam and other claimant nations in the region.

Apparently, the Chinese claim over the territory is mainly guided by its strategic interest in SCS such as: (a) to assert its historical rights including sovereignty over the region and defend its long coastline and territorial integrity. Subsequently, China is emerging as a global power and it seeks to exert greater influence in Asia, particularly the SCS, which is an important backyard to shield the mainland from any sea attack, (b) to secure access to maritime resources and ensure the safety of SLOC for smooth flow of goods and energy, for example, European Union (EU) is the largest importer of Chinese goods and also China's 30 percent of export goes through SCS, thus ensuring free flow of goods, which is vital for China's economy [28], (c) to boost its maritime economy which is around 4.65 trillion Yuan (2011), now inching towards 10 percent of its GDP, (d) to prevent Taiwanese independence and to counter US intervention of supporting development and partnership with claimant countries—subsequently, also to oppose US military surveillance activities in the EEZ, (e) Chinese people believe that other claimants are extracting "China's oil", and catching "China's fishes", while China has not obtained any drop of oil from the Spratly islands, and Chinese fisherman are being captured and driven away [29]—thus, it is time for China to assert its rights over SCS, and (f) many of the Chinese officials argue that ASEAN claimants' activities have forced China to react. This is China's main argument when it accused other claimants of provoking tension and violating China sovereignty in the SCS. All these interests are directly linked to China's economic prospects and great power aspirations. Thus, China's strategy in its quest for dominance over the sea has been a concern for the nearby nations and also for major powers like the US and EU and India.

To counter the ASEAN claimants in the SCS, the Chinese navy has also increased the frequency and level of coordination in conducting naval exercises in the SCS. One of the most significant event happened in July 2010 when the PLA navy for the first time mobilized at least a dozen modern warships from three fleets (the North Fleet, the East Fleet, and the South Fleet) to conduct a large-scale joint naval exercise in the SCS. [30] Significantly, on June 28, 2012, China's Ministry of Defense announced that China commenced combat-ready patrols in disputed waters in the SCS. [31]

In addition, in September 2012, China's establishment of High Level Task Force on Safeguarding Sovereignty and Maritime Rights and Interests launched a program to increase the number of unmanned aerial vehicles (UAVs) monitoring the Scarborough Shoal, Paracel Islands and Spratly Islands. It conducts out regular patrols over the waters in claims over the SCS to secure nation's maritime rights and interests. In January 2013, the Chinese government appropriated US$ 1.6 billion to fortify islands in the SCS. The plan includes construction of airports, piers and other facilities that could have both civilian and military uses; and naval exercises in the Shansa and Spratly areas have become routine affairs. Hence, China continues to assert itself politically and militarily in SCS.

Counter Claims by ASEAN Countries: Apart from China, there are other six Southeast Asian countries involved in the territorial disputes, each claiming rights based on the historical accounts and international laws. Brunei claims two areas, namely Lousia Reef (also claimed by Malaysia) and Rifleman Bank on the basis of extending EEZ; Indonesia asserts 200 miles of EEZ under the provision of UNCLOS; Malaysia occupies three islands that it considers to be within its continental shelf; Philippines, claims eights islets of Spratly island chain; [32] Taiwan's claim of sovereign over Spratly; and Vietnam's claim of entire Spratly island chains.

Apparently, in order to defend their claims, the claimants are engaged in modernization process and entering into defence cooperation with major powers. For example, both Vietnam and Philippines are procuring submarine forces to counter China's aggression and signed defence agreement with US and Russia, to purchase from Russia six *Kilo* class submarines and eight Su-30 MK2V multi-role fighters. Others are also not behind, as Indonesia has contracted to purchase three submarines, costing about US$ 1.2 billion from South Korea and is planning to increase the tally of submarines to 10 by 2024. [33] In November 2011, Indonesia announced its plan to buy 24 F-16 fighter aircraft from the US, which were to be delivered in 2014. It is also in the process of negotiating with UK for buying 3 warships to modernize its naval fleet. Singapore has fully modernized all its three armed services and raised them to the first rank and allocated US$ 9.7 billion in 2012, which was 24 percent of its national budget. In June 2012, Singapore military agreed to allow the US Navy to deploy up to 4 littoral combat ships (LCB) in the city-state. Malaysia has acquired two Lekiu-class fighters (1999), 18 Su-30 MKMs and Scorpene-class submarines in 2009. [34]

Vietnam signed a deal with Russia for 6 Project-636 *Kilo*-class convention submarines and 12 Sukhoi Su-30MK2 fighters in 2009. The first submarine began sea test in early December 2012. Vietnam will have its 6 *Kilo*-class submarines in its waters by 2016-17. The Philippine Congress approved the budget and acquisition process for the acquisition of 12 jet trainer/surface-attack aircrafts; 6 close-air support aircrafts; 2 long-range maritime patrol aircrafts; 2 light-lift and 3 medium-lift fixed-wing military transports; 3 ground-based radars and 10 attack helicopters. This was approved under the country's 1st five years (2012-17) of a 15-year military modernization bill. The budget allocated for 2012-17 is estimated at least 75 billion pesos (US$ 1.8 billion).

In addition to defence cooperation, they have also increased building up of infrastructure in their occupied areas to strengthen their claims. Moreover, countries like Philippines took China to court by filling a case at the ITLOS tribunal—a pleading that challenges China's claim to sovereign rights including all resources and navigational rights. [35] Thus, claims and counter claims have caused a lot of tension in the region. The disputes over the territory have already led to two military clashes between China and Vietnam in 1974 and 1988 and the Chinese occupation of Mischief Reef in 1995 intensified the tension between China and the Philippines. Subsequently, there has been a continued and heated rhetoric exchange between China, Vietnam and Philippines, so much so that China's Defence Ministry had openly warned that "combat ready" Chinese naval and air patrols are ready to "protect our maritime rights and interests" in the South China Sea. [36] Overall, only China has used and continues to threaten other claimant's states, about the use of force to assert its claims, which has intensified the conflict.

Limitation of Regional Organisation: The maritime security has over the years gained prominence in the successive summits of regional organisations like ASEAN, ARF and EAS, in which attempts have been made to resolve the SCS dispute or at least ease the tension in the region. For instance, ASEAN played a useful role in developing and adopting its own Declaration on Territorial Disputes based on the principles enumerated in 1976 Treaty of Amity and Cooperation. Subsequently, the November 2002 Declaration on the Conduct of Parties in the SCS (DOC), which commits parties, to seek peaceful ways to settle territorial disputes in SCS. Again in the July 2010 Bali summit, it adopted the guidelines for the implementation of the DOC of parties in SCS.

Ironically, these measures have failed to resolve the dispute due to various reasons, such as: (a) the ASEAN declaration only commits and does not bind the nations to evolve peaceful settlement at the earliest, (b) China's consistent opposition to any resolution on SCS, as it would not accept any multilateral discussions on this issue. Even the ASEAN Summit in June 2012, for the first time in its 45 year history, closed without issuing a joint communiqué, due to China's pressure on Cambodia, the new found ally into disallowing other countries from presenting their arguments. Subsequently, the Chinese Foreign Minister Yang Jiechi declared there was "no dispute" about China's sovereignty over the reef and warned not to internationalize the issue. He also went on to warn Philippines that "China hopes the Philippine side faces the facts squarely and stops creating trouble" [37], (c) it is difficult for ASEAN to speak in one voice, or mediate, due to many parties to the dispute, which prevents any scope for consensus during the summits [38], (d) ASEAN approach towards the SCS has been conflict management, rather than conflict resolution and has failed to persuade China to enter into dialogue with the Southeast Asian countries for a peaceful resolution of the conflict—like in July 2012, China rejected the ASEAN proposal for talks on DOC, by stating that "the time is not ripe", and (e) ASEAN functions on a modus operandi of non-interference in the territorial disputes and other political upheavals involving member states, thus limiting its role as a facilitator in conflict situations.

In addition, due to the divergent interests and external impact, ASEAN countries have different viewpoints regarding the South China Sea issue. Even claimants in ASEAN, including Vietnam, the Philippines, Malaysia and Brunei sometimes do not share a common voice. For example, both Vietnam and the Philippines had the largest number of collisions/incidences with China. Therefore, both countries are the two most active players who call for ASEAN's solidarity in handling the South China Sea issue. Since the US pronouncement of "Asia's pivot", Philippines has become more confident and proactive, and has frequently proposed new initiatives in ASEAN forums. Despite their status as claimants in the South China Sea dispute, Malaysia and Brunei were not directly intimidated by China on the sea and they often attach greater importance to their relations with China. [39]

Among the non-claimants, Singapore and Indonesia hold a neutral view. They do not support the claim of any party. Singapore Foreign Affairs spokesperson once commented that "Singapore is not a claimant state and takes no position on the merits or otherwise of the various claims in the South China Sea. [40] Indonesia has a tradition of playing a mediator's role, hosting many workshops on managing potential conflict in the SCS over the last 20 years and now actively promotes ASEAN common position on this issue. Laos, Thailand and Myanmar do not have direct interests in the SCS; therefore they rarely express their positions. Having close political and economic ties with China, Cambodia, to a certain extent, supports Chinese principle of bilateral negotiations.

Although ASEAN members have divergent interests on the SCS, all of them share common interests in protecting freedom of navigation, regional stability, respecting international law as well as maintaining the solidarity and centrality role of ASEAN within the regional security (and economic) architecture. All 10 ASEAN member states participated in negotiations and signed the Declaration of Conduct (DOC) in 2002 and are now in the same position to promote the negotiation of the Code of Conduct (COC) with China, in order to effectively manage the disputes and enhance peace and cooperation in the region. [41]

In addition, the ASEAN Maritime Forum, was mooted in ASEAN foreign ministers' meeting in Jakarta in June 2004, and was later launched in July 2010. However, expecting any steps towards resolving SCS dispute is unlikely, as it is non-security centric that looks at promotion of business through maritime cooperation and establishment of maritime linkages to support the ASEAN connectivity, rather than any conflict resolution. [42] The other measures like ARF ISM on Maritime Security (July 2008) and Maritime Security Expert Working Group (October 2010) are yet to make any concerted progress. Nevertheless, over the years, ASEAN and China co-operation have improved in search and rescue operations; sustenance of marine ecosystem and biodiversity; maritime hazard prevention and mitigation; marine ecological environment and monitoring techniques and so on. Although, the growing China-ASEAN relation is yet to resolve the SCS dispute, it has however strengthened the ties in bringing stability in the region.

The ARF on the other hand, has not been able to move beyond phase of confidence building to preventive diplomacy. It is yet to tackle security issues like North Korean nuclear programme and Taiwan Strait. Similar to ASEAN, the ARF is also unable to make any progress in the peaceful resolution of the SCS dispute due to lack of consensus and China's objection. Overall, the regional forums have limited role in initiating any peaceful settlement of the SCS.

In this context, it is important for India and the US to safeguard their interests through cooperation. Subsequently, without an amicable cooperation among all the affected countries, having to secure and stabilize maritime transportations is difficult. Hence, cooperation between the two is inevitable and vital for the regional stability. At the same time, India and the US could be in a stronger position vis-à-vis China in SCS.

Concluding Observations

The energy, territorial, maritime and military security factors have complicated the SCS dispute and led to the interstate rivalries in SCS. This dispute over maritime sovereignty is going for more than four decades, and given the maximalist positions, particularly of China, and to certain extent other claimants, it is unlikely to be resolved in the near future.

Furthermore, it is very unlikely that China will use force in the near future, for two vital reasons: Firstly, the use of force will bring ASEAN countries together and will also draw US, India and Japan, and derail China's plans for sustained economic growth. Subsequently, China does not have a navy capability to challenge US, as China is still in the process of completing its first aircraft carrier. Ironically, its navy is insufficient in size and quality to challenge the mighty America. Secondly, despite the prevailing tensions, China's bilateral trade and ties with the claimant states have improved—like in October 2012, China and Vietnam signed a six-point agreement to contain the SCS dispute, including the opening of a hotline to deal with the potential conflicts and both agreed to hold border negotiations at least twice a year. Subsequently, as of July 2011, China, ranked 14th among Vietnam's foreign investors, having 805 operational projects in Vietnam with a capitalized value of US$ 4.2 billion. [43]

The bilateral trade between the two is valued at US$ 27 billion in 2010. Philippine also continues to attract Chinese investment particularly in the fields of tourism and energy, such that China's overall investment in Philippines was US$ 294 billion in 2011. Furthermore, China is also one of the key investors in Southeast Asian countries and is emerging as the largest trading partner. As a result of the growing bilateral ties between China and ASEAN countries, the former is unlikely to use force, as it would be suicidal for is its own economic growth and peaceful rise.

Against this background, the maritime cooperation between India and US in SCS is the best way out to achieve the strategic interests. Thus, both the countries should:

- Cooperate to ensure security of the SLOCs, as well as to overcome Chinese hegemonic attempt at sea.
- Engage economically and militarily with Southeast Asian nations, despite China's concerns.
- Encourage the efforts and initiatives of Southeast Asian countries or the regional forums like ASEAN and ARF to resolve the disputes over the territorial sovereignty, land features, rightful jurisdiction over the waters and seabed, and the legality of conducting military operations within a country's EEZ, and this will obviously take care of both Indian and US concerns.
- Both should not take sides on the territorial disputes and their policy towards SCS should be based on a clear understanding of what both stand to gain and how their national interests are strengthened.
- Defend their interests and promote status quo in dispute, to ensure access to SLOCs for all for both commerce and for peaceful military activities. Humanitarian interventions

and coastal defense should continue to form the core interest.

- Move away from the maritime cooperation on case to case basis and explore the codified maritime cooperation mechanism for stronger and lasting maritime power. Overall, the India and US maritime cooperation in SCS will go a long way in deepening the bilateral relations.

Although, different suggestions from various quarters have come up through which this dispute can be resolved—such as a push for submission of territorial disputes to the International Court of Justice or the International Tribunal for the Law of the Sea for settlement; encouraging an outside organization or a mediator to resolve the dispute and sharing of the resources of the SCS by establishing 'regional sovereignty' over the islands in the South China Sea among the six claimants, allowing them to collectively manage the islands, territorial seas, and airspace—however, the prospect for success in these cases is slim, given the China's likely opposition.

Nevertheless, dialogue is the only way out for a peaceful resolution of the dispute. If this does not happen at the earliest, then there would be intensification of conflict and strategic rivalries between major powers—China, India and Japan in the Asian landscape and also with the extended role of the US, it will create further instability in the region.

Endnotes

1. Teshu Singh (2012), "South China Sea: Emerging Security Architecture", *IPCS Special Report*, No. 132, August.
2. Patrick M. Cronin (ed.) (2012), "Cooperation from the Strength: The US, China and the South China Sea", Washington D.C: Centre for a New American Security, p. 89.
3. Teshu Singh, op. cit. 1, p. 1.
4. Patrick M. Cronin, op. cit. 2, p. 35.
5. David Brewster (2010), "Australia and India: The Indian Ocean and the Limits of Strategic Convergence", *Australian Journal of International Affairs*, 64(5): 555.
6. S.D. Muni, "The Turbulent South China Sea Waters: India, Vietnam and China, *Institute of South Asian Studies*, October 11,

2011, available at:
http://www.isas.nus.edu.sg/Attachments/PublisherAttachment/IS
AS_Insights_140_The_Turbulent_South-
China_Sea_Waters_13102011121226.pdf.

7. Monish Tourangbam (2009), "India-Japan-South Korea Dialogue China's South China Sea Forays", July, available at: http://www.sarkaritel.com/india-japan-south-korea-dialogue-chinas-south-china-sea-forays.

8. Leszek Buszynski (2012), "The South China Sea: Oil, Maritime Claims, and US China Strategic Rivalry", *The Washington Quarterly*, 35(2), p. 143.

9. "India Makes Waves with South China Sea Oil and Gas Exploration", *People's Daily Online*, September 18, 2011, available at:
http://english.peopledaily.com.cn/90883/7598163.html.

10. Harish V. Pant (2012), "South China Sea: New Arena of Sino-Indian Rivalry", August 2, available at:
http://yaleglobal.yale.edu/content/south-china-sea-new-arena-sino-indian-rivalry.

11. Ibid.

12. Indrani Bagchi (2011), "China Harasses Indian Naval Ship on South China Sea", *The Times of India*, September 2, p. 13.

13. Sandeep Dikshit (2012), "Off This Block, Lock, Stock and Barrel, *The Hindu*, May 22, p. 12.

14. Amit Singh, "South China Sea Dispute and India", available at: http://maritimeindia.org/article/south-china-sea-dispute-and-india.

15. Bonnie S. Glaser, (2012), "Armed Clash in the South China Sea", Contingency Planning Memorandum No. 14, available at: http://www.cfr.org/east-asia/armed-clash-south-china-sea/p27883.

16. Tran Truong Thuy (2013), "The South China Sea: Interests, Policies, and Dynamics of Recent Developments", available at: www.csis.org/files/publication/110629_Thuy_South _China_Sea.pdf and see Michael McDevitt, (2013), "The South China Sea and US Policy Options", *American Foreign Policy Interests*, Volume 35:4, pp. 175-187.

17. Jingdong Yuan (2012), "Emerging Rivalry in the South China Sea", The Report prepared for International Security Research and Outreach Programme, Canada, p. 12 and see Sean Creehan,

(2011), "Assessing the Risks of Conflict in the South China Sea", *SAIS Review*, XXXII(1), Winter-Spring: 126.

18. Toshi Yoshihara and James R Holmes (2011), "Can China Defend a 'Core Interest' in the South China Sea?", *The Washington Quarterly*, 34(20): 55.

19. Joshua Kurlantzick, (2012), "South China Sea: From Bad to Worse?", July 24, available at:
http://www.cfr.org/china/south-china-sea-bad-worse/p28739,
and see Greg Yellen, (2011), "Holding the Tiger by its Tail: Chinese Maritime Expansion and the US hedge Strategy in the Indian Ocean", *The Monitor*, Summer: 31-49.

20. Caitlyn Antrim, "International Law and Order: The Indian Ocean and South China Sea", available at:
 http://www.stimson.org/images/uploads/research-pdfs/IOR_chapter5.pdf.

21. Jayadeva Ranade (2013), "Beijing Strategic Towards South China Sea", *IPCS Issue Brief*, p. 2.

22. Taylor Fravel (2011), "China's Strategy in the South China Sea", *Contemporary Southeast Asia*, 33(3): 293.

23. Mark J. Valencia (1995), "China and South China Sea Disputes", Adelphi Papers, No. 298, London: IISS.

24. Taylor Fravel, op. cit. 22, p. 294 and also see Alice D. (2011), "Staking Claims and Making Waves in the South China Sea: How Troubled are the Waters?", *Contemporary Southeast Asia*, 33(3): 269-91.

25. Jingdong Yuan, op. cit. 17.

26. Taylor Fravel, op. cit. 22.

27. Tran Truong Thuy, op. cit. 16, p. 7.

28. Jacques DeLisle (2012), "Troubled Waters: China's Claims and the South China Sea", *Orbis*, Fall: 609; Also see Joshy M. Paul (2010), "The Role of Energy Security in China's Foreign Policy: A Maritime Perspective", *Maritime Affairs*, 6(2): Winter 49-71.

29. Mingjiang Li (2010), "Reconciling Assertiveness and Cooperation? China's Changing Approach to the South China Sea Dispute", *Security Challenges*, 6(2), Winter, pp. 51-58.

30. "China's Three-point Naval Strategy", *Strategic Comment*, Volume 16, Comment 37, October 2010, The International Institute for Strategic Studies (IISS), available at:
http://www.iiss.org/publications/strategic-comments/past-issues/volume-16-2010/october/chinas-three-point-naval-

strategy.

31. "China Pledges to Protect Maritime Sovereignty", available at: http://www.chinadaily.com.cn/china/2012-06/29/content_15533944.htm.

32. For details see Nien-Tsu-Alfred Hu (2010), "South China Sea: Troubled Waters or a Sea of Opportunity?", *Ocean Development and International Law,* 41:203-213.

33. Leszek Buszynski, op. cit. 8, 152.

34. Felix K. Chang (2012), "China's Naval Rise and the South China Sea: An Operational Assessment", *Orbis*, Winter, p. 21.

35. Zhao Hong (2013), "The South China Sea Dispute and China-ASEAN Relations", *Asian Affairs*, 44(1): 34.

36. Harish V. Pant (2012), "South China Sea: New Arena of Sino-Indian Rivalry", August 2, available at: http://yaleglobal.yale.edu/content/south-china-sea-new-arena-sino-indian-rivalry.

37. Jayadeva Ranade (2012), "High Stakes and Rising Tension in the South China Sea", *DNA,* August 8.

38. Jingdong Yuan, op. cit. 17, p. 21.

39. Tran Truong Thuy, op. cit. 16, p. 3.

40. Ibid.

41. Tran Truong Thuy, op. cit. 16, p. 4.

42. Sam Bateman (2011), "Solving 'Wicked Problems' of Maritime Security: Are Regional Forums up to the Task", *Contemporary Southeast Asia*, 33(1):18.

43. Rukmani Gupta (2011), "The South China Sea Dispute: Why Conflict is Not Inevitable?", *IDSA Comments*, October 17, available at: http://idsa.in/idsacomments/TheSouthChinaSeaDisputesWhyConflictisnotInevitable_rgupta_17101.

6

U.S. and South Asia

Nanda Kishor

The much spoken Asian rebalancing or 'Asia Pivot' of the US is essentially a shift beyond Atlantic to the Pacific; it has many more things to read. One needs to catechize the very hermeneutics used in the whole discourse with the word Asia. With enough appetite of the strategic studies scholars to interpret the rebalancing, it has also led to several apprehensions in the countries within Asia. This is more so in particular case of South Asia. Though the rebalancing strategy directly does not make a reference to South Asia, it makes a mention of India being the linchpin in realizing the strategy. China being the prime target of the US in the pivot to Asia, it cannot ignore the role of South Asia and the influence of China in the region. It is in this context that this research is an attempt to analyse and understand the type of response for the US rebalancing strategy and what the US can expect from the region.

Before attempting to understand the responses from South Asia, it is equally important to understand the nuances of such a strategy. It would be of greater relevance to look at some of the scholarly interpretation of the strategy. Ashley Tellis takes a more unconventional view of the strategy as something which the US is doing as it has become inevitable and is driven by geo-economic compulsions. 'The United States is rebalancing to Asia because that is where the "money and the action is" in contemporary geopolitics' (Ashley Tellis). It also can be analysed as an attempt by the United States to remain as a super power through Hegemonic Stability Theory. One of the main reasons for the sustenance of American predominance in the post-World War has been the ability of Washington to successfully manoeuvre the international political economy by experimenting all the tools and measures available.

In this attempt, the US has not been hesitant and has gone ahead even at the cost of drawing heavy criticism. The understanding of foreign policy dynamics of the US is a typical mix of realism with a more engrained characteristic of neo-liberalism that has been pushing it to become a resident power in many parts of the world. The hermeneutics are built around with a sophisticated language of calling it as a rebalancing strategy and building trust by calling a particular region as very important one.

These language skills are very much visible in statements made by some of the US officials who were part of framing and propagating the strategy. One such example is the language used by Tom Donilon. "The rebalance is ultimately oriented to making certain that international norms and law are respected, that commerce and freedom of navigation are not impeded, that emerging powers build trust with their neighbours and disagreements are resolved peacefully without threats or coercion" (Tom Donilon).

Scholar S.D. Muni makes it all the relevant with his analysis on rebalancing strategy by stating that "the statements of Clinton, Donilon and others suggest that the policy of "pivot to Asia" was a well-considered, thoughtful move and not just a knee-jerk reaction to the decision to withdraw from Afghanistan. This policy move in fact is a continuation of America's long-term strategic and economic stakes in the Asia-Pacific region" as against the distracters of the US mission in Afghanistan and its relation with China. To be very precise, the neorealist prism is apt and applicable in understanding the American rebalancing situation as unlike the Cold War, the competition is not between bipolarity but struggle within multi-polarity which is loaded with surprises in terms of behaviour as well as outcomes.

This can be analysed by what Waltz says, "competition

in multi-polar systems is more complicated than competition in bipolar ones because uncertainties about the comparative capabilities of states multiply as numbers grow, and because estimates of the cohesiveness and strength of coalitions are hard to make" (Kenneth Waltz). One can see rebalancing as an attempt to forge and strengthen partnerships in the Asia-Pacific region with additional countries to fulfil the objectives from other regions too having implication on the Asian continent itself.

Perspective from South Asia

India: This specific work would not be looking into the dominant view of South Asia pertaining to India but rather would take more opulent view from the other remaining nations in the region. The myth of associating anything in South Asia to India is something that this research would want to take as a point of departure. The large geographical area and dominance of India in the region may lead to thinking of having India on the side is equal to that of South Asia, but this can be a failure in strategy as India does not enjoy cordial relationship with any of its neighbours and itself is struggling in finding frequency with the neighbours. There has been much written and debated about the bonhomie shared between the United States and India. Needless to say, the relation though often termed as matured has not fetched anything phenomenon starting from intelligence sharing to bringing nuclear reactors to India.

Apart from all these, the new Prime Minister Narendra Modi has a different style of working and he would not budge to any sort of intimidation from the United States if it wants to use India as a lynchpin against China as Modi has good rapport with China. Modi underlined his government's resolve to utilise the full potential of "strategic and cooperative partnership with China and keenness to work closely with the Chinese leadership to deal with any outstanding issues in bilateral relations by proceeding from the strategic perspective of our developmental goals and long-term benefits to our peoples" (freepressjournal.in). This is a trend that many of the scholars also have envisaged of Modi being a realist but with extreme amount of pragmatism laced within. While courting investment from China, Modi would steer a course between defending the country's security interests, while deepening economic links with the world's second largest economy. Being a great admirer and follower of the BJP stalwart and former prime minister Atal Behari Vajpayee who ordered a series of nuclear tests in 1998, thereby adopting a strategy on both *Shakti* and *Shanti* (power and peace), Modi is likely to adopt a similar approach to deter China from being adventurous (Rajaram Panda, c3sindia.org). Following his recent visit the United States, one only has to wait and watch what steps Modi would take to work with the United States which had kept him away and was vocal on human rights issues pertaining to the Godhra riots.

It needs to be noted that more than India requiring the US, it is the US which is keen in looking at India as a major power for obvious reasons as there have been four major shifts with regard to India: from self-perception as a weak developing country to an emerging power; from autonomy to responsibility in the international system; from third-worldism to democracy; and from non-intervention to a willingness to use force abroad. Each of these shifts is a major change in India's self-perception that will affect how the country behaves in the future (Raja Mohan). These above mentioned shifts have actually been seen with a different lens altogether with the type of clear mandate that the new government has got with absolute majority in the recently held elections in India. Needless to say, India would play a major role in the US rebalancing strategy only if India is treated with dignity and is allowed to stay peaceful in region by US not trying to create new challenges in the form of intimidating SAARC neighbours.

Pakistan: The 9/11 attacks and the subsequent US decision to oust the Taliban regime in Afghanistan permitted

Pakistan to become, virtually overnight, one of the United States' most important allies in what has come to be known as the "global war on terror" or "overseas contingency operations" (Christine Fair).

There are other expectations from Pakistan which would never be realized in the near future. The US government wants Pakistan to be an effective partner in the war on terror. The United States wants to ensure continued use of Pakistani military, police, and intelligence assets to eliminate Al-Qaeda leadership and cells within the territory of Pakistan. The United States would also like Pakistan to make it more difficult for Al-Qaeda and other militants to recruit and train new members. The United States would like Pakistan to deny these groups the ability to operate without fear of reprisal (Christine Fair).

Although the US government has always claimed to support democracy in Pakistan, other goals have often been of greater importance. US administrations have rarely pursued democracy vigorously. They have forged close working relationships with Pakistani military leaders willing to cooperate on other pressing issues. They have tended to subscribe to the idea that the Pakistan Army is a modernizing institution in Pakistan as it was in Turkey (Christine Fair). This complicates the process of having a democratically elected government in Pakistan. However modernized the army may be, at the end of the day another sovereign nation not dealing with political representatives of the people but with military would be a disastrous recipe for Pakistan as they have been victims of military rule time and again and this matrix has direct connection with India-Pakistan conflict. The expectation from the United States is to respect democratic institution and support it in such a way that it feels confident about dealing with extremist elements and bring in stability to the region.

US policymakers have made short-term tradeoffs in favour of supporting the Pakistani military rather than bolstering democratic institutions. They openly concede that they feared abandoning or even diluting support for the military because the United States might lose the benefits that the Pakistani military is able to deliver. This attitude of the US needs to be changed as there has been one experiment it tried in the past to race with the formerly USSR in Afghanistan that subsequently has led to 9/11. Short-term tradeoffs would never fetch results leading to democracy and peace. Promoting military which is directly in link with radical elements will only dilute the very process of war on terror and will have long-lasting effects on the peace and stability of the region.

The US-Indian nuclear agreement seriously discomfits Pakistan. The Pakistani government fears that the agreement may allow India to improve and expand its nuclear weapons arsenal. The new cooperative framework is aimed at making India a global power, at least the regional power to play a vital role in international politics. Collaboration between New Delhi and Washington, particularly, in the nuclear and space fields would disturb the conventional and non-conventional balance of power between India and Pakistan. Pakistan launched a diplomatic offensive to undermine the Indo-US deal, arguing that it would spark an arms race in the subcontinent, which Pakistan cannot afford. Pakistan also objects that the deal is India specific (Christine Fair). The nuclear deal will further enhance Indian capability to have pre-emptive attack against Pakistan.

The Indo-US nuclear deal gave a green signal to India's nuclear programme, raising its status from "unlawful and illegal" to the legitimized nuclear power. Pakistan expressed its desire, time and again to US to sign the similar nuclear deal, but the latter did not pay any response. As a result, Pakistan was compelled to explore a number of options that would best serve its security interests in the face of emerging Indo-US strategic partnership in the region. The prime concern for Pakistan was the acquisition of counter-force capability by India, which put the former's military assets at stake in case of a major conflict. There are apprehensions that India may convert its civilian nuclear program into nuclear arms, which will have serious security implications for Pakistan (Zahid Ali Khan).

The very aspect of the United States supporting India in its nuclear programme is generally attributed to clean track record of India with regard to nuclear technology. In contrast, Pakistan has indulged in proliferation time and again and has invited the wrath of several countries. US is also aware of the complexity involved in dealing with issues such as nuclear and also the cut throat competition between India and Pakistan. The biggest challenge is to curb the unquenching desire of Pakistan to receive the same status as India with the United States. India and the US relations have gone much beyond the normal level. Any government for that matter both in the US and India cannot think to abandon the relation as the relations have matured to a particular level. If at all there is a strain in relation, it can only be in some frequency but looking at sidelining the relation is a ruled out options for both democratically vibrant nations. On the other hand, Pakistan would continue to watch the growing bonhomie with open eyes and wait for an opportunity to attract US even in a negative way if not ever positive.

The past troubles in the US-Pakistan relationship had generated a so-called trust deficit on both sides (Stephen Cohen). Pakistanis felt that Americans had allied with and used their country when it suited them but then abandoned Pakistan to handle the consequences of the US policy. Though traditionally, Pakistan has enjoyed best of its relations with the United States in the past, with the rebalancing strategy, it feels a little cornered due to the importance attached to its arch rival India. Pakistan would never be in a position to digest the new bonhomie between India and the US which is growing stronger day by day. Till date, Pakistan has managed its relation in the best diplomatic way between the United States and China. It has received help from both the countries on different fronts at different times. With the rebalancing and India finding a primordial position, has put Pakistan into an awkward position.

Sri Lanka: The other nation to join the Pakistani concern is Sri Lanka in the region. Though it has no rivalry with India, it has often vented its displeasure in India voting the US sponsored resolution at the UN Human Rights Council (UNHRC). The history of Sri Lanka is marked with the emergence of the civil war which lasted for 26 years. The war was marked by phases of high intensity leading to Eelam War I: June 1983-July 1987; Eelam War II: June 1990-January 1995; Eelam War III: April 1995-February 2002; and Eelam War IV: July 2006-May 2009 which was often interrupted by different efforts to find a negotiated solution, which failed altogether. Rajapaksa strengthened Sri Lanka's military capabilities and established a "highly personalized, authoritarian regime, in which extreme nationalist views were widely accepted" (ICG, 2007).

Not only the LTTE displayed a willingness to provoke the government and to resume the war, but also the government seemed to be keen on a "fight to the finish" (Reddy, 2006): "what was new in the Rajapaksa administration's approach was the goal of defeating, as opposed to weakening, the LTTE militarily and then making the LTTE irrelevant to any political solution to the ethnic conflict" (Uyangoda, 2009). By mid-January 2009, the LTTE had been confined to a small jungle area in the Mullaithivu district, a space that continued to shrink up until the LTTE's military defeat and the death of its leadership in May 2009.

It is important to understand the personality trait of Mahinda Rajapaksa, a socialist in nature and more close to the non-capitalist and non-Western regimes. The very style of his consolidation which came as a great strategy from his first tenure to second tenure is fodder for psychologists to understand him. It is equally important to understand personalities and then deal with them in international relations rather than always trying to dominate through the size of geography and size of the forces. The history is a ready reckoner to showcase the failures of big nations against tiny ones; it is more particular when asymmetric conflicts are rising day by day. Rajapaksa—from a small town of Hambantota—had a unique way of handling the problems compared to his predecessors, with his approach being more radicalized and local in strategy implementation. One question comes up time and again; was the previous Sri Lankan regimes weak in military and had no strength to handle groups such as LTTE? The partial answer is not the strength of military but lack of a personality like Rajapaksa with a strong political will.

One such example which spoke of his skilled politics could be proved by a popular survey conducted by Sri Lanka's popular business magazine *Lanka Monthly Digest* in October 2007, in which more than 70 percent of Sinhalese, Tamils and Muslims supported him and his policy. These internal dynamics needs to be understood. This is not without a well-planned way of conduct of Rajapaksa as it would answer why the President did not go fully offensive on LTTE in the very beginning. He wanted to consolidate himself, become a strong leader, win peoples' confidence in him and then launching the offensive was his motive. This can be understood only when history of his regime is deconstructed by date and year-wise and a reconstruction of events would bring us to logical end.

For any country, when the power is authorized in a particular political party through democratic elections, there are certain expectations and a baggage of hopes. This in turn demands the elected government to act according to peoples' will and protect the nation's sovereignty and integrity, keeping the national interest at the pivotal position. One question that Rajapaksa often throws at his distracters has been that of questioning international action when Sri Lanka was going through a turmoil phase due to civil war and violence for three decades. The easiest way most of the nations escaped was through pronouncing the problem as domestic except may be nations such as India (again with a bad plan of IPKF) and to an extent Norway.

The rebuttal that Rajapaksa gives is the position of legitimacy associated with an elected government of protecting the people. The people in Sri Lanka, though were electing their political representatives, could not find a decisive leader and strong personality who could stand against a rebel group. This paucity was fulfilled by Rajapaksa and he filled the trust deficit that had come against the political class in whole of Sri Lanka by taking on the LTTE. It can be summed up as a prerogative of the government to take stringent action against a group which only believed in violence and which had bought disrepute to Sri Lanka being responsible for the killing of the Prime Minister of India. When national interest becomes paramount for all the nations in the world why not for Sri Lanka?

The US is indulging in reprimanding and intimidating the Sri Lankan government through some international agencies which are under its influence. The US has not learnt by its experience with Iran which was isolated by US through sanctions but was supported by all the NAM countries at a very crucial moment. It is the same case now again as two important members of Security Council, Russia and China, would never support US efforts to corner Sri Lanka. As long as there is no support by these two permanent members of Security Council, nothing substantial is going to happen to Sri Lanka and leadership in Sri Lanka is fully aware of that. Some have observed that a strong effort by the United Nations and the international community to force a criminal investigation into war crimes could be counter-productive as it would further bolster Rajapaksa's popularity on the basis of Sinhalese nationalism.

These observers argue that a focus on building the institutions of civil society and democracy, including freedom of the press and a more open political process, may have a stronger long-term effect on peace, stability, and ethnic integration (Bruce Vaughn). China's aid to Sri Lanka has reportedly increased dramatically since 2005. In the view of some analysts and observers, China is seeking to gain influence with the Sri Lankan government as part of a "string of pearls" naval strategy to develop port access in the northern reaches of the Indian Ocean. Indian defense planners are reportedly particularly concerned with Chinese efforts to develop ports in the region.

The UNHRC resolutions over the last three years have become a major bone of contention in understanding Sri Lanka. Sri Lanka has out rightly rejected the resolution as biased and US sponsored. "It is an established principle of international law that parties seeking remedy for a perceived grievance must exhaust all possible avenues within the domestic jurisdiction, prior to seeking redress in the international arena. Therefore, the State where the alleged violation occurred should have an opportunity to redress it by its own means, and exhaust the framework of its domestic system, before recourse to an international mechanism. It is ironic that with extensive domestic mechanisms in place, a resolution has been brought before the Council. This amounts to an infringement of state sovereignty and pre-judgment of the outcome of domestic processes" (Ravinatha Aryasinha). India decided to abstain from the UNHRC vote on the resolution against Sri Lanka in Geneva in 2014.

India's voting in 2012 and 2013 was a reaction to Rajapaksa government's approach to reconciliation and its reluctance to deliver inclusive political settlement as assured to the Government of India while enlisting India's support in its war efforts (Daily Mirror). India has always regarded any international investigation into conduct of war within a state as illegitimate intrusion into the sovereign sphere of a state. Hence, New Delhi chose to abstain rather vote in favour of the resolution brought by the US in the UNHRC in Geneva (Smruti Pattanaik). If due to Indo-US civil nuclear deal and the bonhomie, if the US pressurizes India to act against Sri Lanka, it would be extremely awful for India in maintaining peace in the neighbourhood.

Rajapaksa commented recently at CHOGM, "people in glass houses shouldn't throw stones', an oblique reference to Bloody Sunday, when 13 civilians were shot dead in Northern Ireland by the British army in 1972. He went on to say that countries should not "dictate" to Sri Lanka essentially referring to the military action he undertook against LTTE. Sri Lanka's hermeneutics in condemning any nation forcing on human rights issues is essentially not to become another Pakistan by accepting drones by countries like the United States in the name of establishing democracy and war on terror by subduing sovereignty. Apart from these pro-Sri Lankan approaches, there is no doubt that there has to be a credible enquiry and institution needs to be promoted to work for maintaining the human rights standards.

Sri Lanka would not want India to become part of the larger strategy of the US to corner Sri Lanka in the name of human rights and IDP's, rather it wants India to remain neutral and allow Sri Lanka to function as a sovereign nation. If the rebalancing has more influence on India to in turn to pressurize Sri Lanka to favour the United States, then Sri Lanka is completely against any such move. The leadership regime in Sri Lanka presently is predominantly socialist-oriented and would look towards East for help rather than West. All the allegations by different agencies across the world have been rubbished by Rajapaksa government.

The recent CHOGM meeting that took place in Sri Lanka also resonates the same. There is a necessity for US to respect institutions established by each sovereign nation as it does on its own soil. US needs to move beyond the rhetoric of Hegemonic Stability Theory of maintaining US supremacy like Cold War times and go beyond to understand that it is operating a more multifarious system with complex interdependency as the basic component in the world. The lesson to be drawn from the type of defiance shown by Sri Lanka reiterates the point of engaging as a primordial component to get better results and have a peaceful world than confronting and intimidating.

On the other hand every wrong step US takes would lead to an effortless campaign for China to enter nations waiting in despair. The startling example is China's presence in Sri Lanka in particular and other South Asian nations in general. It is an established fact that the US cannot take on China due to the type of economic relations they both share. It is wise for the United States to become a smart power and engage with nations rather than getting carried away with super power enigma. Though the US rebalancing is more specific to Asia-Pacific, it is no doubt that Indo-Pacific is going to be a region for the next great game and the role of tiny strategic countries like Sri Lanka would be paramount.

Bangladesh: Bangladesh is a curious case as its Prime Minister Sheik Hasina has also not been pro-US in the recent few months. The fallout between the Jamaat and Awami League regarding the hanging of Abdul Quader Molla has been a case in point where US tried interfering and nationalism prevailed over such a move.

Apart from the typical role US played during the freedom struggle of Bangladesh by supporting United Pakistan, the US-Bangladesh relations were stable until 2013. One of the brightest moments of Bangladesh-US relation was President Bill Clinton's visit to Bangladesh. His visit to Bangladesh proved that Bangladesh would get significant place in the US's South Asian regional calculation. The geostrategic interests that guide the US foreign policy today makes it imperative for it to have presence in areas where it can counter China effectively but in contrast, the recent events between Bangladesh and US have been proving detrimental in realizing the objective of containing China by the US. Every action of the US supporting extremist groups and pro-extremist political parties has been extremely problematic for Bangladesh.

Islamic fundamentalism is on the rise in Bangladesh and the groups identified with or espousing the cause of radical Islamic trends have brought havoc to the country. Far from being a marginal and sporadic element, these extremist groups have grown in strength and reach. The massive victory of Khaleda Zia in the October 2001 Jatiya Sangsad (Bangladesh Parliament) elections was often seen as the beginning of the current wave of fundamentalism and militancy. The BNP made an alliance with Islamic political parties, Jamaat-e-Islami, Jatiya (National) Party, and Islami Oikya Jot (IOJ) (Islamic National United Front), and returned to power in 2001 (Prasant Sahoo).

Now the former Prime Minister Khaleda Zia's Bangladesh National Party's coalition alliance with the Jamaat-e-Islami Party of Bangladesh has led to a "Faustian bargain" that brought Jamaat officials into the government. These officials, he argued, in turn have allowed Taliban-styled squads to operate with increasing impunity. Jamaat's entry into the former BNP government also reportedly led to fundamentalist control over large parts of the Bangladesh economy with Islamist Madrassa schools acting as fronts for terrorist activity (Selig Harrison). The most astonishing aspect of the issues is that on one hand, US is waging war on terror against terrorist organisations in other parts of the world as well as South Asia but the same time, US is supporting a political party led by Khaleda Zia supported essentially by Jamaat-e-Islami, which is known for its extremist views and heinous acts against freedom during 1971 to keep Pakistan united.

US questioned the election of Sheik Hasina and demanded for re-election. The statements made by the State Department Deputy Spokesperson Marie Harf was evident when she said, "We have been very clear about our strong concerns about the selection and what we think the way forward should be. We believe Bangladesh still has an opportunity to demonstrate its commitment to democracy by organising free and fair elections that are credible in the eyes of the Bangladeshi people". In contrast to this, India and China supported and appreciated Hasina's efforts to reconcile all the political parties and control extremism.

The worry for India is about the fundamentalists in Bangladesh motivating and biasing poor people in the name of enemy to Islam. They have been motivating and mobilizing people against India and supporting the anti-Indian elements. There is also report that they have been sponsoring terrorism against India and supporting insurgency movements in North-East India (Prasant Sahoo). Hasina has learnt lessons from Pakistan with regard to extremist organisations and their presence among the public, as Pakistan has become a victim of its own policy. India has been the most benefited nation from the Hasina regime with regard to containing terrorism and extremism affecting India.

There have been some reports that the United States was trying to use Mamata Banerjee to stall the peace process between India and Bangladesh with stalled issues such as Teesta, which has been detrimental for Hasina as she feels this was a plot to bring in BNP led by Zia with the help of Jamaat to power. Experts are of the opinion that US funded Mamata heavily for her campaign against the Left to come to power in West Bengal in 2011. This was a fruit that US thought of getting by hitting a single stone. On the one hand it was able to realize its revenge against the left for having stalled the Indo-US civil nuclear deal and on the other by trying to bring Khaleda Zia to power, again using Mamata by stalling the Teesta settlement (Subhir Bhaumik).

Though this sounds predominantly like a conspiracy theory, it cannot be ruled out completely. If US thinks that India should play the role of a lynchpin in Asia strategy, then for India, there is a necessity for having peaceful neighbours and go closer to being free from extremist elements. This can happen only when there is a pro-India and anti-extremist regime in the form of Hasina government. If the US does not rectify its working strategy, probably it will lose out to China even in Bangladesh which has been a trustworthy nation for a long time. China has been making its presence felt in Bangladesh heavily along with Myanmar. Though Bangladesh is another small country for US but it can be one more Sri Lanka in making and would add up to the negative popularity of the United States in South Asia. The success of US rebalancing strategy in Asia would be a triangle of US-India and another country. Without understanding this matrix, there can be no success for the US in its ambitious strategy.

Afghanistan: The position of Afghanistan is well known with regard to the 'Asia Pivot'. The United States has a continuing interest in the stability and development of Afghanistan.

However, advancing the valuable bilateral relationship with India, achieving a sustainable and effective policy towards Pakistan, and developing a regional policy that understands how South Asia connects to other parts of Asia are of even greater consequence.

The nation-building objective of the US has not fetched the expected results in the last one decade. The problem was of senior policy makers and US military leaders in 2001, and in later years too, with absolutely no expertise on Afghanistan and who were involved in making hasty decisions and establishing many poorly planned and disjointed initiatives.

Throughout much of the War, many policy makers and US military leaders had a Pollyannaish attitude towards winning the war and "sorting out" Afghanistan…The protracted US mission in Afghanistan shifted from overthrowing the Taliban leadership and its Al-Qaeda allies to denying safe haven to terrorists to democratization to fighting an insurgency to open-ended nation building" (Alexander Evans).

The question continues to remain as to what has been achieved so far by the United States in Afghanistan at large. Taliban and Al-Qaeda continue to threaten and challenge US every now and then. The drone strikes have not fetched the results as expected. Afghanistan would have a greater role in the US Asia rebalancing strategy as the respect towards the US also depends on its debacle in Afghanistan. There is no doubt in the fact that US will be haunted and would be made to remember Vietnam again in the form of Afghanistan.

Though no one knows whether the move to negotiate with the Taliban is part of the rebalancing with an expectation of having Taliban ruling in Afghanistan, the present Afghan government is literally upset with any such move. Afghan President made statements such as, "United States hardly kept his nation's best interests in mind during the 12 years of war in the country. The United States was much more concerned for the US security and for the Western interest, I felt "extreme anger" toward the US government for perceived betrayals by US forces who pursued Taliban insurgencies in Pakistan more than in villages of Afghanistan. Afghans died in a war that's not ours", (washingtontimes.com). Somewhere the Afghan President has felt that the plan did not go the way he anticipated; rather it undermined Afghanistan as a sovereign nation. Karzai's statement, "We want a good relationship with America; we want friendship, but friendship between two sovereign nations" (bbc.com) proves it right. US needs to move beyond its own geostrategic interests when it is in another sovereign soil. Afghans have better opinion on India which is involved in development activities than the US, though both the nations are investing with keeping their national interest as primordial. The US needs to work on its image building in Afghanistan as fear is not equal to respect".

Nepal and Bhutan: Since 2007, thousands of Bhutanese refugees have been leaving squalid camps in eastern Nepal and departing for new homes in the West. Though the older generation has long aspired to return to Bhutan, many younger refugees are excited to move to Western countries. The US is one of the seven Core Group countries taking the initiative on the third country resettlement of Bhutanese refugees. More than 65,000 Bhutanese refugees from Nepal and other regions have been resettled in the US until the end of 2012 (mofa.gov.np).

Recent reports, however, say the American dream might have turned sour for the Bhutanese refugees. A 2012 report by the US Center for Disease Control and Prevention revealed that the rate of suicide among Bhutanese refugees is 20.3 per 1,00,000 people—higher than the global average of 16 per 1,00,000 people. A 2014 report, 'Invisible Newcomers', explains some of the challenges faced by Bhutanese and Burmese refugees, who make up the two largest groups of recent refugee arrivals in the US (Aljazeera.com). Nepal and Bhutan have been two nations which do not have any major concern with the United States. Both being landlocked nations, have interest in the Unites States as it is one of the destinations for many of their refugees—though Bhutanese government would not accept the Nepali origin Bhutanese, accusing them of ethnic cleansing.

The Tibetan community in Nepal has, according to Human Rights Watch, been subject to numerous abuses at the hands of Nepali authorities as Nepal has reportedly come under pressure from China to quell any protests in Nepal over Chinese rule in Tibet. Nepali authorities reportedly made an estimated 8,350 arrests of Tibetans, out of an estimated total population of some 20,000 Tibetan refugees, exiles, and asylum seekers, during the period between March 10 and July 18, 2008. Human Rights Watch accused the government of Nepal of unnecessary and excessive use of force, arbitrary arrest, and sexual assault of women during arrest, arbitrary and preventative detention and beating of Tibetans in detention, and unlawful threats to deport Tibetans to China (Bruce Vaughn).

The only tension that has sandwiched Nepal is the issue of Tibetan refugees. US has been vocal in its support to Tibetan refugees in the form of making provision for 5,000 visas to Tibetan refugees to enter the United States for three years from 2013, citing "terrible" and increasing oppression by Chinese authorities against Tibetans—Senator Dianne Feinstein offered the matter as an amendment to the vast legislation aimed at fixing the US immigration system (tibet.net). This has certainly notched up the anger in China against the United

States but China would use Nepal to show that anger. China has been wooing Nepal with hydroelectricity projects. There has been a major shift in China's foreign policy towards Nepal since the Maoist ascendance to power. China had earlier adopted a policy of 'non-intervention' in the internal matters of Nepal and largely stayed out of Nepalese internal politics. In fact, twelve high-level Chinese delegations, including two military teams, visited Nepal in the course of 2008-2009.

During these visits, China has repeatedly assured economic, technological and military aid to Nepal. The Maoist-led government was also asked to adopt a 'One-China' policy, not to allow Nepalese land for anti-China activities, take strong action against Tibetan refugees and grant special facilities for Chinese investments in strategic sectors (Nihar Nayak). The United States needs to keep this in mind and engage with Nepal so that Nepal does not fall into the Maoist-China nexus. The best way to have Nepal in its rebalancing strategy is by making investments and encouraging and supporting Nepal to realize MDGs on human development front.

Conclusion

The most often accusation on the United States has been on the lines of having different standards for itself in all aspects of sovereignty, democracy and human rights and having different standards for other nations. This has led US being called as the most important factor in failing the Westphalia system and making it a West failed system. Though reacting to international affairs at the very first instance is the prerogative of being a super power, the US needs to learn to respond rather than reacting. It needs to learn to respect smaller nations and nations which require handholding support of being late to the grand subjects such as democracy and human rights. There are several other measures the use of which would yield better results.

The use of force should always be the last resort, certainly not the first. The US rebalancing strategy in South Asia can be carried forward only when US understands the intricacies of issues pertaining to growth and development of each nation and thinks beyond the national interest and behaves as the real super power, aspiring for global peace.

References

Bajpai, Kanti (2003), "Managing Conflict in South Asia", in Diehl, Paul F. and Joseph Lepgold (ed.), Regional Conflict Management, Oxford: Rowman & Littlefield, 209-238.

Bhasani, Avtar Singh (2003), "India-Bangladesh Relations", Documents-1971-2002, New Delhi: Geetika Publishers.

Bhaumik, Subir (2007), "Insurgencies in India's North East: Conflict Cooperation and Change", East West Centre Working Paper, No. 10. Washington: East West Center, July.

Chellaney, Brahma (2002), "Fighting Terrorism in Southern Asia: The Lessons of History", *International Security,* 26(3), 94-116.

Datta, Sreeradha (2004), "Attack on Sheikh Hasina", *Strategic Analysis,* 459-463.

Dixit, Jyotindra Nath (2003), "Sri Lankan External Affairs: Cross-Border Relations", New Delhi: Roli Books.

Fair, C. Christine (2010), "Pakistan: Can the United States Secure an Insecure State?", Santa Monica: RAND Corporation.

Gokhale, Nitin A. (2009), "Sri Lanka: From War to Peace", New Delhi: Har-Anand.

Hagerty, Devin T. (2008), "Bangladesh in 2007: Democracy Interrupted, Political and Environmental Challenges Ahead", *Asian Survey,* 177-183.

Kapila, Subhash (2003), "Bangladesh-China Defence Co-operation Agreement's, Strategic Implications: An Analysis", SAAG Working Paper, Chennai: South Asia Analysis Group, January 14.

Karlekar, Hiranmay (2005), "Bangladesh: The Next Afghanistan?", New Delhi: Sage Publications.

Lunn, Jon, Claire Taylor, and Ian Townsend (2009), "War and Peace in Sri Lanka", Research Paper, London: UK House of Commons Library.

Mohan, C. Raja (2003), "Crossing the Rubicon: The Shaping of India's New Foreign Policy", New York: Viking.

Noronha, Dos Santos and Anne (2007), "Military Intervention and Secession in South Asia: The Cases of Bangladesh, Sri Lanka,

Kashmir, and Punjab", London: Praeger Security International.

Pant, Harsh V. (2010), "The New Battle for Sri Lanka", July 23, available at:
www.isnethz.ch/isn/layout/set/print/content/view/full/73?id=11.

Rajagopalan, Rajeswari Pillai (2011), "US-India Strategic Dialogue: 'Sky's No Limit' for Space", New Delhi: Observer Research Foundation.

Ramanna, Deepa Ollapally and Raja (1995), "US-India Tensions: Misperceptions on Nuclear Proliferation", *Foreign Affairs.*

Reddy, B. Muralidhar (2006), "Water War", *Frontline,* August 12.

Saran, Shyam (2007), "The India-US Joint Statement of July 18, 2005: A Year Later"; Mohta, Atish Sinha and Madhup (2007), "Indian Foreign Policy: Challenges and Opportunities", New Delhi: Foreign Service Institute, 759-766.

Schaffer, Teresita C. (2002), "Building a New Partnership with India", *Washington Quarterly,* 41.

Schaffer, Teresita (2011), "Continued Primacy, Diminished Will: Indian Assessments of U.S. Power"; Cohen, Craig (2011), "Capacity and Resolve: Foreign Assessments of U.S. Power", Washington: Center for Strategic and International Studies.

Selig, Harrison (2006), "A New Hub for Terrorism? In Bangladesh, An Islamic Movement with Al-Qaeda Ties is on the Rise", *The Washington Post,* August 2.

Senanayake, Darini Rajasingham (2009), "From National Security to Human Security: The Challenge of Winning Peace in Sri Lanka", *Strategic Analysis,* 820-827.

Talbott, Strobe (2004), "Engaging India: Diplomacy, Democracy, and the Bomb", Washington: Brookings Institute.

Vaughn, Bruce (2011), "Nepal: Political Developments and Bilateral Relations with the United States", Washington: Congressional Research Service.

7

U.S. Rebalancing Strategy in the Indo-Pacific Region

B. Mohanan Pillai

Introduction

The rebalancing strategy of the US in the Indo-Pacific region has been on the scanner of the strategic community the world over in general and India in particular, ever since President Obama and his team in the administration have issued a series of announcements to step up and intensify the US presence in the region. These announcements have received worldwide attention because of its implications for both China and India. In his address to the Australian Parliament on November 17, 2011 Obama said, "As it has been to our past, our alliance continues to be indispensable to our future. So, here, among close friends, I'd like to address the larger purpose of my visit to this region—our efforts to advance security, prosperity and human dignity across the Asia-Pacific. For the United States, this reflects a broader shift. After a decade in which we fought two wars that cost us dearly, in blood and treasure, the United States is turning attention to the vast potential of the Asia-Pacific region"…"as President, I have therefore made a deliberate and strategic decision—as a Pacific nation, the United States will play a larger role in shaping this region and its future, by upholding core principles and in close partnership with allies and friends" (*Text of Obama's address in the Australian Parliament*).

In his view, security is the foundation of peace and prosperity. While re-emphasizing the strategic rationale of pivot to Asia initiative, he has in unequivocal terms articulated the economic imperatives of the new policy. He said, "The world's fast growing region—home to more than half the global economy—the Asia-Pacific is critical to achieving my highest priority and that is creating jobs and opportunities for the American people. With most of the world's nuclear powers and some half of humanity, Asia will largely define whether the century ahead will be marked by conflict or cooperation, needless suffering or human progress".

President Obama's announcement got the shape and status of a doctrine on Asia-Pacific when it was further explained, fine-tuned, projected and popularised by Hilary Clinton, US Secretary of State, Leon Paneta, US secretary of Defense and their junior colleagues in the US strategic establishment.

From the announcements of the President and other key players in strategic policy-making in the Obama administration, one could glean three clearly defined objectives of the pivot strategy. Firstly, the US wants to reinforce traditional alliances with Japan, Australia, South Korea, The Philippines, Singapore and Thailand. Secondly, it aims to build new partnerships and capabilities in the region with India, Vietnam and Burma. Thirdly, Obama wants to develop a new regional strategic architecture. According to Muni, "the present policy looks like an attempt to preserve and reinforce that predominance which seems to be sliding down in the face of China's rise, difficulties in the US economy both at home and abroad, and the unwinnable involvement in the war against 'global terror' in Afghanistan. It looks like an attempt to extricate the US from the vicious conflicts in Afghanistan and the Middle East without giving an impression that the US can no longer afford such involvements".

Obama said, "We see America's enhanced presence across Southeast Asia, in our partnership with Indonesia against piracy and violent extremism and in our work with Malaysia to prevent proliferation, in the ships we will deploy in Singapore and in our closer cooperation with Vietnam and Cambodia... and in our welcome of India as it looks east and plays a larger role as an Asian power…the United States will continue its efforts to build a cooperative relationship with China. All our nations—Australia, the US, all our nations—have a profound interest in the rise of a peaceful and prosperous China…We have seen that China can be a partner, from reducing tensions on the Korean peninsula to preventing proliferation. And we will seek more opportunities for cooperation with Beijing, including greater communication between our militaries to promote understanding and avoid miscalculation. We will do this, even as we continue to speak candidly to Beijing about the importance of upholding international norms and respecting the universal human rights of Chinese people (*Text of Obama's speech*).

Along with the statement of President Obama, we have also read the pronouncement of US Defense Secretary Leon Panetta, "after a decade of war, we are developing a new strategy—a central feature of which is a 'rebalancing' towards the Asia-Pacific region. In particular, we will expand our military partnership and our presence in the arc extending from the Western Pacific and East Asia into the Indian Ocean Region and South Asia" (quoted in Muni, *Obama Administration's Pivot*). Secretary of State Hillary Clinton and Panetta had referred the region as 'Indo-Pacific'.

According to American Policy analysts, the Obama administration's policy towards the Asia-Pacific region has evolved over time and has gone through two distinct phases. When the policy was first rolled out in 2011-12, much of the emphasis was placed on military initiatives in the region. China disapproved of these initiatives and Beijing took steps to demonstrate its power in maritime territorial disputes with the US allies. The Obama administration adjusted its approach in late 2012, playing down the significance of military initiatives, emphasizing economic and diplomatic elements, and calling for closer U.S. engagement with China (Sutter et al.).

From the above, it is very clear that although much attention has been paid on the military aspects of the pivot to

Asia strategy, it is important to note that the strategy is multidimensional in pronouncements and in implementation. Three sets of elements are inbuilt into the strategy viz. security elements, economic elements and diplomatic elements (Sutter et al.).

In the rebalancing strategy, an important juncture has been the weeklong trip of President Obama to Japan, South Korea and Malaysia in April 2014. It is to be kept in mind that during his reassurance trip to the region, all the original architects of the 'pivot' strategy, including Hillary Clinton, Defense Secretary Robert Gates, National Security Advisor Thomas Donilon and Assistant Secretary of State for East Asian and Pacific Affairs Kurt Campbell, left the Obama administration.

One Indian analyst has written, "Obama spoke to different audiences simultaneously. On the one hand, he tried to reassure the US allies of its commitment to remain supportive at a juncture when there are fears that China could exploit the prevailing international climate to become even more assertive or even belligerent on the Pacific Rim. On the other hand, while vowing to defend the allies, the US would expect them to show restraint themselves and even insisted that Washington sought solid relations with Beijing and hoped to enlist the latter to find solutions to various issues" (Bhadrakumar).

It is very clear that US counts India as an active partner in the rebalancing strategy to counter the rise of China. The Philippines, Japan, South Korea, and Singapore have been quite explicit in their support for a greater US presence in the region. It is noteworthy that both Australia and New Zealand have welcomed the US strategy in such a way without upsetting the existing economic ties with China. In what way did India respond to the pivot strategy? What are the implications of the US strategy for India's national security?

This paper examines these issues from a political economy perspective. The study is divided into three sections. The first section presents the theoretical and analytical framework of the study. The second section deals with India's response and the last section offers the author's own concluding remarks based on his analysis of the pivot strategy and India's response from the political economy perspective elaborated in the first section.

Theoretical and Analytical Framework

The social structure of accumulation (Kotz and McDonough) that came into being in the capitalist world to regulate macro economy as well as to provide a set of social programmes under the mixed economy rubric in the aftermath of the Great Depression and World War II had gone through dramatic transformations from the beginning of the 1980s. The world order that had been erected through the Brettonwoods agreements such as UN, IBRD, IMF etc. and a blend of state, market and democratic institutions to guarantee peace, inclusion, well-being and stability had also been reorganized. In other words, the world capitalist system has undergone a dramatic shift from welfare capitalism of the post-World War II period to a new phase of finance capitalism by the end of 1980s.

The social structure of capital accumulation has simultaneously witnessed a shift from accumulation through the expansion of wage labour in industry and agriculture to accumulation by dispossession, which in fact entails a very different set of practices. The former form of capital accumulation which dominated the scene during the 1950s and 1960s was not hostile to the culture of opposition that appeared in the form of trade unions and working class political parties. The contemporary form of capital accumulation, on the other hand, is fragmented and hostile to oppositional culture. Techno-capitalism manifested its ability to fragment production across borders and reintegrate the process through trade and transnationalisation of production relations. A multi-layered system of transnational governance has emerged under the protective shield of the international political economy managed by the Wall Street-WTO-World

Bank complex under the overarching politico-military dominance of the US.

In fact, the US as the lone super power has a global strategy to dominate the world. The rebalancing strategy is very much a part of it and a remodelled version of the project that the US ruling class has been cherishing since 1945 which now has five objectives as noted by Samir Amin: (i) to neutralize and subjugate the other triad partners (Europe and Japan) and to minimize their capacity to act outside the American fold; (ii) to establish military control over NATO and to 'Latin Americanize' the former parts of the Soviet world; (iii) to assert undivided control over the Middle East and its oil resources; (iv) to break-up China, to ensure the subordination of the other major states (India and Brazil), and to prevent the constitution of any regional blocs that might renegotiate the terms of globalization; and (v) to marginalize regions in the South that are of no strategic interest (Amin).

From the above, it is very clear that the US re-engagement in Asia-Pacific is nothing but the extension of the good old Monroe Doctrine to the Asia-Pacific region.

World Capitalist System and the Rhetoric of Non-alignment

During the decades of welfare capitalism, the newborn India followed a policy of non-alignment that got incubated in the nest of freedom movement. The experiments in diplomacy and foreign policy on the platform of non-alignment with its core value of strategic autonomy were to protect and promote the national interest of the newborn nations. Precisely, right from the Nehruvian era, the recurring theme in India's foreign policy has been "strategic autonomy". The seemingly autonomous space that was carved out of non-alignment policy facilitated the growth of domestic capital in the age of "embedded liberalism" (Harvey). But actually it was not autonomous as it was projected. In fact, the foreign policy of a country can never be independent and autonomous. It exhibits the complexity and interplay of relations that emanate from the national and international political economies.

India's foreign policy during the Nehru era was dominated by the question: how to sustain a full-fledged capitalist development legitimately under state patronage? Ideologically non-alignment's argumentation was couched in the fine language of counter-hegemony. But India never delinked itself from the world capitalist system. In fact, Nehru's proclaimed policy of non-alignment was a strategy aimed at augmenting adequate infrastructure facilities from both sides of the bipolar power bloc to accelerate native capitalist development. By adding socialist flavours, the Indian bourgeoisie embarked on a strategy of domestic capital development under state protection (Pillai). Import substitution industrialization was ensured under the protectionist umbrella of the state. From a political economy perspective, non-alignment never enjoyed strategic autonomy in the true sense of the term.

The objective of non-alignment was to facilitate import substitution strategies to help the growth of domestic capital within the overall framework of welfare state—the dominant paradigm of development of the period. "Embedded Liberalism" always allowed a bit of flexibility within its extended boundary. Nehru, and later Indira Gandhi, made use of this extended boundaries of embedded liberalism to promote economic growth and development through import substitution strategies.

The world capitalist system has moved out of its welfare capitalist phase to the brand new corporate techno-capitalist phase—a decisive shift from embedded liberalism to neo-liberalism. In its new phase, the world capitalist system forced the countries of the South to structurally adjust their economies to the requirements of finance capital. In the present phase of global political economy, the native bourgeoisie is inclined towards more cooperation with foreign capital and the state is attuned to an outward looking growth strategy. The neo-liberal reforms in the Indian economy coincided with the formulation of the celebrated 'Look East

Policy' (LEP) and strategic partnership with the US.

The post-Cold War period witnessed replacement of the bipolar balance of power of embedded liberalism period with the overarching dominance of finance capital controlled by global conglomerates. Side by side, the domestic Indian capital too has grown strong enough to take up roles beyond the territorial limits of India and naturally turned out to be subservient to global finance capital on the domestic front.

During the period of 'embedded liberalism'—precisely during the period of Cold War—India's security concerns revolved around the threats emanating primarily from Pakistan. On a conventional analytical frame, China is also perceived as a threat to India's national security.

Turning the international and domestic situations favourable to India's security architecture is a daunting task. The post-Cold War international power structure, is symptomatic of the overarching politico-military dominance of the US which turned out to be the protective shield of the international political economy managed by the Wall Street-WTO-World Bank complex. The US initiatives to curb international terrorism and actions against state sponsored terrorism suits New Delhi's official positions on India's foreign policy objectives which were reformulated in the aftermath of the collapse of the Soviet Union. In official parlance, India's relations with the United States have acquired remarkable maturity and dynamism in the post-Cold War period. Many developments created a conducive atmosphere for such a transformation, including the end of the Cold War. India's emergence as a dynamic economic force and an objective assessment of the strategic implications of a world dominated by knowledge-driven societies, have also led to the same.

Under the UPA government headed by Manmohan Singh, India-US relations moved beyond a bilateral partnership towards a global partnership, which were anchored not only on common values but also on common interests of the dominant sections. The strategic dimension of India's relationship with the US underlines their common interest in combating terrorism, proliferation of weapons of mass destruction and enhancing global peace. There has been a convergence of views on strategic and security issues which extends to cooperation in defence, science and technology, health, trade, space, energy and environment. Therefore, it is a logical extension that the US counts India on its side in the execution of the newly crafted 'rebalancing strategy in the Indo-Pacific region'.

Nature of the state and class configuration in the society and its relations with the world capitalist core are the major determinants of the foreign and security policy of a nation. In the case of India, native capital is inclined to have more cooperation with foreign capital. India's foreign policy establishment is now closely aligned with the interests of business groups and corporates which are exporting capital and welcoming foreign capital. Since India has been fully integrated to the global governance architecture controlled politically and militarily by the US, India has no other way to go but to perform a subordinate role in the pivot strategy of the US. Thus, the US rebalancing strategy and India's response need to be assessed against the backdrop of the dominance of finance capital in global political economy.

India's Response

India naturally appeared in the pivot to Asia-Pacific calculations of US strategists due to its geopolitical location and commendable military capabilities. Defence cooperation with India had been made a key component of the pivot strategy as explicated by President Obama and Secretary of State Hillary Clinton. India has also shared with the US a strong commitment to a set of principles that help India to enhance its power position in the region. Officials in the Indian foreign and strategic establishment and a section in the strategic community have seen that the pivot strategy converge with India's 'Look East Policy' (LEP). The initiation of LEP represented a reorientation of India's foreign economic policy strategy after the Cold War. The LEP signalled the end of India's precious pursuit of self-reliant concise development, and the start of an era which India strived to take advantage of, following new opportunities from international trade and investment.

On several counts, US's rebalancing strategy in the Indo-Pacific region finds strategic convergence with India's 'Look East Policy' which was drawn up in the 1990s to cement further its relations with the countries of Southeast and East Asia in the context of the disappearance of India's most trusted friend Soviet Union from the political map of the planet. More than an external economic policy or a political slogan, the 'Look East Policy' is a strategic shift in India's vision of the world and its place in the evolving global political economy. It is also a manifestation of India's belief that developments in East Asia are of direct consequence to its security and development. Therefore, India is actively engaged in creating a bond of friendship and cooperation with East Asia, and this has a strong economic foundation and a cooperative paradigm of positive inter-connectedness of security interests. Thus, LEP represents a reorientation of India's foreign economic policy in the aftermath of the demise of the Soviet Union and it signalled the end of the era of self-reliant growth strategy. The economic and foreign policy elites of the country facilitated the business class of India to take advantage of the new opportunities thrown open by neo-liberalism in the form of international trade and investment.

India thought that positive response to pivot strategy would help the country on a number of issues such as military, civilian and nuclear technology transfers, securing a deserving place in global decision-making, including the UN Security Council and high tables of nuclear decision-making, strengthening trade and investment flows and for support on regional security issues related to Pakistan and Afghanistan. Ever since the conclusion of 'Framework Agreement' in 2005, it has been acknowledged that defence cooperation between India and US has been put on firmer footing.

However, no consensus has been found among the Indian

strategic community about India's role in the pivot strategy. The debates in India has been summarised and grouped into four different categories by the Sigur Centre for Asian Studies. According to the Sigur Centre, the Indian views represent four distinct schools of thought: Soft Nationalists, Great Power Realists, Hard Nationalists and Bandwagoners (Sigur Centre for Asian Studies).

Ideologically, Soft Nationalists are not in favour of any kind of alignment with any of the great powers. According to this section, President Barack Obama's pivot is an attempt by the declining hegemon to "wrestle control of power transitions occurring in the Asia-Pacific and represents a strategic concern". They advocate that India should address the pivot question by maintaining strategic autonomy and equidistance from both US as well as China.

Great Power Realists prescribe greater strategic engagement with the US in terms of diplomacy and defence cooperation. Hard Nationalists talk about 'strategic independence' from great powers. They visualise a possibility of a grand accommodation between the US and China. Bandwagoners stand for a close strategic partnership with the United States. According to Sigur Centre, the domestic debate in India is fractured by the lack of consensus.

The Sigur Centre further observes that a lingering theme that has influenced the Indian debate very much is that the United States is not a reliable long-term ally. Sigur Centre has, no doubt, captured a very vital aspect of Indian position on the whole issue.

There is broad agreement in India that a strengthening of the US presence in the region will generally support India's interests and aspirations. Yet, when it comes to actually embracing the US rebalance, India has been cautious—to the consternation of many Americans. India's stand is driven by its aversion to provoking China, its attachment to strategic autonomy, and doubts about the extent of the US commitment to India (Ollappally).

It is noteworthy that major newspapers in India like *The Times of India*, *The Indian Express* and *The Hindustan Times* have viewed the rebalance strategy favourably. Influential analysts like Raja Mohan think that the US rebalance strategy has thrown open geopolitical opportunities for India. On the face of it, the US pivot to Asia is an extraordinary strategic opportunity for India. The unfolding Sino-US rivalry has the potential to end India's prolonged isolation from Asian geopolitics and offer Delhi a chance to insert itself as an indispensable element of the new regional balance of power. That India has long sought to balance Chinese power is beyond doubt. India's expanding security cooperation with the United States and its allies in the last few years and the attempts to raise its independent profile in East Asia points a clear Indian intent to balance China" (Raja Mohan).

"The realists in New Delhi's policy establishment have no problem recognizing the geopolitical significance of the US pivot to Asia. They appreciate the possibility that the pivot could compel Beijing to be more reasonable towards India as China begins to focus on the US military challenge from the east. The greater the US pressure in the Pacific, the more likely that China would want to keep its south-western frontiers tranquil. New Delhi's realists also understand that the gap in defence and strategic capabilities between India and China is widening in Beijing's favour. China's GDP is currently four times to that of India and its defence spending is nearly three and half times larger. India thus cannot merely rely on internal balancing to cope with China's rise; rather, the United States and its Asian allies must be central to any Indian strategy of external balancing" (RajaMohan).

India's Ambassador to the United States, Nirupama Rao, were among the few officials who made statements on the US rebalance. Lecturing at Brown University in February 2013, Rao said, "We welcome the US engagement in Asia for the Indo-Pacific…It is a space that impacts our destinies, whose security and prosperity is vital to both of us, and where we have an increasing convergence of interests". Ambassador Rao then turned to China, "Many observers are tempted to view the India-US engagement in this region, as directed at China. I do not believe that such a construct is valid or sustainable, given the significant overlapping interests that bind us in the region and globally…China is our largest neighbour". The ambassador went on to endorse an Asian "Concert of Powers" including the United States that would require mutual accommodation between countries. She termed it 'inclusive balancing' where the US simultaneously engages all the regional powers like China, India, Japan and Russia working to see a multipolar order" (quoted in Ollappally).

According to Ollappally, realists close to the Indian government prefer to express their views privately. For instance, former ambassador to the United Nations, T.P. Sreenivasan, was quoted as saying, "We do not want to be identified with US policy in Asia, even if we secretly like it".

One of the best studies on India's response to US pivot to Asia Strategy is that of S.D. Muni. He has analysed the statements of President Obama and other key policy makers in the US Administration. He has also examined statements of key leaders of the Indian Government. On the basis of such an extensive study, Muni has concluded that India positively responded to the pivot strategy with certain reservations. "What then is expected out of India in relation to the US 'pivot'? Some analysts compared the evolving strategic partnership between India and the US to the complex affair between the Egyptian queen Cleopatra and the Roman General Mark Antony, which was masterfully portrayed by Shakespeare. They were both charmed by and longed for each other but were not prepared to compromise with each other on their respective turfs, imperial possessions and areas of influences.

Likewise, India and the US have found their strategic partnership valuable and are trying their best to expand and reinforce it, but would not like to compromise on their respective autonomy, leadership and strategic spaces. This would likely to be the benchmark, guiding their engagement in relation to the US 'pivot" (Muni).

Another major analysis on India's response is that of Deepa M. Ollapally of the Sigur Centre of Asian Studies. As noted above, she has concluded that there is a broad agreement in India about the US rebalance strategy. However, India is very cautious in the matter of openly embracing it.

According to the present writer the scholars referred above have not taken into account the political economy aspect. The duality that was found by them in the foreign policy behaviour of India with respect to the pivot strategy could be the end product of the dynamic interplay of international political economy and the domestic political economy. That is why we argue that India's foreign policy behaviour is required to be analysed from a political economy perspective. Such an analysis would help us to unravel the fact that, right from the Nehruvian days, India's foreign policy making has been within the orbit of global capitalism. Viewed thus, all the talks about strategic autonomy is just a political rhetoric.

Concluding Remarks

The attempt in this paper has been to analyse the US pivot strategy in the Indo-Pacific region and the Indian response to it from a political economy perspective. To get an in depth understanding of India's foreign and strategic policy positions, the nature of international political economy has been discussed initially, and against the backdrop of it, India's policy framework of non-alignment has been discussed briefly. The author's argument is that despite the rhetoric of strategic autonomy, India has always been a part of the international political economy.

Therefore, India got adjusted and readjusted to the shifts and trends in international political economy with ease. Because of that, India did not find much difficulty in embracing the new phase of capitalism. Viewed thus, the flexibility of non-alignment permits India's integration into the contemporary international political economy with a subordinate status. At the same time, the rhetoric of strategic autonomy will continue to echo in official statements and will never explicitly acknowledge that India welcomes the pivot strategy.

References

Amin, Samir (2006), "Beyond US Hegemony: Accessing the Prospects for a Multipolar World", New York: Zed Books.

Harvey, David (2005), "A Brief History of Neo-liberalism", New York: OUP.

Kotz, David M., and Terrence McDonald (2007), "Global Neo-liberalism and the Contemporary Social Structure of Accumulation", in Terrence McDonough, David M. Kotz and Michael Reich (ed.), Understanding Contemporary Capitalism: Social Structure of Accumulation Theory for the Twenty-First Century, CUP, December 18.

Muni, S.D. (2013), "Obama Administration's Pivot to Asia-Pacific and India's Role", ISAS Working Paper 159, August, pp. 1-13.

——(2012), "Rebalancing-Obama 2.0: India's Democratic Differential", ISAS Insights 191, November 6, pp. 1-6.

Ollapally, Deepa M. (2013), "India's Response to the U.S. Rebalance", in Robert G. Sutter et al., Balancing Acts: The U.S. Rebalance and Asia-Pacific Stability, Sigur Centre for Asian Studies, August.

Sutter, Robert et al. (2013), "Balancing Acts: The U.S. Rebalance and Asia-Pacific Stability", Sigur Centre for Asian Studies, August.

8

Indo-U.S. Economic Relations after Global Financial Crisis

Shaijumon C.S.

Introduction

Indo-US bilateral relations have always been under the global scrutiny, particularly because India is now the second fastest growing economy in the world and US is the world's largest economy. Since 2004, Washington and New Delhi have been pursuing a 'strategic partnership' based on numerous shared values and improved economic and trade relations. Indian economy is growing at an ever increasing speed and US companies view the Indian market as a lucrative option and a candidate for foreign investments. For its part, the current Indian government sees itself continuing the economic reforms aimed at transforming a quasi-socialist economy into a more open, market-oriented one.

The world has been witnessing a financial and economic crisis following the sub-prime mortgage in the United States (Nanto, 2009; Bosworth and Bosworth, 2009). While exact reasons are yet to be known at a fundamental level, the crisis could be ascribed to many factors including gross financial irregularities, excessive risk taking and large and persistence global imbalance. The crisis threatens to undo the economic development achieved by many countries and to erode people's faith in an open international trading system (Lamy, 2012). This is the first global recession of the new era of globalization (Stiglitz, 2008). Over the past decades of globalization, India had grown rapidly till the financial crisis appeared in mid-2007. This acceleration of growth, in which international trade has played an important role, has helped Indian economy make impressive strides in economic development.

The unfolding global financial crisis comes in various forms and presents many challenges as well as opportunities, even though it is too early to predict any specific outcome. However, the fact remains that the international system of trade, investment and power relations are undergoing a shift. This has serious implications for a developing country like India and its relations with major powers like United States of America. The impact of the global crisis on India can broadly be divided into three different aspects: (i) the immediate direct impact on its financial sector; (ii) an indirect impact on economic activities; and (iii) potential long-term geopolitical implications.

Fortunately, India, like most of the emerging economies, was lucky to avoid the first round of adverse affects because its banks were not overly exposed to subprime lending. With the increasing integration of the Indian economy and its financial markets, there is recognition that the country does face some downside risks from the developments in economic crisis of US. The crisis imbalances, when combined with the monetary, fiscal and regulatory policies in the United States, exposed the risks of disintermediation, corporate governance practices and financial innovations, and contributed to a housing bubble. Given the magnitude of the US economy and the seriousness of the financial shock in the US, the crisis reverberated back across countries like India with potentially important implications in the economic relationship between the two countries.

India-US economic relations in the form of bilateral investments and trade constitute important elements in India-US bilateral relations. Economic reforms introduced since 1991 have radically changed the course of the Indian economy and led to its gradual integration with the global economy. Benefits of the reform process are visible in the form of better growth rates, higher investment and trade flows and accelerated decline in income poverty. Until late 1990s, United States often ignored India, treating it as a regional power. India is now an important economic power on track, and marching towards to become one of the top five global economies by 2030. The effects of these reforms on trade and investment relations with the United States have been profound. US is a major investing country in India in terms of FDI approvals, actual inflows, and portfolio investment. US investments cover almost every sector in India, which is open for private participants.

India's investments in US are picking up. Since 2000, the two countries have been making efforts to strengthen institutional structure of bilateral economic relations by means of the "India-US Economic Dialogue" that aims at deepening the Indo-American partnership through regular dialogue and engagement. The financial crises experienced by the international system have serious geopolitical and economic implications. It has brought in new players like India and China, and it has exposed the domestic economic policy compulsions of the United States. However, the extent to which the challenges engendered by the crisis can be converted into opportunities by a country like India, remains to be seen.

Global Crisis and Indo-US Trade Relations

One of the first transmission channels of the international financial crisis was foreign trade financing and the rapid drop in world trade. In India, as in most countries that are reasonably integrated into the global economy, the first adverse impact of the crisis on the real economy was on its exports. India was the 13th largest goods trading partner of US with US$ 57.8 billion in total (two ways) goods trade during 2011 (Table 8.1).

Merchandise exports shrank by more than 17 percent from October 2008 to May 2009. The decline in exports accelerated, with a drop in May 2009 of 29.2 percent compared with May

2008. Likewise, exports of services also faced a steep downturn. US was India's largest trade partner before the crisis and it came down to third in 2013. Total bilateral trade in goods touched US$ 62.8 billion in 2012, registering a growth of about 9 percent over the previous year. Indian exports accounted for US$ 40.5 billion, resulting in a trade surplus of around US$ 18 billion. The merchandise trade in first seven months (January to July) of 2013 was US$ 38.4 billion, growing at 7.4 percent over the same period last year. India was the United States 17th largest goods export market and 13th largest goods supplier in the year 2011.

Table 8.1: India-U.S. Goods Trade (US$ billion)

Year	Exports	Imports	Total Trade	Trade Balance
1980	1.1	1.7	2.8	- 0.6
1985	2.3	1.6	3.9	0.7
1990	3.2	2.5	5.7	0.7
1994	5.3	2.3	7.6	3.0
2000	10.7	3.7	14.4	7.0
2006	18.9	11.7	30.6	7.2
2008	25.7	17.7	43.4	8.0
2009	21.2	16.4	37.6	4.7
2010	29.5	19.3	48.8	10.3
2011	36.2	21.6	57.8	14.5

Source: Compiled by the author from various reports.

India's total trade with US in the year 2008, the year of global crisis, was US$ 43.4 billion and it declined to US$ 37.6 billion in 2009. The slump in trade of merchandise goods after the crisis was very deep in India's exports to US although it did recover in the year 2009. The point to be noted here is that India has been experiencing a positive trade balance with US since 1985.

Indo-US Investment Relations

FDI inflows from USA constitute about 8 percent of actual

FDI inflows into India in rupee terms. U.S. is the fifth largest source of foreign direct investments into India; as per the official statistics of September, 2013, the cumulative FDI inflows from the US from April 2000 to March 2013 amounted to about US$ 11.6 billion constituting nearly 6 percent of the total FDI into the country. During the financial year 2014-15 (from April 2014 to March 2015), the FDI inflows from US into India were US$ 1,824 million contributing 6 percent of the total FDI inflow during this period. In recent years, growing Indian investments into the US has been a novel feature of bilateral ties.

A recent study of 68 Indian companies which have invested in the US, conducted by the Confederation of Indian Industry (CII), has found that these companies invested nearly US$ 17 billion in the US; and, about one-third of the companies were actively engaged in research and development (R&D), having spent over US$ 340 million in R&D activities, thus contributing to innovation in this country. Indian investments in the United States have risen from US$ 200 million to US$ 5 billion between 2000 and 2010, and further rose to US$ 11 billion in 2012. This led to a mentionable growth in the US economy and created more than 100,000 jobs.

Services sector have accounted for the highest share of cumulative FDI equity inflows from US with a share of 22 percent amounting US$ 2.1 billion (this was about 7 percent of total FDI equity flows to services sector in India).

The Indian government is making a concerted effort to integrate its economy with the rest of the world. To help Indian firms raise capital abroad, the government will allow unlisted Indian companies to list on overseas markets without having to be publicly traded on domestic exchanges.

Indian companies have aided the turnaround of struggling US firms, saving jobs and improving company's performance. They have also made important new investments, stimulating innovation and production in the American economy. For example, Essar Group invested over US$ 1.6 billion in the declining Minnesota Steel Industries and now employs over

7,200 people in almost a dozen states. The Tata Group has invested more than US$ 3 billion in the US and now employs nearly 19,000 throughout the country. Jubliant Organsys Total Capital invested US$ 246 million in the US and now employs nearly 900 employees throughout the country.

Wockhardt, a pharmaceutical company, acquired Morton Grove for US$ 37 million. The deal preserved the jobs of all 200 original Morton Grove employees. Crompton Greaves, an entity of the Indian conglomerate Avantha Group, has invested and partnered on a US$ 20 million project to launch a Centre for Intelligent Power with the University of Albany. The deal will create 100 high-tech jobs in upstate New York. According to a report by Ernst & Young and the Federation of Indian Chambers of Commerce and Industry (FICCI), the largest share of investment capital from India to US has been allocated to industries associated with the knowledge economy. This inflow of capital will expand the US economy across a wide variety of fields, creating jobs and keeping the US competitive in the global markets.

India's sizable population and growing middle class makes it a potentially large market for US goods and services. But the major impediments to expanding the trade and investments into India for US are the constraints in FDI in many sectors, poor infrastructure, bureaucratic procedures, poor enforcement of dispute resolution mechanisms, unfavourable labour policies, tariff and non-tariff barriers to trade, meagre enforcement and inadequate laws in intellectual property rights and corruption. While maintaining high tariff rates on imports, India also levies high surcharges and taxes on a variety of imports.

Major non-tariff barriers include sanitary and phyto-sanitary restrictions, import license, regulations, discriminatory government procurement practices, export subsidies etc. which are still prevalent the economy. Almost 2 million people of Indian origin are living in US. Their participation in the Indian economy has been largely confined to remitting money or investing in equity and bank deposits rather than into more productive investments. Interestingly, research has shown that immigrants have been the key founders in one of every four US engineering and technology firms, with overseas Indians involved in 26 percent of these.

The combined Indian market in defence, aerospace and homeland security sectors is projected to grow to US$100 billion in the next five to six years with India becoming one of the top 10 defence markets globally. Business opportunities for the US companies are galore since they could be key suppliers of advanced fighter jets, modern surveillance technologies, unmanned aerial and ground vehicles, sophisticated guns and missiles, etc. US aerospace companies are already gunning for the US$ 10.8 billion project to supply 126 medium multi-role combat aircraft (MMRCA) to the Indian Air Force (IAF), which is touted as India's single largest defence deal ever. India requires investment to the tune of US$ 1 trillion during the 12th Five Year Plan ending March 2017 for development of various infrastructure projects. The share of infrastructure investment in GDP is planned to be increased to more than 10 percent by the end of the 12th Plan. These are some of the opportunities.

India should play a more proactive role for filling the economic vacuum created by the global financial crisis. It should look for more engagement with US for attracting capital and technology which will help to diversify its exports for the world market. India has to focus on an agenda to create productive jobs outside of agriculture, which will help it reap the demographic dividend and also improve livelihoods in agriculture. The country needs to examine carefully whether regulations constrain businesses excessively and, if so, strip away the excess regulations while ensuring adequate protection and minimum safety nets for the workers. India should relax the restrictions in imports and exports. India is chronically short of electric power, yet equipment imports are restricted. Firms not producing in India often cannot compete for tenders. For solar equipment and materials, India requires joint ventures. It is vital that the trade goal should have an ideal set of rules, not an ideal set of results. The ability of American firms to compete in India should neither be ruined nor assured by government action, but by their own competitiveness.

Three main reasons which explain the resilience of the Indian economy to the recessionary impacts of the global crisis are outlined here. The first is that Indian foreign exchange regulations, in spite of being relatively open to investments in the stock market, are still highly restrictive to investments in both government treasuries and most fixed-income assets. Therefore, under a regime which somewhat restricts external financial integration—a rare situation in most developing countries in the late 2000s—policymakers were able to restore positive expectations more effectively, even though the global economy was being driven in the opposite direction.

The second reason is related to the speed and intensity with which the RBI reduced the basic interest rates. This decision was essential to signal to markets that the priority was to prevent a sharp slowdown or even a possible shrinking of economic activity. The third reason is that the first round of fiscal stimuli was adopted quicker and with much more intensity. The global financial and economic crisis has brought to the fore the role of governments and public administration in preventing such crises in the future. The assumption, widely prevalent, that we pause and reset the button is neither borne out by experience nor is safe to rely on. The objectives of regulation should include the assessment of the safety of financial products and the stability of the financial system, including assessment of the risks of unrestricted integration of financial markets, domestically and internationally.

With its emergence as an economic powerhouse, India is now in the "priority markets" list of US investors since they are lured by ample and diverse business prospects available in India. The US is capital-rich and land-rich, India is labour-rich. Due to skills and education gaps, India does not make full use of its labour, but the comparatively high cost of American labour and the raw size of the Indian labour force, even in some high-margin sectors, leave huge potential gains from trade. Yet the top Indian export to the US and the top American export to India were both jewellery with a combined revenues of US$ 10 billion. Instead of an approximation of a traditional alliance relationship founded on presumed common geostrategy, New Delhi and Washington should focus on pragmatic cooperation on the basis of the intersection of their narrower respective interests.

References

Amit Gupta (2005), "The U.S.-India Relationship: Strategic Partnership or Complementary Interests?", available at: http://www.carlisle.army.mil/ssi.

Arvind Subramanian (2013), "Deepening US-India Trade Relations", Testimony before the Ways and Means Committee of the United States Congress, hearing on "US-India Trade Relations", Congressional Testimony, March 13.

B. Bosworth and A. Flaaen (2009), "America's Financial Crisis: The End of An Era", A paper presented at the ADBI conference Global Financial and Economic Crisis: Impacts, Lessons, and Growth Rebalancing, Tokyo, April 22-23.

Dick K. Nanto (2009), "Global Financial Crisis: Analysis and Policy Implications", Congressional Research Service, CRS Report for Congress, USA.

George Perkovich (2010), "Towards Realistic US India Relations", Carnegie Endowment, Washington D.C.

Joseph E. Stiglitz (2008), "Making Globalisation Work", Research Series, Economic and Social Research Institute (ESRI), Number GL35, December.

Madan Lal Goel (1999), "Indo-American Relations in a New Light", Lecture at the Annual Meeting of the Indian Association of American Studies, University of West Florida.

Pascal Lamy (2012), "The Future of the Multilateral Trading System", Richard Snape Lecture, Commonwealth of Australia, Melbourne.

Prabir De (2011), "Trade Facilitation in India: An Analysis of Trade Processes and Procedures", Working Paper No. 95, Asia Pacific

Research and Training Network on Trade.

Richard C. Holbrooke and Vishakha N. Desai (2009), "Delivering on the Promise: Advancing US Relations with India", Asia Society.

Robert A. Buckle (2009), "Asia Pacific Growth: Before and After the Global Financial Crisis", *Policy Quarterly*, Volume 5, Issue 4.

S. Paul Kapur and Sumit Ganguly (2007), "The Transformation of US India Relations: An Explanation for the Rapprochement and Prospects for the Future", *Asian Survey*, Volume 47, Issue 4, pp. 642-656, University of California.

Special Report from the Asia Study Centre (2013), "Beyond the Plateau in U.S.-India Relations", *The Heritage Foundation and the Observer Research Foundation,* Washington D.C.

Swaminathan S. Anklesaria Aiyar (2012), "India and the United States: How Individuals and Corporations Have Driven Indo-U.S. Relations", *Policy Analysis*, No. 713, CATO Institute.

Uma Purushothaman (2012), "India US Defence Trade Relations: Trends and Challenges", ORF Seminar Series, Volume 1, Issue 7, April, Observer Research Foundation.

Wayne Morrison and Alan Kronstadt (2004), "Indo-US Economic Relations", CSR Report for Congress, *Foreign Affairs*, Defence and Trade Division, The Library of Congress, USA.

9

Indo-Japanese Strategic Relationship

Anil Kumar P.

The realist paradigm reigns supremacy in international relations theories. This is because it has core features that exert strong appeal beyond the academy: explanatory parsimony and the use of historical analogy. Realists place great emphasis on Europe's experience of great power politics, and for those like the Kenneth Waltz, John Mearsheimer and Australia's Hugh White, 'secondary' powers have little agency in an anarchic international system. Great powers call the shots and other states have few options but to fall in line. Yet Asia's geopolitical order, mid-way through the second decade of the 21st century, is not mirroring the realist script. The region is characterised by great-power rivalry between the US and China, but there is little evidence that non-great powers feel under pressure to 'choose sides'. And there are few indications this will change in the future. Indeed, small and middle powers are demonstrating a degree of agency in shaping geopolitics that undermines the validity of the realist model for predicting how states in Asia will behave.

Middle Powers: The Conceptual Debate

Middle power theorists can be divided into classical and the revisionist schools of thought. Classical school scholars, writing throughout the Cold War, argue that a state's material position in the international system determines its status as a middle power. This approach derives a state's hierarchical rank, based on structural factors including resources such as population, territory and economy, as well as power capabilities such as power projection or nuclear weapons. Despite the analytical ambiguity of his approach, Holbraad did make a valuable contribution to middle power theory through his observation that the middle power's propensity to act as mediators is contingent upon the structure of the international system.

Competitive balance of power situations, for example, allow a larger scope of action for middle powers, while a unipolar order stifles their foreign policy freedom. [1]

The likelihood of middle powers to balance or bandwagon, Holbraad argues, 'depends on a number of factors, such as [their] geographical position, political tradition, the nature of the issue, and norms of the states' system'. [2]

An alternative has been presented by Cooper, Higgott and Nossal, who reject the structuralist approach of the classical school and instead present a model where the behaviour of states, rather than their position in an international hierarchy, determines middle power standing. [3]

They offer a typology of middle power behaviour, which became the basis for future revisionist work. Cooper et al. portray middle powers as: (i) catalysts and policy entrepreneurs; (ii) facilitators, building coalitions and setting agendas; and (iii) managers, building institutions, confidence and credibility.

Middle powers, they argue, are most appropriately defined by 'a particular style of behaviour in international politics', whereby they tend to pursue multilateralism and compromise on notions of 'good international citizenship'.

According to the revisionist framework, states with a range of relative material capabilities may qualify for middle power status, as long as their foreign policies demonstrate elements of middle power behaviour, as outlined by the Cooper et al., typology. [4]

Middle powers are best understood through an approach that combines material, behavioural and ideational factors. The refined middle power concept developed over the time considers middle powers to be states that: (i) have mid-range capabilities and are medium sized; (ii) perceive multilateralism and soft power as the optimal way to maximize their foreign policy interests; and (iii) self-identify as middle powers to domestic and international audiences. [5] All three components must be present for a state to qualify for the recalibrated definition of a middle power. Unlike small and great powers, middle powers are generally not expected to engage in combative diplomacy, preferring instead constructive engagement and consensus building in pursuit of peace and conflict management, multipolarity, and rules-building.

In short, the *middle level powers* are those which by reason of their size, their material resources, their willingness and ability to accept responsibility, their influence and stability are close to being great powers. [6] They are not superpowers or great powers, but still have large or moderate influence and international recognition.

Middle Level Powers in Asia

Whichever way we define middle powers, the fact is that Asia has a large number of countries which have fairly large populations, significant resources and strong economic growth. Many of them in the region have significant military and other power potential and, unlike in Europe, many of these countries are not going to simply sit back and accept what the great powers are going to do.

India and Japan belong to this middle power groups. They are strong middle powers in Asia. Middle level powers and there relations are very important in Asia because they have the capability to influence the rebalancing strategy in Asia and have capability to change the course of rebalancing. This middle power alliance will also enhance their mutual security and development. Given this large number of middle powers in Asia, they can, in one way or another, try and influence the environment around them rather than merely submit to the logic that the Sino-American rivalry presents itself. Middle power alliance will create more space for the nations by reducing the dependency over major powers.

Middle powers are demonstrating a degree of agency in

shaping geopolitics. Indonesia, Thailand, and Malaysia have resisted bandwagoning with the new rising powers in Asia, nor have they joined the US, Japan, and Australia to balance against China. Far from being pressured into choosing camps, all three have been highly adept at exploiting benefits from close relations with Beijing and Washington. The two Koreas are showing signs of serious hedging strategies. Seoul's intimate economic relationship with Beijing has led to closer politico-strategic ties, but there are few indications that South Korea is weakening its alliance ties with Washington. For its part, Pyongyang has reasserted foreign policy autonomy in relation to Beijing by engaging in direct talks with Tokyo and effectively ignoring China's warnings about the need to exercise restraint.

Asian Rebalancing

The rise of Asia in all its dimensions has profound implications for the world. Asia is in a state of flux and uncertainty. Obama administration's rebalancing strategy is a well calibrated attempt to deal with the emerging Asia. They assume that a close co-operation with Asian powers is central to America's interests. Four of the world's emerging military powers—Russia, Japan, China and India—and five of the world's nine nuclear powers (six if Israel is counted as part of Asia) and some of the fastest growing economies are in this geographical area. The US continues to be a super power although there is a strong expectation that the US pre-eminence is waning in relative terms. At the same time, Asia appears ripe for strategic conflicts, competition and power rivalry due to some of the inherent characteristics and problems. Some of the factors that contribute to conflict and rivalry include unsettled boundary and territorial issues; distrust among major Asian powers; uncertainties surrounding China's growing military might, competition for resources and competition for dominance and changing power dynamics in the region.

Beginning in the fall of 2011, the Obama administration has issued a series of announcements and taken a series of steps to expand and intensify the already significant role of the United States in the Asia-Pacific region. Explicitly identifying the Asia-Pacific region as a geostrategic priority for the United States, the Obama administration has accorded significant attention to the region across a wide range of issue areas.

The story of the rebalance is not a story of US disengagement and then re-engagement in Asia. It is a matter of emphasis and priority, building on an elaborate foundation of US-Asia relations. The Obama administration's policy toward the Asia-Pacific region has evolved over time and has gone through two distinct phases. When the policy was first rolled out in 2011-12, much of the emphasis was placed on military initiatives in the region. China disapproved of these initiatives, and Beijing took steps to demonstrate its power in maritime territorial disputes with the US allies. The Obama administration adjusted its approach in late 2012, playing down the significance of military initiatives, emphasizing economic and diplomatic elements, and calling for closer US engagement with China.

It is generally argued that the rebalance was designed to contain China. US policymakers are certainly aware of China's economic rise and its growing military power, but the rebalance has been driven by a much broader set of strategic, economic, and political considerations. Following more than a decade of war in Afghanistan and Iraq, the Obama administration has been trying to place more emphasis on Northeast, Southeast, and South Asia—parts of the world that will be of growing strategic and economic importance in the first half of the 21st century. In geostrategic terms, the rebalance is the Obama administration's grand strategy for US foreign policy.

It is also an important fact that rebalance is also driven by a desire to reassure US allies, friends, and other countries in the region that the United States has not been exhausted after a decade of war, that it has not been weakened by economic and political problems at home, and that it is not going to disengage from Asia-Pacific affairs. Even though the basic goals of the new US policy are to broaden areas of cooperation beneficial to the United States with regional states and institution; emergence of China in the international field as a potential competitor to United States became a real catalyst for this rebalancing strategy.

The rebalance is a region-wide, multidimensional policy initiative. In regional terms, the shift includes a stronger emphasis on Southeast Asia and South Asia to complement traditionally strong American attention to Northeast Asia. In policy terms, the rebalance entails three sets of initiatives—security, economic, and diplomatic elements.

Regional Responses to Rebalancing
China has reacted at two levels to the Obama administration's rebalancing of US-Asia relations. At the official level, Chinese government representatives and official media have levelled measured criticism of the new US policy, especially its military aspects. In China's non-official media, criticism of the rebalance and the United States has been vociferous. Some commentators have alleged that the United States is engaged in a conspiracy to develop a Cold War-style "containment" of China. Almost every other regional power in Northeast, Southeast, and South Asia holds to two positions. First, most regional powers have been publicly or privately pleased to see the stronger US commitment to the Asia-Pacific region. Second, regional powers are also keen to avoid having to choose between the United States and China. They very much want to have good relationships with both countries. A few regional powers, including Indonesia, Thailand (a formal US ally), and Malaysia, have been "straddling the fence"— avoiding any public sign of tilting toward either the United States or China.

The Philippines, Japan, South Korea, and Singapore have

been exceptions to the generally muted official reactions in the region; their support for a greater US presence in the region has been quite explicit. Australia and New Zealand also have warmly welcomed the US rebalance, though both have taken pains to avoid upsetting China and their important economic ties with Beijing. Many other key countries in the region—including India, Vietnam and Burma—have taken significant steps to improve relations with the United States in recent years. Although governments in these countries have been careful to preserve their close economic ties with China and to avoid offending the region's rising power, they have found it strategically reassuring to position themselves a few steps closer to the world's pre-eminent superpower. In the face of a rising and increasingly assertive China, many countries in the Asia-Pacific region have drawn on classic balance-of-power thinking and "rebalanced" their positions closer to the non-threatening great power.

The challenge for the United States is to provide strategic reassurance to allies, friends, and other regional powers without provoking a strategic backlash from China. The United States will continue to be important economically and as a provider of strategic reassurance. If Beijing continues or intensifies its assertive policies on maritime and territorial disputes, many countries in the region are likely to favour even closer ties with the United States. Most regional powers will continue to want good relations with both China and the United States. China will continue to be vitally important to many Asia-Pacific countries economically.

Regarding India, most Indians have welcomed the renewed attention to Asia by the United States. The worst possible outcome for New Delhi is the emergence of a China-centric Asia, something that many Indian government officials and policy analysts worry will be the case if the United States vacates the region. There is broad agreement in India that a strengthening of the US presence in the region will generally support India's interests and aspirations. The Japanese government and mainstream foreign policy community have generally welcomed the US rebalance because it demonstrates that the United States at least has the intention of maintaining and even enhancing its military presence in Asia in the context of a rising China.

At the same time, however, Japanese officials and experts are concerned that fiscal problems will prevent Washington from fully implementing this new policy and that, as a global power, the United States might once again focus its attention on other regions such as the Middle East.

India-Japan Strategic Relations

As a region located at the cusp of anarchy, competition and inter-dependence all at the same time, Asia presents an interesting locale of great and emerging power competition. More importantly, the region assumes critical significance as a chessboard with multiple consequential and vital middle level players—each with its own strategic posture and outlook towards its rightful place in the international arena.

Perhaps the most noteworthy development in this regard is the emergence of India and China which combines with the presence of Japan and the external influence of the United States. It is, therefore natural that the three major regional powers—India, Japan and China—have to devise strategies to have a balanced response to all three contradictory but intertwined trends. There is also the presence of players like a resurgent Russia, SAARC and ASEAN countries, which have become potent powers in themselves, especially in multilateral and regional organisations.

The rise of China and the power shift in Asia becomes a *primary* factor in bringing Tokyo and New Delhi together. There is much more substance to the relationship which has grown by leaps after 2001. Therefore, mere maintenance of balance of power vis-à-vis China is not the sole driver of foreign policy and bilateral relations between India and Japan. There are other forces like functional need, inter-dependence and simply the prospects of mutual gain, which shape relations between the two sides, even though these have not been fully realised and exploited.

Historically, India-Japan relations have existed for more than a thousand years. It is said that Japan first came into contact with India during the reign of Emperor Kimmei (539-571 A.D.). [7] Buddhism was the first common link between both sides, although it did not really find its way directly between the two countries. Another vital connection between both sides was a result of the common feeling of Pan-Asianism. During the period of the Indian Renaissance (1881-1905), India was keenly looking at building a spirit of Asian oneness. Organisations like Oriental Youngman's Association formed in 1900 served as a platform for increased interaction between Japanese, Indian and other Asian students in Japan.

Despite Japan's aloofness with the rest of the world, the connectivity between India and Japan remained with the fast-growing Japanese spinning industry, which found India as a source of raw cotton. India also became a destination for finished Japanese goods. Perhaps the most significant bilateral contact was that of Indian industrialist J.N. Tata who visited Japan in 1893 and set up an office there. The initiation of trade ties led to the establishment of a Japanese consulate office in Bombay and consulate general office in Calcutta. An Indo-Japanese Trade convention was also signed in 1894 which marked the beginning of "opening of regular ocean transport" between the two sides. [8] After its war with Russia, Japan became a role model for Indians to fight against colonialism. The formation of Indo-Japan Frienship Association (1903), Indian Club (1921), India's affinity towards Japan even in the midst of Swadeshi Movement [9] and the role played by Indian revolutionaries like Rash Bihari Bose and Subhash Chandra Bose [10] were very important in creating intimate links with Japan and the Japanese. On the cultural and literary front, the legendary friendship between Okakura Tenshin and Indian poet Rabindranath Tagore accelerated this process.

But with Japan's militarisation and imperialist lash-out in the 1930s, relations between India and Japan began to deteriorate. Japan's advancement into China—the Manchurian Incident, its actions in Korea (1910-1911) eroded the positivity which defined and underlined bilateral relations between both sides. Attempt for a good friendship and Nehru's interest give a new impetus to India-Japan relations with the signing of the bilateral treaty in 1952.

The distance between India and Japan grew wider during the time of Cold War. India, despite choosing to follow a policy of non-alignment, had a definitive tilt towards the former Soviet Union. Japan, on the other hand, had become an ally of the United States, placing both sides in opposite camps. In addition to this, India's Nuclear Tests in 1974 became a huge shock for Japan. South Asia was largely a "distant region" for Japan till the late 1990s and did not fall within its definition of the Asia-Pacific or Asia.

Historically, India and Japan shared much in terms of religion and culture, which should have ideally provided enough bedrock for a stable superstructure of relationships. There were a number of potential binding factors which could glue the two sides more effectively than they did. Japan had an important indirect participatory role in the Indian National Movement. However, the post-War period was underscored by a chill in relations which summed up to be a considerable loss for both sides in terms of opportunities which they could have possibly built upon.

Japan's strategic thinking changed a lot in the post-Cold War period in the midst of the Gulf War. It became a milestone in Tokyo's strategic thinking as it came under censure from Washington over its inability to contribute manpower to assist its ally. Despite making a significant contribution to the tune of US$ 13 billion, Japan was criticised for mere "chequebook diplomacy". Other developments which shook up Japan were the North Korean missile tests in 1993, the US-North Korean nuclear crisis in 1994 and firing of a

Pyongyang's missile which flew over Japan's Honshu island in 1998. The rise of China during this decade also became a challenge for the region and actors therein—including India and Japan. What is obviously and lucidly apparent is the common concern over China's growing assertion, rapid military modernization, claims and conflict over territory and arms build-up which had begun sprouting during this period and continues unabated till today.

India-Japan relations began to change in the early 1990s with launching of India's 'Look East Policy' in 1991, liberalization of the economy, and the international situation of post-Cold War period. As bemoaned by former Foreign Secretary J.N. Dixit, "Japan was identified as one of the most important sources of both investment and technology by the Government of India". [11] But the nuclear tests of India in 1998 had a negative impact on India-Japan relations. But Delhi's announcement of having a moratorium on conducting further tests revoked the position of the bilateral relationship on a positive track.

However, major changes began to reflect in the bilateral ties only in 2000 with the historic visit of Japanese Prime Minister Mori Yoshiro to India in August, marking a new chapter in relationship. The relations between India and Japan got fresh impetus going beyond economic and trade relations with gradual improvement in US-India relations and the signing of the US-India nuclear deal in 2005. Several factors including China's rise and other security concerns such as maritime security influenced the changing nature of the relations between the two. Even though the initial rationale for this eastward foray by India was economic, strategic imperatives also played a significant role in it.

For India, Southeast and East Asian countries provide an avenue not just for economic integration but also for strategic linkages. New Delhi has had increased defence exchanges, joint exercises, joint patrolling of sea lanes of communication and dialogues between security establishments of both sides.

This was India's response to what it viewed as China's challenge to its interests in the Indian Ocean. For instance, the Indian Navy was called upon to participate in a multinational navy exercise in the Philippines named "Team Challenge" in 2002 involving Australia, Brunei, Indonesia, Japan, Korea, Malaysia and Singapore among others. What was significant was the fact that it was the first-ever exercise by the Indian Navy in the East Asian security region. [12]

Similarly, India conducted joint passage exercises with the Japanese Maritime Self Defence Force in the East China Sea in October 2008. [13] The Malabar 2007 exercises, which also included trilateral exercises between the United States, Japan and India, were also a landmark event. The "extended neighbourhood" formulation encompassed both Southeast and Northeast Asia as well. China's economic threat, military modernization and converging demands and issues of India and Japan came as a booster towards bilateral relationship between them. The recognition of India's emergence as an economic powerhouse became evident. In a Yomiuri Shimbun poll taken in July 2006, as many as 20 percent of Japanese chose India as the third most important country in the future of world economy after China and the United States. [14]

The warming up of Washington's relations with New Delhi especially since the late 1990s also led Japan to take a more positive note of India. The 2002 U.S. National Security Strategy called for close ties with India for a "strategically stable Asia". [15] Besides, there seemed to be some realization trickling in Japanese strategic community on the ability of India's nuclear status to balance China in some way. The terrorist attacks in the United States also kindled the Japanese urge to assist India and the region in its combat against terrorism. Finally, Japan started recognising the advantages of bringing New Delhi in its fold especially in inter-government institutions mushrooming in the region.

There is a certain realisation between both sides that they share a number of areas of common concern. There is, therefore, a resultant cooperation in areas including safety and security of sea lanes of communication and a permanent seat in the UN Security Council. Two, there are economic complementarities between both countries with India's human resource capital and manpower complementing Japanese "money power" and technical prowess. Japan's ageing society is a severe problem today and the country lacks young and active workforce. India's abundant cheap and skilled workforce can make up for this gap. Third is the oft-mentioned value based connectivity—democracy, freedom and human rights which combine with rich cultural and historical links. The legacy of history has perhaps become the most important variable which continues to eat away and corrode Japan's ties with most of its Asian neighbours. Tokyo has had problems with Asian neighbours like China and South Korea over the history issue with offshoots in the Yasukuni Shrine issue, the textbooks issue and differing positions over the Nanjing "massacre" and wartime history. The fact that there is no such historical irritant with India makes it easier for the two sides to work towards building the relationship further. A positive public opinion has only bolstered bilateral relations between India and Japan.

For India, Japan is a critical source of capital and commercial technology. Indeed, there cannot be a better partner for India's development than the country that was the first non-western society to modernise and emerge as a world power, spearheading Asia's industrial and technological advances since the 19th century. India has underscored the importance of also building security collaboration with it, saying Indians "see Japan as a natural and indispensable partner in our quest for stability and peace in the vast" Indo-Pacific region.

Japan and India, as energy-poor countries are heavily reliant on oil imports from the unstable Persian Gulf region, and are seriously concerned over mercantilist efforts to assert control over energy supplies and the transport routes for them.

So the maintenance of a peaceful and lawful maritime domain, including unimpeded freedom of navigation, is critical to their security and economic well-being. That is why they have moved from emphasising shared values to seeking to protect shared interests, including by holding joint naval exercises. Japanese and Southeast Asian investors consider India as a potential location for their export-oriented investments as a hedge against their perceived over-dependence on China. India offers a large domestic market, industrial depth, urban centres, and sophisticated financial services.

India and Japan boast of the fastest-growing bilateral relationship in Asia today. Since they unveiled a "strategic and global partnership" in 2006, their political and economic engagement has deepened at a remarkable pace. Their free trade pact, formally known as the Comprehensive Economic Partnership Agreement (CEPA), came into force in 2011. They have even established an alliance to jointly develop rare-earth minerals so as to reduce their dependence on China. The level and frequency of India-Japan official engagement have become extraordinary. In addition to holding an annual Prime Minister-level summit, the two also conduct several yearly ministerial dialogues: A strategic dialogue between their Foreign Ministers; a security dialogue between their Defence Ministers; a policy dialogue between India's Commerce Minister and Japan's Minister of Economy, Trade and Industry; and separate ministerial-level energy and economic dialogues. And, to top it off, they also hold a trilateral strategic dialogue with the United States.

Today, the confluence of Modinomics and Abenomics is now a common refrain. They (Modi and Japanese Prime Minister Shinzo Abe) are decisive leaders aiming at accelerating faltering growth momentum. This is evident during the maiden visit of Indian Prime Minister Narendra Modi to Japan in September 2014, which has been touted as the crown jewel in India's East Asia diplomacy this year. New Delhi not only secured unprecedented economic investment from Tokyo but also found a partner for economic growth. India's need for a financial boost for its economy cannot be overstated and the trip has clearly bolstered bilateral ties.

To realize its full economic and demographic potential, India needs a partner that can provide multi-sector support. On this recent trip, however, Modi and Abe went further, discussing their nascent military engagements, triggering speculation over a gradually solidifying Indo-Japanese strategic alliance, particularly through the prism of the "China threat". [16] All the above mentioned factors solidify the argument that India-Japan relations are reaching unprecedented heights due to the international compulsions, common concerns and shared strategic interests.

Japan, India and Asian Rebalancing

US Asian rebalancing strategy has raised many questions among the minds of the scholars regarding its intention. Does it aim at containing China or for providing a foundation for peaceful coexistence between the United States and China and thereby avoiding the upheaval that marks the rise of a new power? But an analysis in this regard highlighting the factors like concerns of US regarding China, the desire to reassure US allies, friends, and other countries about the strength of US after a decade of war and its capability to ensure and keep the world order in this era of strategic competition, are the primary factors behind this rebalancing. The middle level players identified this situation and they are finding a bargaining space in their relations with the US and the China.

Japan and India are the two largest democracies in the most populous and dynamic region in the world and they are most powerful middle level players in Asia. Both countries are also facing the challenge of dealing with rapidly changing security as well as economic realities and have converging interests more in this international situation. While Japanese Prime Minister Shinzo Abe has looked increasingly towards greater multilateral cooperation to ensure regional stability,

Indian Prime Minister Narendra Modi is seeking to develop closer ties in East Asia through Japan. Japan and India share many common concerns, including the prospect of accommodating China's rise and broader changes in regional geopolitics, as well as meeting energy needs and ensuring continued economic growth.

Beijing's rise and an effective balance of power strategy in this rise becomes threatening and is one of the primary drivers catalysing India-Japan ties. There are four primary actors in the puzzle of power transition in Asia—the United States as a declining hegemon, Japan as a declining ally, China as an emerging perturbing "challenger" and India as a somewhat "swing state" and a suitable candidate to be propped up as an effective balancer against what many perceive to be the "menacing" rise of China. [17]

India, of course, can best be perceived as a "limited challenger" keeping in mind its several problems. It has been seen as a vital balancer against the absolute dominance by China at different points in time. Perhaps the Indian membership of the East Asia Summit (EAS) is one of the most significant examples of this strategy. Keeping these dynamics in mind, it is clear that the United States, Japan and India are all cautiously watching the rise of China. Nevertheless for both countries as well as for the United States, alternatives like bandwagoning, neutrality and containment would not be preferred options considering that they have stakes in maintaining ties with Beijing. This strategy was perhaps echoed in the words of Joseph Nye, when he stated, "It is in the interest of the US, Japan and China that China's rise be peaceful and harmonious (in the words of their leaders). That is why the strategy of integration plus a hedge against uncertainty makes sense for both the US and Japan. In the words of Robert Zoellick, it is in our interests to welcome the rise of China as a "responsible stakeholder".

If by some mishap, China does turn aggressive, it will find that Asia contains others such as India and Australia as well as

Japan that would contain its power. But it would be a mistake to turn to containment under current circumstances. If we treat China as an enemy, we guarantee enmity. Integration plus a hedge against uncertainty is a better approach". [18]

A closer examination of the China factor in India-Japan relations reveals that purely realist balance of power concerns is perhaps not wholly accurate. The other side of the coin reveals that both Tokyo and New Delhi are cautious, aware and sensitive not to be abrasive in their respective equations with China. These countries are therefore choosing to hedge and practise soft balancing against the potentially precipitous fallout of Beijing's rise in case it gets threatening. It is here that other factors behind foreign policy decisions such as functional cooperation and economic complementarity and inter-dependence have come into play, which has led them to tread gingerly. This has become evident in various points in time. As middle level players and emerging great powers of the Asian region, any kind of alliance between these regions is important to US and China. That is why US in their Asian rebalancing come forward with the strategy of making alliance with India and Japan through all possible means. The benefit for India and Japan in this context, depending on their leadership in playing a greater role and as middle powers and their alliance will be more meaningful in making the world order more multi-polar and peaceful.

Endnotes

1. Carsten Holbraad (1971), "The Role of Middle Powers, Cooperation and Conflict", Volume 6, No. 1, p. 88.
2. Carsten Holbraad (1984), "Middle Powers in International Politics", New York: St. Martin's, p. 121.
3. Andrew F. Cooper, Richard A. Higgott and Kim Richard Nossal (1993), "Relocating Middle Powers: Australia and Canada in a Changing World Order", Vancouver: UBC Press, p. 32.
4. Ibid., pp. 24-25.
5. Anton Bezglasnyy (2013), "Middle Power Theory, Change and Continuity in the Asia-Pacific", Columbia: The University of British Columbia, p. Ii.

6. R.G. Riddell (1969), cited in R.A. MacKay, "The Canadian Doctrine of Middle Powers" in H.L. Dyck and H.P. Krosby (eds.) *Empire and Nations,* Toronto, University of Toronto Press, 1969, p. 138.

7. T.R. Sareen (2007), "India and Japan in Historical Perspective", Lecture Series on Japan, Issue No. 4, New Delhi: The Japan Foundation, January, p. 9.

8. Ibid., pp. 10-11.

9. When Indians decided to follow the *swadeshi* system of boycotting foreign goods, Japanese goods were excluded from the banned category. In fact, a prominent Indian newspaper *Kesari* clearly called on people to choose Japanese goods over all other foreign manufactured ones. For more details see Birendra Prasad (1979), "Indian Nationalism and Asia, 1900-1947", Delhi: B.R. Publishing Corporation, pp. 44-45.

10. Rash Bihary Bose who came to be known as the "Bose of Nakamuraya" not only took political asylum in Japan, married a native woman, but also spent his entire life in the country as a Japanese citizen (from 1924) till his death in January 1945.

11. J.N. Dixit (1996), "My South Block Years: Memoirs of a Foreign Secretary", New Delhi: UBSPD, p. 254.

12. Shibashis Chatterjee (2007), "Conceptions of Space in India's Look East Policy: Order, Cooperation or Community?", *South Asian Survey,* Volume 14, No. 1, p. 72.

13. As cited in David Scott (2009), "India's 'Extended Neighbourhood' Concept: Power Projection for a Rising Power", *India Review,* Volume 8, No. 2, April-June, p. 125.

14. As cited in Takio Yamada (2008), "Japan-India Relations: A Time for Sea Change", in K. Kesavapany, A. Mani and P. Ramaswamy (eds.), Rising India and Indian Communities in East Asia, Singapore: Institute of Southeast Asian Studies, p. 150.

15. "The National Security Strategy of the United States of America" (2002), September, available at: http://merln.ndu.edu/whitepapers/USnss 2002.pdf. Accessed on January 2, 2014.

16. Swati Arun, "No, India Should Not Seek an Alliance With Japan", available at: http://thediplomat.com/2014/09/no-india-should-not-seek-an-alliance-with-japan. Accessed on September 26, 2014.

17. Arpitha Mathur (2012), "India-Japan Relations: Drivers, Trends and Prospects", RSIS Monograph No. 23, Singapore: S. Rajaratnam School of International Studies, p. 119.
18. Testimony by Joseph S. Nye, Jr., House Foreign Affairs Committee, Subcommittee on Asia, the Pacific and the Global Environment, *Hearings on Japan's Changing Role*, Thursday, 25 June 2009, Kennedy School of Government, Harvard University.

10

Indo-U.S. Defence Co-operation

Ninan Koshy

Indo-US defence cooperation is a post-Cold War development. Though, the US was eager to rope in India as an ally after the Second World War, Nehru's aversion to bloc politics and military alliances and adherence to non-alignment rendered any defence cooperation between India and US practically impossible. The only occasion of Indo-US defence cooperation was during the Chinese war in 1962 which got evaporated in the 1971 Bangladesh war. The signing of the Indo-Soviet friendship treaty and emergence of USSR as the major defence supplier to India ended the possibility of any defence cooperation between India and the US during the Cold War. But the recent international developments, particularly the rise of China as a challenger to the US hegemony, has evolved a peculiar geopolitical context in the Asia-Pacific, where India and the US find themselves as natural strategic partners with convergence of interests in a variety of fields. Indo-US defence cooperation is a corollary to these developments and Asian rebalancing by the US.

The January 2012 Pentagon document on strategic guidance, entitled "Sustaining Global Leadership: Priorities for Twenty First Century", has inaugurated a new cold war in the Asia-Pacific region between the United States and the China. The document affirms that the United States will of necessity rebalance, or "pivot", towards the Asia-Pacific region. The goal of the rebalancing is American "global leadership", to be maintained by military superiority. The document gives a prominent place for India in the US strategy. In his maiden visit to India in the first week of May, US Secretary of

Defense, Leon Panetta piled on, calling defence cooperation with India "a linchpin in US strategy" in Asia. The United States has been exhorting India to move from its "Look East" policy to an "Act East" policy. Washington expects India to go beyond forging bilateral relations with countries in the region and to get involved in their critical issues even militarily. This, the United States believes, is essential for the integration of the Asia-Pacific region under a US umbrella.

Towards a Military Alliance

While India has provided assistance to the United States in Afghanistan and continued defence cooperation on other fronts, the two countries have operated under a formal framework only since 2005. The Framework Agreement on Defence Cooperation, signed on June 28, 2005, in Washington by then defense secretary Donald Rumsfield reflected these US objectives.

The agreement said that the two countries were entering a new era and transforming the relationship "to reflect our common principles and shared national interests". Important parts of the agreement were, "defence relationship would support and be part of the larger bilateral strategic partnership...conducting joint exercises and exchanges and collaborating in multinational operations"..."strengthening the military capabilities to combat proliferation of weapons of mass destruction" and "expanding collaboration in missile defence".

The agreement signalled an important stage in the implementation of the policy of the US "to help India become a major world power", declared by George W. Bush administration. It assigned the place for India as a junior partner in the grand US-led coalition. This framework was the basis of the nuclear deal between India and the United States that gave India the *de facto* recognition as a nuclear-armed state, which was announced just weeks afterward. A series of defence-related agreements followed in 2007.

Although India remains unwilling at this juncture to sign pending defence agreements that might be construed as opening the door for an official military alliance with the United States, there has been considerable progress on US-India arms transactions. The United States has bagged the largest number of arms contracts—about $8 billion worth in the last five years—despite its stringent and intrusive end use monitoring requirements. The increase in the import of weapons from the US has been so high that the United States recently surpassed Russia as India's largest supplier of arms. India has fundamentally reoriented its defence procurement, moving away from its traditional reliance on Russia. In fact, nearly half the value of all Indian defence deals in recent years has been in US transactions alone.

Naval Co-operation
In addition to a booming arms trade, India and the United States have conducted more than 50 joint military exercises in the last seven years. Against this, India's joint exercises with other countries appear to be mere tokens. Military-to-military relations have especially deepened in the realm of naval cooperation. The US and Indian navies have cooperated operationally on four separate occasions: in the Strait of Malacca after 9/11, in disaster relief efforts after the Indian Ocean tsunami in 2004-2005, in a non-combative evacuation operation in Lebanon in 2006, and counter-piracy operations in the Gulf of Aden since 2008.

In December 2001, the two countries reached an agreement on naval cooperation to secure the maritime routes between the Suez Canal and the Malacca Straits known as "chokepoints". During the US invasion of Afghanistan, naval ships were provided by India to safeguard US non-combatant and merchant ships transiting the Straits of Malacca, which freed US naval ships for service off the coast of Pakistan. This has been officially acknowledged by Washington as a contribution by India to the "war on terror". India was also one of the very few countries to join the "core group" set up by Washington in the wake of the 2004-2005 Indian Ocean tsunami. The "core group" was actually a Pentagon plan to assess the geostrategic implications of the tsunami and to gain US military access to areas where it had not previously been permitted. It was disbanded because of sharp criticism from the United Nations and European nations like France.

But India is apparently not the only South Asian nation being courted by the United States. The *Times of India* reported in June that Washington is in the process of stationing a naval base in Chittagong, Bangladesh. "Worried by the increasing presence of Chinese naval bases in the South China Sea," the paper reported, "America now eyes a counter-strategy as it wants an overall presence in Asia—right from Japan to the Diego Garcia base in the Indian Ocean". The Bangladeshi government has denied the report, but if it is true, it could cast a shadow on India's own security strategy and on US-Indian naval cooperation. However, such an initiative would be perfectly in tune with Washington's ongoing quest for more naval facilities in the region.

Extension of Defence Co-operation Agreement

The decision by India and the United States to renew and extend for 10 years, the 2005 defence cooperation agreement between India and the United States was announced in September 2014, during Indian Prime Minister Narendra Modi's visit to Washington. US President Barack Obama and Modi stated their intention to "expand defence cooperation to bolster, national, regional and global security". The two leaders asked their defence teams to develop plans for "more ambitious programs and activities".

Renewal of the agreement assumes special significance today in view of the US's continuing military entanglement in West Asia and its "pivot" to Asia-Pacific, a region of which South Asia has been made an integral part by Washington's cartographers. Leaders and senior officials of the US had repeatedly stated from September 2001, when India declared whole-hearted support to the "War on Terror", that the India-US strategic relationship is essentially a military relationship on American terms and primarily in American interests. Ambassador Robert Blackwill made it abundantly clear on May 12, 2003, in a lead page article in *The Hindu* on the eve of the end of his assignment in India, "The strategic objective is to have an Indian military that is capable of operating effectively alongside its American counterpart". The cooperation is for "future joint military operations". All this, he candidly admitted, was "in America's interest".

The United States and India will work to include defence transactions, not solely as ends in and of themselves, but as a means to strengthen our security, reinforce our strategic partnership, and achieve greater interaction between our defence establishments. The agreement also goes far beyond defence matters. Several of the provisions go against the tenets of India's foreign policy. For example, take "collaboration in multinational operations". US officials have repeatedly mentioned the US objective of Indian and American military joining in military operations in third countries. In US strategic parlance, "multinational operations" means US-led military operations outside the purview of the authorization or permission of the United Nations.

The implications of India agreeing "to collaborate in multinational operations" are serious. The Indian public was kept in the dark about such a major agreement and there was no hint that such a momentous pact would be made during the visit of the Indian Defence Minister to Washington in June 2005. In fact on the eve of his visit, Mukherjee downplayed its significance, saying that the trip was "exploratory in nature". Considering the pivotal role the agreement had in the making of the nuclear deal, it is evident that there was a deliberate move on the part of New Delhi to keep away from public scrutiny and the links between the different parts of the strategic alliance between the two countries.

Commenting on the new defence pact, Siddharth Varadarajan wrote, "The new military agreement with the US will help advance Washington's strategic goals in Asia and expand the global market for American defence contractors. But it is not clear what good it will do for India and Asia... India is being cultivated as its (America's) lever for realising a more fundamental goal to remain firmly embedded in Asia at a time when the continent is emerging as the world's new centre of gravity and Beijing as Washington's challenger nonpareil". It is important to note that the defence agreement was made just 20 days before a joint statement of President George W. Bush and Prime Minister Manmohan Singh on a nuclear deal, and in fact provided its basis. There is reason to believe that it was the condition precedent for the nuclear deal.

The Joint Statement of July 18, 2005, which is often presented as dealing only with the civilian nuclear deal, began by declaring the American President's and the Indian Prime Minister's interest to "transform the relationship between the two countries and establish a global partnership". It specifically "expressed satisfaction at the New Framework for the US-India Relationship as a basis for future cooperation". Siddharth Varadarajan in an article, "US Cables Show Grand Calculations Underlying the 2005 Defence Framework", opined, "Leaked US Embassy cables accessed by *The Hindu* through WikiLeaks provide an unparalleled insight into the military and strategic considerations that drove and continue to drive [the] US administration towards seeking close ties with India".

There is the sheer size of the Indian market for weapons imports, estimated by US diplomats to be worth more than $27 billion in the near term. There is also the promise of a clear working relationship with the Indian armed forces in the Asian region". In the run-up to Mukherjee's crucial visit to the US in June 2005, American diplomats, eager to assess the extent to which India might be willing to enter into a close military embrace, were unnerved by the generally sceptical tenor of

Indian media coverage. Varadarajan continues the cable saga, "In a meeting with Assistant Secretary of State Christina Rocca, Ministry of External Affairs Joint Secretary S. Jayashakar said, "the actual changes [in the bilateral relationship] are more profound than the optics of change. He urged a greater focus on changing the Indian optics which he described as being "more entrenched in scepticism than in the US".

On the eve of the defence minister's visit to Washington in June 2005, the US Embassy sent a "scene-setter" cable to secretary of defence Donald Rumsfield, saying that Mukherjee was "in effect the Deputy Prime Minister and we believe that he aspires to the top job. By demonstrating our understanding of his influence beyond the military realm, it may be easier to advance on defence related objectives"...."Signing the Framework for US-India Strategic Defence Relationship was the deliverable", the cable identified. The word "strategic" did not find a place in the final title of the agreement.

India and the US have taken unprecedented steps in recent years to boost their bilateral defence ties. India conducts more military exercises with the US than with any other country and has joined the Rim of the Pacific Exercise (RIMPAC), the world's largest international maritime exercise. Since taking office, Modi has raised caps on foreign investments in the defence sector to permit greater participation of foreign firms, especially from the US. Given the potential for future contingencies in the Indian Ocean and the West Pacific, both countries have an interest in continuing to deepen the defence cooperation.

The January 2012 Pentagon document on Strategic Guidance, entitled "Sustaining Global Leadership: Priorities for 21st Century", gives a prominent place to India in the US strategy. While India is singled out with specific reference to strategic partnership, long-standing allies such as Japan, Australia and South Korea are clubbed together under existing alliances. In his visit to India in the first week of May 2012,

Leon Panetta as the then secretary of defense, called "defence cooperation with India a linchpin in the US strategy". The response of New Delhi appeared to be lukewarm at that time. During US Secretary of Defense Chuck Hagel's visit to New Delhi in August 2014, he seemed to have received a more positive response with regard to India's policy on the US "Asian pivot" strategy.

For the first time in an India-US joint statement, the situation in South China Sea is specifically mentioned. This is highly significant. The two leaders expressed concern about "rising tensions over maritime territorial disputes in the region". They affirmed the importance of safeguarding "maritime security and ensuing freedom of navigation and over-flight throughout the region". The problem with this formulation is that the US is not an impartial actor in the scene. It rejects the maritime territorial claims of China. It supports the claims of Vietnam and Philippines and is strengthening military alliances with these countries in their confrontation with China. The US has not ruled out the option of use of force in safeguarding maritime security in South China Sea. The joint statement of the leaders of the US and India tends to give the impression that India is ready to be drawn deeper into the muddled waters of South China Sea. There is every chance that India would be used as pawn in the US power games in Asia to maintain its hegemony and serve its interests.

References

Robert D. Blackwill (2003), "US India Cooperation", *The Hindu*, May 13.

Siddharth Varadarajan (2005), "India Entering Uncharted, Risky Territory", *The Hindu*, July 1.

Siddharth Varadarajan (2011), "US Cables Show Grand Calculations Underlying 2005 Defence Framework", *The Hindu*, March 28.

11

Politics of Climate Change

Anu Unny

Introduction

Climate change has emerged as a major issue of concern in international politics since 1970s. The increased concentrations of greenhouse gases (GHGs) and thereby extraordinary warming of the earth, has already resulted in climatic consequences such as acid rain, unpredictable weather pattern, and rise in sea level. However, even in the midst of all these emerging concerns, unfortunately there is no consensus among world nations especially among India, China and the United States over who should take the responsibility for climate change and what all measures should to be taken to mitigate the effects, and how to implement it. Even in the Warsaw Conference that concluded in 2013, major developed and developing countries were busy engaging in hard bargaining in pursuit of their narrow self-interests and relative power gains rather than rationally seeking the larger interests of the humanity. Harris (2013) has termed this self-centred behaviour of the states-the 'Westphalia cancer'.

At present, Kyoto Protocol is the only existing legally binding emission reduction treaty that offers a top-down approach at the international level to redress the problem of climate change. Though the 2012 Doha Conference had extended the validity of the Kyoto Protocol till 2020, the Protocol has become virtually ineffective due to the disengagement of some of the major players from the treaty. [1] Japan, Canada, Russia and above all the United States of America which is the second largest greenhouse gas emitter in the world have expressed their unwillingness to take up binding emission reduction targets even in the second phase of the treaty. Southern countries including India and China maintain that any emission reduction treaty would be less effective without the participation of key emitter countries such as the US.

India has stated in many climate change negotiations that since developed countries bear the historical responsibility for global warming, they have also the responsibility for taking up emission reduction burden; especially United States which has an active role in polluting the global atmosphere since the period of industrial revolution (Agarwal, 2002). On the other side, United States which blames China and India for their growing emissions argue that, these countries need to take binding emission reduction targets, considering their current level of emissions and potential for future emissions. [2] United States' chief climate change negotiator Mr. Todd Stern recently indicated that China and India have already become the world's first and third largest greenhouse gas emitters and therefore without ensuring the participation of these key developing countries, negotiations to frame a new treaty would be worthless (Stern, 2013). In this scenario, in order to understand this issue from the perspective of South and North and to analyze the nature of bargaining between India and the US in climate change negotiations, a study of the stance of both the countries is extremely important since these countries constitute a major share of the global greenhouse gas emissions.

Key Issues

Climate change is a global issue. To prevent the catastrophic effects of climate change, average temperature needs to be kept in between 1.5-2.0 degree Celsius above the pre-industrial levels (Watkiss et al., 2005). The challenge before the world today is how they can produce a legally binding framework which can set national limits on the greenhouse gas emissions from states. Giddens (2008) opines that, in responding to climate change we must concentrate a good deal of attention on the states. Kyoto and Bali-style agreements, the EU targets together with carbon markets, the activities of business and NGOs will no doubt be extremely important in this regard. However, it is indispensable that the state will have a major role in setting up a framework for these endeavours. The part it has to play in the developed societies is especially important, since these countries must be in the vanguard in reducing their emissions (Giddens, 2008).

In a detailed analysis of the US foreign policy on climate change, there are criticisms that US position is always self-protective and inward-looking. It is a fact that US, compared to all other nation states has more responsibility in polluting the atmosphere. No nation has emitted more greenhouse gases than the United States. Vandana Shiva, a prominent Indian environmentalist points out, "I think it is time for the United States to stop seeing itself as a donor and recognizing itself as a polluter, a polluter who must pay for its pollution and its ecological debt. This is not about charity. This is about justice" (Roberts, 2009).

Historical Responsibility
According to the 1992 United Nations Framework Convention on Climate Change (UNFCCC), "responsibility" and "capability" are the twin bases for determining who should take action and by when (UNFCCC, 1992: Article 3.1). [3] The question of responsibility states that those who have caused the problem are responsible for solving it. It implies that, in the context of climate change debate, the responsibility for coping with this problem rests with those countries that emit the largest amount of greenhouse gases (GHGs), namely the developed countries. UNFCCC (1992) preamble notes, "the largest share of historical and current global emissions of GHGs has originated from developed countries". GHG emission level of United States and other developed countries reflects this.

Table 11.1 based on the data brought out by the World

Resources Institute (WRI, 2011) portrays the top 10 nations as measured by their cumulative emissions (historical emissions) between 1850 and 2007. As per the statistics, 28.8 percent of the total greenhouse gas emissions were from US during the period from 1850 to 2007, whilst just 2.4 percent were from India. Though China stands at second place in terms of the total greenhouse gas emissions, its emission is just 9 percent, i.e. 1/3rd of the total US emissions. This reveals that, United States cannot move away from its historical responsibility for polluting the atmosphere.

Table 11.1: Cumulative Greenhouse Gas Emissions from 1850 to 2007

US	3,39,174 Metric Tonnes (MT) or 28.8 percent
China	1,05,915 MT or 9.0 percent
Russia	94,679 MT or 8.0 percent
Germany	81,194 MT or 6.9 percent
UK	68,763 MT or 5.8 percent
Japan	45,629 MT or 3.87 percent
France	32,667 MT or 2.77 percent
India	28,824 MT or 2.44 percent
Canada	25,716 MT or 2.2 percent
Ukraine	25,431 MT or 2.2 percent

Source: World Resource Institute, 2011.

Former US President Bill Clinton had acknowledged the United States historical responsibility for climate change problem during the 1997 Kyoto negotiations. He remarked, "the United States has less than five percent of the world's population, enjoys 22 percent of the world's wealth, but emits more than 25 percent of the world's greenhouse gases" (Warick and Baker, 1997). Roberts and Parks (2007) also indicate towards the historical responsibility of US when they argue that 'with only four percent of the world's population, US is responsible for over 20 percent of all global emissions. That can be compared to 136 developing countries that together are only responsible for 24 percent of global emissions'. During 1850-2000, US contributed 30 percent to CO_2 emissions, EU 25 percent, China 7.3 percent and India only 2 percent (Roberts and Parks, 2007). Hence, India and China argue that US has the ethical responsibility to take up emission reduction obligations.

India has always stressed that, for the successful framing of any climate change treaty inequity element and mistrust in the existing North-South negotiations needs to be addressed at first. India upholds the 'Polluter Pays Principle' (PPP) as a necessary condition of equity in the climate change regime. [4] The polluter pays principle specifies that the countries which pollute the atmosphere should bear the cost of pollution and take up atmosphere clean up obligations. In the 2009 Copenhagen Conference, India had maintained that developed countries have benefited from past emissions of greenhouse gases; so that it is the responsibility of the developed industrialized countries to reduce their emissions of greenhouse gases, while they allow the developing countries of the South to focus on their economic development (Agarwal, 2002).

Even though the United States has already accepted its responsibility factor for causing global warming, US's Special Envoy for Climate Change Todd Stern's statement on December 9, 2009, leaves some room for doubts on US's climate change commitment and accountability. Todd Stern had stated, "We absolutely recognize our historic role in putting emissions in the atmosphere up there that are there now. But the sense of guilt or culpability or reparations—I just categorically reject that. Developed nations did not always know that they were causing global warming by burning fossil fuels and emitting greenhouse gases into the atmosphere. This knowledge only began to form in the 1980s and 1990s, over a century after the industrial revolution had begun. It is inappropriate therefore to hold developed nations morally accountable for starting the industrial revolution and causing global warming" (Stern, 2009).

This US stand is a departure from the 'Beneficiary Pays Principle' (BPP) in international relations. As per the beneficiary pays principle, agents who have benefited from historic polluting have to bear the moral responsibility for dealing with the problem caused by that pollution. According to this rationale, because of the benefits and costs associated with historic polluting which are beyond current agents' control and are unequally distributed, the fairest way to rectify this is to assign the moral responsibility to deal with the problems caused by historic polluting to the agents who have benefited out of it (Boston et al., 2010).

As per this view, the United States cannot move away from its ethical responsibility in polluting the atmosphere because US has attained the current economic development, emitting tonnes of greenhouse gases into the atmosphere. US is near the top of national greenhouse gas emitters on a per capita basis, and it is second only to China in total tonnes of greenhouse gas emissions (Brown, 2013). Therefore, for a fair distribution of greenhouse gas burdens, developed countries, especially US, have to accept their moral responsibility for causing the problem first. Unfortunately, United States unwillingness to shoulder its historical responsibility by committing itself to binding emission reduction targets has become one of the most contentious issues in the global climate change regime.

Equal Per Capita Emission Right

The second important issue in the climate change debate is the question related to 'per capita emission right'. It denotes that each and every individual in this world has equal right to certain minimum social and economic welfare. This norm is also related to the principle of egalitarianism. Egalitarian principle in climate change indicates that individuals have the right to emit an equal amount of greenhouse gases. Individuals should therefore receive an identical amount of allowances, permits or quotas to emit greenhouse gases (Ringius, 1998).

However differently from this, the per capita emission level varies drastically from country to country and in developing countries usually, the per capita emission level is very low compared to that of the developed countries.

The UNFCCC (1992) notes that "per capita emissions in developing countries are relatively low and that share of global emissions originating in these countries will grow to meet their social and development needs". As per the International Energy Statistics (2011), per capita emissions of a US citizen was 17.3 tonnes compared to that of 1.4 tonnes of an Indian. Table 11.2 shows that, while countries with small population (like Qatar) tops in the list of countries which are having high per capita emissions, populated stated such as China and India rank low in the list. That is, if the per capita emission of Qatar, US and Australia is 36.9, 17.3 and 17 tonnes respectively, per capita emissions from China and India are just 5.4 and 1.4 tonnes respectively.

Table 11.2: Per Capita Emissions of Countries, 2011

Qatar	36.9 tonnes
United States	17.3 tonnes
Australia	17.0 tonnes
Russia	11.6 tonnes
Germany	9.3 tonnes
UK	7.8 tonnes
China	5.4 tonnes
India	1.4 tonnes

Source: International Energy Statistics, 2011.

Upholding the egalitarian principle, India demands for an equal per capita emission entitlement in UN climate change negotiations. India was the first country to suggest officially the equal per capita emission entitlement demand at the UNFCCC in 1995. In 1997 Kyoto Conference, the then Minister of Environment and Forest, Saifuddin Soz, had said, "Per capita basis is the most important criterion for deciding the rights to environmental space. This is a direct measure of human welfare. Since atmosphere is a common heritage of humankind, equity has to be the fundamental basis for its management" (Soz, 1997). Quoting former Prime Minister of India, Smt. Indira Gandhi in the 2011 Durban summit, the then Indian Minister of Environment and Forest Smt. Jayanti Natarajan also stated, "Poverty is the greatest polluter and development is the greatest healer. Equity has to be the centrepiece of climate discussion and our negotiations should be built on it" (PTI, 2011).

While releasing the National Action Plan on Climate Change (NAPCC), former Indian Prime Minister Manmohan Singh had stated (2008), "every citizen of this planet must have an equal share of the planetary atmospheric space. Long-term convergence of per capita emissions is, therefore, the only equitable basis for a global compact on climate change". India views that it is hardly fair that a poor nation with a huge population is required to adhere strictly to its current emission levels, whereas some developed states with small population size are permitted to emit far more" (Posner and Sunstein, 2009). Based on 'per-capita' emissions, India was ranked one hundred and twenty-second in the world (WRI, 2008).

If the per capita approach is not followed, India points out that the developing nations might possibly have great difficulty in achieving the levels of development which has already been attained by the developed nations. After the Durban conference in December 2011, Indian Environment Minister Jayanthi Natarajan had stated in the Parliament that "there is no question of signing a legally binding agreement at this point of our development. We need to ensure that our development does not suffer" (Rajya Sabha, 2011). [5]

On the other side, United States expressed its concern towards developing countries' demand for an equal per capita emission right stating that it is unfair as it rewards only highly populated states like India and China. The per capita approach would establish that the most highly populated states would obtain the greatest benefits from international cooperation, and the states with the larger population would be able to claim a larger portion of the surplus. Secondly though this demand seems desirable, its adverse effect is that, governments that adopt policies with an aim to promote economic growth would be penalized by this principle. Therefore, United States observe that India's per capita emission approach cannot be justified either on grounds of fairness since it rewards only highly populated states or on grounds of welfare principle because it restricts economic growth (Posner and Sunstein, 2009). Even though the per capita approach suffers from some drawbacks while setting emission cap for developing and developed countries, each country's population size and the national circumstances should be taken into consideration. Rich nations should limit their emission level providing more room for developing countries' to grow.

Ability to Pay Principle

'Capacity' or 'ability to pay' is an important factor in mitigating the effects of climate change problem. It means that, countries that have greater capacity to solve a joint problem and thus provide a common good, should contribute more than countries with less capacity and ability. This ability to pay principle (APP) places the share of the burden of coping with climate change on northern countries. No one can deny that most of the industrialized countries especially United States and Britain owe their current prosperity to years of historical emissions. Industrialized countries are responsible for 60 percent of the greenhouse gas emissions that causes global warming, however developing countries like India suffer the 'worst and first' effects of climate-related disasters, including droughts, floods, and storms, because of their geographical locations (Stern Review, 2006).

In this context, in order to fight this common menace and reduce the vulnerability to climate change, enabling developing countries especially least developed countries with technology and finance, becomes crucial. 2007 Bali Conference was an important landmark in the technology and finance related debate in climate change. The Bali Action Plan which is centred around 4 building blocks like mitigation, adaptation, technology and financing, recognized that countries can take different nationally appropriate actions in accordance with common but differentiated responsibilities (CBDR) and respective capabilities (RC).

Article 2.5 of Kyoto Protocol (1997) also emphasizes the 'ability to pay' principle. It states that "the industrialized countries are required to take all practical steps to promote, facilitate and finance the transfer of environmentally sound technology and other resources to the developing countries". In the Protocol, clean development mechanism (CDM) was introduced in order to facilitate technology transfer to developing countries. However, the projects implemented through CDM are too small-scale to deliver technology to the extent required for rapid climate change mitigation. [6]

Apart from that, issues related to carbon trading mechanism and intellectual property rights (IPRs) also remain unresolved. India and China have been vocal that compulsory patent licensing should be expanded to cover clean technologies. [7] The United States has raised its opposition to compulsory licensing, arguing that such a scheme will discourage companies from investing in innovation. Moreover, there is no clear global regime governing clean technology investments. In this context, in order to resolve this global crisis, US, being the largest contributor to GHGs, dominant power in international relations and a front runner in financial and technological capacity, should take the lead in transferring the resources to the less advantaged developing countries such as India and China.

Unilateral Decision-making
Treatment of countries at the negotiation table is one important factor that influences the course of negotiations. In

majority of the UNFCCC conferences, agenda of the meeting is decided by the US and the EU. The history of climate change conferences from 1972 reveals this. Most of the time, least developed countries, especially small island states do not get adequate representation in these conferences and their voices are suppressed by the key developed industrialized countries. The Kyoto Protocol itself was not the outcome of a fair process (Ashton and Wang, 2003). There were no agreed criteria for assigning obligations to countries in the 1997 Kyoto Conference. Some commitments were blatantly imposed on developing countries and they were pressed into accepting a deal made in their absence, among their industrialized partners. This practice of taking decisions in the closed green room meetings among the developed country parties has invited criticism from various quarters, especially from G77 countries including India.

US Non-ratification of Kyoto Protocol
The Kyoto Protocol (1997) which came into force in 2005 classified countries into three groups based on their emission reduction commitments. The Annex I group included the industrialized countries that were members of the OECD in 1992, plus countries with economies in transition (EIT Parties) including Russian Federation, Baltic States and some Central and Eastern European states. [8] Annex II parties consisted of the OECD members of Annex I but not the EIT Parties. This Annex II group was mandated by the Convention to provide financial resources to developing countries and environment-friendly technology to both EIT parties and developing countries. Non-Annex I Parties included the members of developing countries. Under the Protocol while Annex I group was forced to take up binding emission reduction targets and to minimize the emissions, on the other hand non-Annex I parties were exempted from taking up any binding emission reduction commitments. Kyoto Protocol was opened for ratification of the states in 1997.

Critics argue that, US is the rogue nation when it comes to Kyoto Protocol (Karon, 2001). United States opposed to ratify the treaty pointing out the exclusion of key developing countries such as India and China from the binding provisions of the Protocol. The Byrd-Hagel Resolution passed in US Senate in 1997 stated, "United States would not be a party to any protocol, unless the protocol also mandates new specific scheduled commitments to limit or reduce greenhouse gas emissions for developing country parties within the same compliance period" (US Congressional Record, 1997). Responding to the Byrd-Hagel Resolution, President Bill Clinton stated a few months before the staring of Kyoto Conference that "key" developing countries (especially China and India) must take "meaningful" action, to reduce their level of greenhouse gas emissions in the atmosphere. Unless and until these developing countries take up binding emission reduction goals, US won't be a party to any binding emission reduction agreement" (The White House, 1997). These US demands marked a departure from the CBDR principle, which was accepted by the US earlier at in the 1992 Rio de Janeiro Conference. Though US signed the Protocol later, it never ratified the treaty.

On March 29, 2001, Bush Administration officially declared the withdrawal of the United States from the Kyoto Protocol. In his speech on June 11, 2001 on global climate change, President Bush stated, "Kyoto Protocol is a 'fatally flawed treaty in fundamental ways and it is a dead treaty for US" (The White House, 2001). Under the Obama Administration, US is once again rejecting the possibilities to be part of the Kyoto Protocol. US has not taken up any commitments in the second phase of the Kyoto Protocol. US asserts that, China and India being the first and third largest GHG emitters have the responsibility to commit themselves to binding emission reduction targets along with other developed countries. On the other hand, developing countries view United States' non-ratification of Kyoto Protocol as a violation of the 'common but differentiated responsibility principle'. [9]

India proposes that, for the framing of any future climate change treaty, three principles need to be accommodated—CBDR principle, polluter pays principle (PPP) and equal per capita emission entitlement principle. India and China point out that any climate change treaty would be unequal and asymmetrical without the participation of the United States. They demand that for the successful framing of any climate regime, United States should take up binding emission reduction; because US has the historical responsibility and capacity (financial, technological and political) to meet this daunting challenge.

Conclusion

In the context of growing emissions from developing countries, India and China may be pressurized to come under a global emission cap in the near future. It was in this scenario, that parties to the 2011 Durban Conference agreed to frame a new legally binding climate change treaty by 2015 which includes not only the developed countries but also the key developing countries like India and China. However, this does not necessarily guarantee that China, India, Brazil, South Africa and US would come on the same platform because of the existing equity issues among them (in terms of the responsibility for climate change, capacity for burden sharing etc.).

In order to break the deadlock in negotiations between the North and South, various proposals have been mooted. Considering the different levels of consumption, and historical responsibility across populations, Agarwal and Narain in their 1991 essay 'Global Warming in an Unequal World: A Case of Environmental Colonialism' have called for a rights-based approach to decide what constitutes fair share of atmospheric space. They argue that, the efforts of the developed countries to impose emissions upon developing countries which are less responsible for climate change is unequal, unfair and even imperialist (Agarwal and Narain, 1991). There are critics who point out that US's insistence on China and India to take up legally binding emission reduction obligations under a new Protocol that may come into effect after the expiration of Kyoto Protocol by 2020 is a part of the deliberate strategy to undermine the economic growth of these countries they otherwise enjoy. China and India are emerging as economic super powers in the Asian region. Indian economy was one of the few economies that overcame the effects of global crisis of 2008. In this context, southern environmentalists point out that Northern countries' especially United States call to India to take up binding emission reduction is part of a strategy to undermine the South's economic growth and to maintain US hegemony.

Rajamani (2007) argues, "India's position on climate change burden sharing is legitimate; it is not a sagacious position to hold". She points out that 34.7 percent of Indians live on less than US$ 1 a day and a vast majority of India's poor are in rural areas and are dependent directly on climate-sensitive natural resources. However, she holds the position that "India needs to undertake commitments at a global level, if not now at some time in future, for it is only cumulative global emission reductions that can eventually make an impact upon the trajectory of climate change" (Rajamani, 2007).

To frame a new legally binding emission reduction treaty, constructive engagements from all parts of the world is needed, especially from the United States. Ashton and Wang (2003) point out four conditions for the successful functioning of any climate change regime: first is action by the United States itself; second one is the positive engagement of the top industrialized countries in resolving climate change crisis; third is, emission reduction by key developing countries and fourth, financial and technology transfer to the South from North (Ashton and Wang, 2003).

As a principal actor in global affairs, United States can play a crucial role in addressing various equity issues prevailing in the current climate change regime. The United States must step up by agreeing to emission limitations and then combine forces with the rest of industrialized countries in convincing developing nations on emission controls; it cannot wait for developing countries like China and India to accept emission cuts before it does the same. It has the 'responsibility' (as the 2nd largest emitter), capacity (political, financial and technological) and the manpower to cut back emissions drastically. As Harris (2001) notes, "because the US economy is so large, its diplomatic influence is so great and its contributions to environmental problems are so extensive, the United States must be a part of international solutions to environmental change".

Endnotes

1. Kyoto Protocol is an international legally binding emission reduction treaty that came into effect in 1997. It set binding emission reduction targets for Annex I Parties (mainly developed countries) and voluntary emission reduction obligations for non-Annex I countries (developing countries). In the second phase of the Kyoto Protocol, it has almost become ineffective due to the disengagement of major emitter countries such as United States, Canada, Japan and Australia.

2. According to the 2011 data compiled by the Netherlands Environmental Assessment Agency (2011), China tops the list of the highest CO_2 emitters with 28.6 percent of emissions, while US and India stand at the second and third positions respectively with 16 percent and 5.8 percent emissions.

3. The United Nations Framework Convention on Climate Change (UNFCCC), 1992 is an international environmental treaty that was produced at the United Nations Conference on Environment and Development at Rio, which is also known as the Earth Summit or Rio Summit.

4. The polluter pays principle advocates that those polluter countries primarily developed countries of the North have the 'responsibility' to take up binding emission reduction commitments than Southern states.

5. However, differently from this, Minister Jairam Ramesh, successor to Smt. Jayanthi Natarajan had stated in the 2009

Copenhagen Conference that "all nations must take on binding commitments in an appropriate legal form". He was referring to the need for taking more pro-active stance by India on this issue.

6. The Clean Development Mechanism (CDM) defined in Article 12 of the Protocol, allows a country with an emission reduction commitment under the Kyoto Protocol to implement emission reduction projects in developing countries. Such projects can earn certified emission reduction credits (CERs), which can be counted towards meeting the Kyoto targets.

7. Compulsory licensing refers to a government's permission to make, use, sell, import and otherwise practice a patented item or process without the consent of the patent owner where such consent would otherwise be required.

8. Annex I countries are developed countries and countries with economies in transition; and non-Annex I countries are mostly developing countries. This classification is based on the 1997 Kyoto Protocol.

9. CBDR (common but differentiated responsibility) principle is reflected in the 1992 Rio Declaration which states that "in view of the different contributions to global environmental degradation, states have common but differentiated responsibilities. The developed countries acknowledge the responsibility that they bear in the international pursuit of sustainable development in view of the pressures their societies place on the global environment and of the technologies and financial resources they command".

References

Agarwal, Anil (2002), "A Southern Perspective on Curbing Global Climate Change", in Stephen H. Schneider et al. (ed.) Climate Change Policy: A Survey, US: Island Press.

Agarwal, Anil and Narain, Sunita (1991), "Global Warming in an Unequal World: A Case of Environmental Colonialism", Centre for Science and Environment, New Delhi.

Ashton and Wang (2003), "Beyond Kyoto: Advancing the International Effort against Climate Change", in Joseph E. Aldy, Richard Baron, Daniel Bodansky, Steve Charnovitz, Elliot Diringer, Thomas C. Heller, Jonathan Pershing, P.R. Shukla, Laurence Tubliana, FernandoTudela, Xueman Wang (eds.) ,Pew Centre on Global Climate Change, Arlington, USA.

Boston, Jonathan, Bradstock, Andrew, Eng, David (2010), "Public Policy: Why Ethics Matters", Canberra: ANU Press.

Brown, Donald, A. (2013), "Climate Change is Real, Yet the US Press is Not Reporting on the Urgency and Magnitude of the Problem", *Ethics and Climate*, February.

CDIAC (2010), "List of Countries by Carbon Dioxide Emissions Per Capita: 1990-2008", Carbon Dioxide Information Analysis Centre, US.

Giddens, Anthony (2008), "The Politics of Climate Change: National Responses to the Challenge of Global Warming", Policy Network Paper. London: Policy Network.

Gore, Al (1993), "US Support for Global Commitment to Sustainable Development", Lecture delivered at the meeting of the Commission on Sustainable Development, United Nations, New York.

Harris, Paul G. (ed.) (2001), "The Environment, International Relations and U.S. Foreign Policy", Washington: Georgetown University Press.

Harris, Paul G. (2013), "What's Wrong With Climate Politics and How to Fix It", UK: Polity Press.

International Energy Statistics (2011), "Per Capita Emissions of Countries, 2011", US.

Joy Warick and Peter Baker (1997), "Clinton Details Global Warming Plan", *Washington Post*, October 23, A6.

Karon, Tony (2001), "When it Comes to Kyoto, US is the Rogue Nation", *Time*, July 24.

Kyoto Protocol to the United Nations Framework Convention on Climate Change (1997), December 10; U.N. Doc FCCC/CP/1997/7/Add.1, 37 I.L.M. 22 (1998).

Natarajan, Jayanthi (2011), "India Not for Legally Binding Pact", Lecture delivered in Rajya Sabha, New Delhi.

Posner, Eric A. and Sunstein, Cass R. (2009), "Should Greenhouse Gas Permits Be Allocated on a Per Capita Basis?", *California Law Review, 51*.

PTI (2011), "Natarajan Stresses Equity at Durban Climate Talks", Policy Brief, Press Trust of India, New Delhi.

Rajamani, Lavanya (2007), "India's Negotiating Position on Climate Change: Legitimate but Not Sagacious", CPR Issue Brief, 2/2007, New Delhi.

Ramesh, Jairam (2010), "Ramesh Calls for Legally Binding

Commitments", *The Hindu*, available at:
http://www.thehindu.com/news/national/article943477.ece.

Ringius, L. (1998), "Equity and Social Considerations of Anthropogenic Climate Change", *Climate Change, Human Systems and Policy,* Volume III.

Robert, J. Timmons and Parks, C. Bradely (2007), "A Climate of Injustice: Global Inequality, North-South Politics and Climate Policy", Cambridge, Massachusetts: MIT Press.

Roberts, David (2009), "Is the 'Climate Debt' Discussion Helpful?", available at:
http://grist.org/article/2009-12-17-is-the-climate-debt-discussion-helpful/,%20Dec.%202009.

Singh, Manmohan (2008), "National Action Plan on Climate Change", Lecture delivered on release of Climate Change Action Plan, New Delhi.

Soz, S. (1997), "India Rejects Incorporation of New Environmental Commitments for Developing Countries", Lecture delivered at the 3rd Session of the Conference of the Parties to the Framework Convention on Climate Change, Kyoto, Japan, available at:
http://www.indianembassy.org/policy/Environment/soz.htm.

Stern, N. (2006), "The Stern Review: The Economics of Climate Change", Cambridge, UK: Cambridge University Press.

Stern, Todd (2009), December 9, at Copenhagen Climate Change Conference, available at:
http://environmentaljusticetv.wordpress.com/2014/04/10/cop15-us-envoy-todd-stern-rejects-the-idea-of-climate-debt-or-climate-reparations.

Stern, Todd (2013), "The Shape of a New International Climate Agreement", US Department of State, Chatham House: UK, October 22.

The White House (2001), "President Bush Discusses Global Climate Change", June 11, available at:
http://www.whitehouse.gov/news/release/2001/06/20010611-2.html. Accessed on March 8, 2008.

White House (1997), "Remarks by President Clinton on Global Climate Change", Policy Brief, The White House, Washington, D.C.

UN (1992), "United Nations Framework Convention on Climate Change", FCCC/INFORMAL/84, United Nations, New York.

US Congressional Record (1997), "105th Congress, Senate Resolution 98", S8113-S8139, Library of Congress, Washington, D.C.

Watkiss, Paul, Downing, Tom, Handley, Claire, Butterfield, Ruth, (2005), "The Impacts and Costs of Climate Change", AEA Technology Environment and Stockholm Environment Institute: Oxford.

World Resources Institute (WRI) (2011), "Cumulative Greenhouse Gas Emissions from 1850 to 2007", World Resources Institute, Washington D.C.

WRI (World Resources Institute) (2008), "Climate Analysis Indicators Tool", available at:
http://cait.wri.org/cait.php?page=yearly.

12

Indian Diaspora and Indo-U.S. Relations

Sandhya S. Nair

The Indian diaspora in United States today is one of the known ethnic minority groups among many ethnic communities which have been increasingly visible in the last few decades. The Indian diaspora in US is a culmination of different phases of Indian migration to the United States. Though a major portion of the present day Indian diaspora is result of the post-1960s, it has its roots way back in the later part of the eighteenth century to the mid-nineteenth century. The story of Indian immigration is distinct from the expatriates of religious or political persecution witnessed in some other countries. Indian immigrants like other hyphenated American ethnic groups have shown greater attachments to their country of origin. Their linkages with the home land has spread through wide areas of economic activity i.e., investment, philanthropic activities etc. and also as political means, most importantly bridging the oldest democracy and the largest but nascent democracy. Devesh Kapur pointed out that any diaspora's ideational effect depends upon its size, socio-economic characteristics and its access to points in power structure in the country of origin.

Along with this, the community's influence in the political sphere of host country is also important. Here it is worthy to examine the impact that the Indo-American community has had on transforming the historic hostile bilateral relationship between India and the US. It is argued that the role of Indian diaspora in the US is significant in altering perceptions of decision makers in both the countries. The diaspora's socio, economic and political achievements as well as their linkages with the homeland are important while considering the role of diaspora as a factor in Indo-US relations.

Socio-economic and Political Profile of the Community

In the beginning, the community was very small, uneducated, unskilled or semi-skilled and their impact on foreign policy was negligible. The community grew from small beginnings and became one of the fast growing ethnic groups in the United States. According to US Census 2010 reports, the total Asians numbered 14,674,252 and the Asian Indians constituted 28,43,391. Accordingly, the population of Asian Indians in the United States grew from almost 1,678 765 in 2000 to 2,843,391 in 2010: a growth rate of 69.37 percent, the highest for any Asian American community. They are represented virtually in all professions including agriculture, biotechnology, journalism, management, medicine, university teaching, information technology and various other branches. Indian community in US is one of the financially powerful and highly educated ethnic groups in the US. The following data clearly reveals the socio-economic status achieved by the Indian diaspora in the United States. [1]

- Almost 67 percent of all Indian Americans have a Bachelor's or higher degree (compared to the national average of 28 percent; and 44 percent average for all Asian American groups).

- About 40 percent of all Indian Americans have a Master's, Ph.D. or other professional degree.

- 65 percent of US born Indian Americans have received a college education.

- 104,897 Indian students enrolled in US universities in 2009-2010.

- Average yearly income of an Indian worker is US$ 51,904.

- US$ 69,470—the median income of Indian American families, nearly double the median income of all American families—US$ 38,885.

- Indian companies played a crucial role during the

recession by employing 60,000 people across 40 states.

- 15 percent of Silicon Valley start-up firms are owned by Indian-Americans.
- Nearly 10 percent of the physicians in the US are of Indian origin.
- Around 35 percent of the hotels in the country are owned by Indians.
- More than 300,000 Indian Americans work in the information technology sector.
- 43.6 percent are employed in managerial and professional specialities.
- There are over 8,000 Indian American faculty members across American universities.
- Indian origin engineers account for 34 percent of the total engineers in the Silicon Valley.

It is generally believed that financial power and security which provides freedom from other burdens is conducive in making political participation relatively easy and attractive. Considering the Indian diaspora, presently being one of the highest income groups in America, has acquired a critical mass in terms of economic clout. This provides them freedom from other burdens, enabling them to join politics, if they are willing. Higher levels of formal education and higher status occupations viz. managerial positions, skilled occupations, academic positions, are also related factors providing a convenient perspective for the political involvement. In spite of all these positive circumstances, the most important would be the subjective factor, i.e., willingness in playing a political role. The studies about the Indian American political participation showed that their political participation is not commensurate with their economic success.

But while analyzing the recent trend in political participation, greater emphasis should be given to the number of Indians who came forward to participate in the electoral contests, rather than how many of them were/are successful in winning the elections at different levels. Recent picture of electoral candidates shows an increasing number of Indian American candidates. If forty years have taken for the election of second Indian American to the American Congress, within the seven years, the third Indian American is elected to the House. This success and the growing number of Indian American candidates show the renewed interest and participation in American politics.

Another noticeable representation of Indian Americans in the American political sphere is the representation in the most important departments of administration. President Barack Obama recognised the immense talent and potential of this community, not only appointed a record number of Indian-Americans to his administration, but also there is hardly any major wing of the US government ranging from his own White House to Departments of State, Treasury, Defence and Commerce that some of the key positions are not being held by an Indian American. Above all, Indian Americans have traditionally exercised the most political influence through their campaign contributions, and are actively involved in fund raising efforts of political candidates on the federal and local levels.

Analysts argue that the recent dramatic growth in India-US relations has been motivated by some factors. Globalization policies and India's economic liberalization, which facilitated foreign investment in India, international terrorism and the consequent 'war on terror' created the tactical need to coordinate strategies with India—the belief that India could play a role in the long-run as a strategic partner of the United States; the China factor etc. are influencing factors in the relation between the two countries. Along with this, the importance of Indian diaspora in Indo-US relations is recognized by policy makers of both the countries and has generated much discussion in the public and academic sphere.

In the early phase of immigration, the Indian diaspora in US with small numbers were facing the restrictions of numerous anti-immigration laws such as Immigration and

Regional Restriction Act also Known as the Barred Zone Act (1917), the California Alien Land Law of 1913 (which was tightened in 1920 and prohibited ownership of property and even leasing of property being banned for Asians), the Asian Exclusion Act of 1924 etc. Naturally, the community effort mostly focused on the problems of these immigration acts and racial riots against them. Even then, the Gadar movement and Indian publications also focused on the cause of India's independence and tried to keep Americans apprised of the independence movement. Under the circumstances, advocates for better relations such as J.J. Singh, the president of the India League of America, could make little progress in his attempt to secure backing from the Roosevelt administration for Indian independence. Although US was sympathetic to the anti-colonialism championed by the Indian National Congress, Washington yet felt it necessary to support its ally Great Britain, rather than the nationalist movement that was demanding independence from Britain.

Later, the community came to realize that managing the core of Indo-US differences was of significance to them, partly, due to their dual roots. Many also carried the burden of Indo-Pakistan relations and continued to voice opposition to the United States assistance to Pakistan as detrimental to US interest in regional stability. The Indian diaspora community staged a demonstration against the AWACS to be sold to Pakistan. Myron Weiner studied about the community and hoped that the growing presence of the affluent Indian American expatriate community in the United States would make a difference for future bilateral relations. [2] As will be seen, the diaspora's influence in the United States has grown as its skills, education, income, and size have increased. It is apparent that the prosperous and demographically significant Indo-American community, typified by physicians and Silicon Valley computer technicians, has remarkably changed not only its image, but also the perception of its home country in the United States. [3]

Capitol Hill discovered new South Asian markets for US goods and Congressional thinking about the region slowly began to shift. For the first time, members of the Senate and especially the House of Representatives concluded that increased attention to the Indian subcontinent could bring benefits in the US political arena. This realization had two immediate results. First, it prompted greater congressional interest in South Asia. Second, it accelerated the dramatic shift in congressional sympathies already underway. A considerable proportion of US lawmakers moved away from the pro-Pakistan stance that had prevailed throughout much of the Cold War, and especially during the war in Afghanistan, and toward a perspective tilted much more towards India. [4]

Formation of India Caucus
The rising prominence of Indian Americans has played a crucial role by creating a new channel of pressure for the United States to pay greater attention on Capitol Hill. One barometer of India's growing profile in Washington is the growing number of the US House of Representatives in the Congressional Caucus on India and Indian Americans. [5] With the help of US law makers, India Caucus was formed in 1993 in the House of Representatives. Pallone, a shrewd politician who due to redistricting had a large Indian American population in his new Congressional district, persuaded six other Democrats and Republican Bill McCollum to join him in organizing a Congressional Caucus on India and Indian Americans. The India Caucus soon became one of the most important links between Indian Americans and Congress and serves as a forum to bring up issues and discuss political options and solutions. Together with its growing importance, the India Caucus experienced a steady expansion. [6]

In an interview with the Indian American newspaper *India Abroad*, Congressman Joe Wilson (Republican, South Carolina) stated, "It's a great tribute to the Indian American community that the India Caucus is the largest caucus in the

US Congress". In 2004, a counterpart of the India Caucus was founded in the US Senate. The Caucus Friends of India had close to 40 members and was headed by Senator Hillary Clinton (Democrat, New York)—another sign for the growing political importance of the Indian American population. [7] The Indian diaspora is thus in a position to act as a lobby— particularly by financing the "Indian Caucus" in the House of Representatives and the Senate, but also as a showcase for India, whose image has changed considerably in the United States. [8]

It was formed with the official objectives of pushing the Indian American community's agenda on the Hill and promote better Indo-US ties. Asian Indians like Kapil Sharma, Himanshu Shekhar etc. were the leading personalities behind the formation of the India Caucus. The Congressional Caucus on India and Indian Americans primarily focused on US-India relations—to include trade, security, cooperation, global terrorism and economic and humanitarian assistance, issues of interest to the Asian Indian community and developments in India and on the Indian subcontinent. [9] As Arthur G. Rubinoff noted, by enlisting floor speakers, lining up votes and placing material in the Congressional Record, the India Caucus had for the first time provided India with an institutional support on Capitol Hill. [10]

The activism of India Caucus includes promoting pro-India legislations and defeating anti-India resolutions and amendments. This was most evident in what happened to the Burton Amendment, introduced by Dan Burton, who used to be a very vigorous critic of India. Finding no support for his move, the Republican from Indiana, Dan Burton, withdrew his amendment to the Foreign Operations Bill which would have slashed development assistance to India by 25 percent. But he did so only after making the usual noises against India— especially on its human rights violations in Kashmir, Punjab and Nagaland. [11]

During a brief debate, Frank Pallone, Democrat from New

Jersey, pointed out that the Burton Amendment made no sense before and it made less sense now. The co-chairman of the Congressional Caucus on India and Indian Americans, Gray Ackerman, argued that the Burton Amendment "is the wrong amendment at the wrong time". [12] As one of the first Congressional caucuses devoted to promoting relations with a single country, the group grew more rapidly than Pallone could have envisioned. The Indian American press gave considerable coverage and encouraged its readers to urge their congressional representatives to join the organization.

Lobbying

The formation of the Congressional Caucus on India has been a milestone for the lobbying efforts of the Indian American community. Lobbying became an important tool for political participation and influence. It includes efforts to influence legislators and top government officials. Lobbying is a common practice in the United States, especially during general elections. Indian Americans and Indian American Associations now play a prominent role in this game. On many occasions, they have mobilized their opinion on important issues and played a crucial role in generating a favourable climate of opinion in the Congress by defeating anti-Indian legislations and lobbying effectively on other issues of concern to the Indian community. In fact, the first lobbying efforts of the Indian diaspora in the US to support India came as early as 1987 when the National Federation of Indian American Associations (NFIA) mobilised large parts of the community and managed to stop the sale of American Airborne Warning and Control System (AWACS) planes to Pakistan. [13]

The importance of Caucus group and lobbying can be witnessed after the Indian nuclear tests of 1998. The 1998 nuclear tests of India made a setback in Indo-US relations. Economic sanctions were imposed on India by the Glenn Amendment Act. On November 13, 1998, the Bureau of Export Administration of the US Department of Commerce released a list targeting a number of Government of India organisations, institutes and Indian private sector companies. The American companies were not allowed to trade with these Indian companies. If they wish to export goods to the listed Indian companies, they have to obtain licences. The list was exhaustive and included 40 parent entities in India and 46 in Pakistan. Through this list the US hoped to break many Indian public sector and private sector organisations like the Atomic Energy Commission, Centre for Development of Advanced Computing, Defence Research and Development Organisation, Bhabha Atomic Research Centre, Mumbai, Indira Gandhi Centre for Atomic Research, Kalpakkam etc. [14] Even some of the companies which had no direct link to nuclear and missile proliferation were put into the entities list.

Living in an atmosphere of sanctions and technology denial regimes has been a normal affair for India. In the US, the Democratic Congressman and former Co-Chair of the India Caucus, Frank Pallone admitted, "the Administration has cast too wide a net in listing entities, including private research institutions that do not threaten US security interests. Particularly, after the recent partial lifting of sanctions, this step seems to indicate an inconsistency in US policy towards India". Pallone added, "the entities list only adds to the negative trend in US-India economic relations. The negative tone that this move creates will cause US companies to lose opportunities to do business with India. America's loss could well be the European Union's or Japan's gain". [15]

These sanctions became crucial for American business firms also. A coordinated effort was made by political interest groups and economic Indian American organisations like the US-India Business Council or the India Interest Group. President Bill Clinton in the first place waived "some sanctions" in the economic domain, both for India and Pakistan. Finally, President George W. Bush lifted all sanctions of the Glenn Amendment. It may be noted that almost all sanctions imposed in the aftermath of the 1998 nuclear tests were lifted, notwithstanding the fact that the action also has to do with the larger foreign policy calculations of the United States.

During the Kargil crisis in 1999, the community 'flooded' the offices of important members of Congress with countless e-mails. This 'e-mail blitz' was a major success in motivating Representatives to urge President Bill Clinton to call for a withdrawal of Pakistani troops from the disputed territories—a classical example of an indirect lobbying effort. [16] The growing importance of the community and its lobbying efforts are recognized and received great momentum in India also. 'For the first time, India has a constituency in the US with real influence and status. The Indian community in the United States constitutes an invaluable asset in strengthening India's relationship with the world's only superpower...They have effectively mobilized on issues ranging from the nuclear tests in 1998 to Kargil, played a crucial role in generating a favourable climate of opinion in Congress and defeating anti-India legislation there, and lobbied effectively on other issues of concern to the Indian community'. [17] This statement by the High Level Committee on the Indian Diaspora rightly summarises the growing importance of the Indian American community.

Not all times have the Indian Americans and their American law maker friends succeeded. There had been some criticism of the India Caucus, as it did not do significant work after the first four or five years. Indian ethnic media in the US reported as to how after 1997-98, the Caucus "was content to just bandy its growing numbers and send out press releases about what it was doing to promote US-India relations, but hardly doing anything substantive or tangible with regard to the growth of US-India relations, and more importantly to help to address the Indian-American community's issues and concerns, but taking them for granted". [18] Lot of factors have influenced the ineffectiveness of the India Caucus. In the first place, it has influence in the House only. The Senate members were resisted to align themselves so decidedly with what is still a numerically modest US ethnic group. Second, although the Caucus claims a membership of more than 100, only a couple dozen of these members take an active interest in the affairs of the Indian American community.

Although most Caucus members cast pro-India votes, their activities on behalf of the community do not extend much beyond that. Indeed, some legislators appear not even to know that their staffs have signed them up for caucus membership. [19] The inaction can be gauged from the fact that Joseph Crowley failed to get the support of 100 fellow Congressmen to enact a resolution on honouring Dalip Singh Saund, the first Asian Indian in the US Congress. At that time in 2003, the Caucus had 163 members, but only 33 signed in favour. The bill to honour Saund was finally passed on February 2, 2005. Personal rivalries may also have undercut the organization's effectiveness, although by its very nature, this development is difficult to document. The ability of the community to influence the Caucus's was limited due to the fact that Indian American community was not a significant voting constituency. Congressional observers expressed concern that the Caucus was being used as a 'fund-raising vehicle' for its members and that the Indian American community was being exploited.

In spite of these shortcomings, the diaspora and most importantly the Indian associations continued its relation with Caucus group members and engaged in the art of lobbying. The Indian American Forum for Political Education (IAFPE) has made many achievements, such as establishing an effective bipartisan liaison with the Democratic and Republican National Committees and opening communication channels between Indian Americans and the White House executive agencies, including the US State Department. One of the objectives of the IAFPE is facilitating and promoting ongoing Indo-US relations. [20] The promotion of Indo-US relations was deemed most crucial to the success of the IAFPE and other such political organizations. This includes working with government officials on both the Indian and the American side.

Additionally, issues such as the property rights of Indian Americans in India, their travel-related problems, concern for their families' interests in India, educational programmes, and business-related matters have dominated the agenda. Philanthropic acts are also included prodding the United States in stepping up its aid to India on specific events. [21] In addition to the efforts by the Indian diaspora itself, Congress approved considerable financial aid packages to India following the 2001 Gujarat earthquake, the 2004 tsunami disaster and the earthquake catastrophe in the Kashmir region in October 2005. This is, at least partly, the result of the sustained drive of the Indian American community to create a positive image of India among US politicians and, equally important, among the American people. [22]

India has been using some powerful lobbyists in the US for furthering its interests. It has also been actively engaged in anti-Pakistan propaganda in the US. The primary group in the Indian lobby is the US India Political Action Committee (USINPAC), a group that was formed after 9/11 with the close support and encouragement of the American Jewish Committee (AJC) and the American Israel Political Action Committee (AIPAC). The US-India Business Council, primarily working for trade and investment in the two countries, has lavished big money on lobbyists, too. In just five years, USINPAC has become the most visible face of Indian American lobbying. [23]

The US Congress received a personal letter from Sanjay Puri, Chairman and founder of USINPAC with an online petition signed by over 16,000 citizens calling to cut off funding to Pakistan if it does not shut down the terror training camps. Indian lobby is active in blocking every move that is favourable to Pakistan like sophisticated weapons for countering insurgency in the tribal belt of Pakistan. [24] Indian American Forum for Political Education (IAFPE), which has twenty-eight chapters across the United States, and the Indian American Political Advocacy Council(IAPAC), the American Association of Physicians, the Indian American Friendship Council and other important Indian Associations in US have transformed their financial and political clout for lobbying and better Indo-US relations.

Diaspora Involvement during Indo-US Nuclear Deal

The diaspora lobbying was also witnessed during the discussions of India US nuclear deal. Using the rubric of a US-India "global partnership", USINPAC spearheaded the national lobbying effort in Washington—preparing widely distributed issue briefs for members of Congress, sponsoring frequent receptions and fundraisers for legislators, and utilizing electronic communications media to mobilize Indian-Americans across the country to sign a petition and to directly contact their lawmakers. [25] In late 2005, USINPAC worked with Eni Faleomavaega, the House's non-voting delegate from American Samoa and co-chair of a Congressional Task Force on US-India Investment and Trade Relations, to organize a discussion of the nuclear agreement attended by Indian Ambassador Ronen Sen and key members of the Congress.

At the forum, long time India champion Pallone remarked, "The agreement strengthens energy security for the US and India, and promotes the development of stable and efficient energy markets in India to ensure adequate and affordable supplies…its implementation is important for US-India relations". Congressman Chris Cannon was both more expansive and more specific, "I am pleased to stand with you this evening and welcome India as a global partner. I commend my good friend, Sanjay Puri and USINPAC, for their visionary leadership in bringing together the Indian-American community, the embassy, and key members of the U.S. Congress to discuss ways in which we can begin to address issues of critical importance including the civil nuclear cooperation agreement". [26] The USINPAC stressed the trade potential in the civilian nuclear sector, and maintained always that the nuclear deal was part of a broader strategic partnership—suggesting the possibility of issue-linkage and expanded trade in other sectors as well. It also argued that with a freer nuclear hand, India could diversify its energy sources away from coal and petroleum, at a time when its rapidly growing consumer class is contributing to unprecedented demand for global resources. While economic and environmental arguments were placed at the fore, USINPAC also continued to stress India's solidarity with the US against terrorism. [27]

Community publications and websites, such as *India Abroad*, offered extensive coverage of the draft agreement, and also named individual members of Congress who had expressed support or opposition to the bill. Traditionally, professional-minded organizations such as the American Association of Physicians of Indian Origin got involved, hosting a panel discussion in Washington that featured Assistant Secretary of State Richard Boucher and other administration officials. The AAPI and other community organizations took out a full-page advertisement in The Washington Post on April 5 to champion the draft bill. Bulk emails to legislators and their staffs carried briefs and electronic petitions in favour. In reality, the most effective face of Indian diaspora lobbying was witnessed in the matter of India-US Nuclear deal.

Indian Diaspora Perspectives on Indo-US Relations

Generally, Indian Americans are interested in American public policy issues, particularly issues related to Indo-US cooperation. The diaspora members identified certain important areas of co-operation between India and the United States. The most important aspect is cooperation in combating international terrorism. It became important in the context of September 11 terrorist attacks and terrorist attacks on India as well. More than 96 percent have identified combating international terrorism as an important policy area in which India and US can cooperate with each other. Some of the respondents mentioned about the illegitimate Pakistan support to terrorist groups and pointed out that the joint efforts of India and US is essential.

Other areas of cooperation include global environment protection (53 percent), promotion of globalization of trade and commerce (52 percent), protection of ethnic minorities in plural societies (51 percent), combating world poverty (49 percent), and fighting illegal drugs.

Respondents further pointed out other areas of cooperation; focus on democratic values—both the governments should promote spread of democracy and good government, travel and visa related issues, tourism, spiritual enlightenment and affiliate events, technology, education, defence, business, people to people contact, health care, educational exchange between both the countries, cultural exchanges-film, arts etc.

They specified the importance of strategic relations between the two countries and stated that cooperation in the above mentioned areas will bring the two democracies closer. They also pointed out that the worsening relations with Pakistan and China threat will push the United States to associate more with India.

The US-India cooperation in civilian nuclear energy, initially announced in 2005, during the visit by Prime Minister Singh to Washington, and which came into effect in 2008 is considered as a watershed in the history of Indo-US relations. The deal had generated much discussion in both the countries.

Majority of the respondents believed that Indo-US relations had improved because of nuclear trade and commerce. The role of Indian-American citizens' groups in the United States, and the efforts of an increasingly professional and well-funded "India lobby" on Capitol Hill, were critical in pressing members of Congress to support the agreement. [28] Despite the long odds against winning congressional support, the Indian-American community mobilized around the nuclear agreement issue as never before. Walter Anderson, a close observer of Indian-American political activity on Capitol Hill, notes, "This controversial proposal of the Bush administration galvanized the usually fractured Indian American community into united action like no previous issue...[Indian-Americans] played hard ball politics and used sophisticated lobbying tactics to focus community attention on the proposed legislation". [29] The USINPAC stressed the trade potential in the civilian nuclear sector, and maintained always that the nuclear deal was part of a broader strategic partnership suggesting the possibility of issue-linkage and expanded trade in other sectors as well.

An important question which arises here is that how can the Indian community contribute to the betterment of Indo-US relations? About 90 percent of the respondents pointed out the importance of diaspora's political involvement and participation in the US political process. They have provided some insightful suggestions for better relations between the two countries, outlined below:

- Develop business contacts, people to people contact, and cooperation in key areas of development.
- Business collaboration and political forums to exchange ideas for better relations between India and the US.
- The general public in US is either ignorant or obvious of India or have a poor or narrow image of India. The Indian community needs to bring more public awareness of what India exactly is, her contributions, her greatness and question the stereotyping that news media or others sometimes tend to make about Indians. This awareness needs to be carried out from grassroots level to the top. Overall, the Indian community needs to develop their appreciation of their homeland, communicate and educate folks about India in a positive light whenever the opportunity presents. This can be done through promoting more Indian studies in colleges and universities, talking to

neighbours, colleagues or friends, contributing articles to news and social media and emerging as a true cultural ambassador of India. A new think tank in Washington called US-India Institute was recently set up to achieve this goal.

- Active involvement in the national politics of United States and being engaged in policy and political issues.
- A positive and enterprising presence and getting involved in non-Indian issues that are important to American lives.
- More and more people from Indian origin should get elected in political offices in state or federal levels.
- Political activism to be promoted locally and nationally. Political dialogue with political parties and business in India are required.
- Live a life that is acceptable to the people by promoting Indian culture and take part in the political system very actively.
- Demonstrating the quality of work, tourism and interest in Indian culture, art, music, movies and culinary delights.
- On the whole, the community have provided very generous and concrete suggestions for better relations between the two countries. The extent to which these respondents are thoughtful in Indo-US cooperation seems very important. More than 95 percent of the respondents believe their economic and political success can be converted to political gains and consequently their role in bridging the two democracies.

In essence, it is clear that the diaspora can play an important role in improving the relations between the two countries. The study rightly pointed out that the diaspora's socio-economic achievements and political participation is important in this context. Along with this, creating better awareness about India and the Indian culture is also important. This should be intended not only for the American public but also the second and third generation Indians. In this perspective, diaspora's media, journalism efforts, literature, film and music have great impact in reflecting the immigrant's life and Indian culture. The contributions of international figures such as V.S. Naipaul, Salman Rushdie, Shashi Tharoor and talented writers like Jhumpa Lahiri, Bharti Mukharjee, Pankaj Mishra, Anita Desai etc. are praiseworthy. The themes of their writings often relate to Indian social, political and economic issues, Indian culture, Indian immigrants and their American reared children, assimilation, cultural conflicts, identity etc. The musicians like Pandit Ravi Shankar, Ali Akhbar Khan, Zakir Hussain etc. made Indian music popular. Indian films screened overseas help to shape and reshape cultural practices and social attitudes among the diasporic communities. All these contributions have helped to create an increasing knowledge and awareness about India and Indian culture in the United States and a changing perception towards India.

Another important factor is the growing presence of American educated Indian law makers (who were once a part of diaspora community), in the Indian political spectrum. Reflecting increased cooperation between American and Indian legislators, a recent parliamentary delegation included Palaniappan Chidambaram, Finance Minister in the UPA government, who earned a Harvard MBA, Congress leader Sonia Gandhi's son Rahul Gandhi, who studied at Harvard, Milind Deora, son of veteran Mumbai Congress politician Murli Deora, Sachin Pilot, son of the late Congress leader Rajesh Pilot, B.J. Panada of the Biju Janata Dal, and the Bharatiya Janata Party's Manvendra Singh, son of former external affairs minister Jaswant Singh, Dayanidhi Maran, the son of former Industries Minister Murasoli Maran of the Dravida Munnetra Kazhagam (DMK); Jyotiradithya Scindia, the son of the late Madhav Rao Scindia, Dushyant Singh, the son of Vasundhara Raje etc. [30] Ajit Singh, son of former Prime Minister Charan Singh, who actually became a US citizen, and later renounced his American citizenship in order to return to India and run for election.

The emergence of Shashi Tharoor in the Indian politics is also worth mentioning here. He was elected from Thiruvananthapuram Lok Sabha Constituency in 2009 with a thumping majority. George Abraham, the founding General Secretary of the Indian National Overseas Congress, [31] wrote letter to Mrs. Sonia Gandhi expressing the strong support from the part of diaspora. He states that "NRIs are constantly asked to invest financially, offer our services or technological skill-sets, and advocate further socio-economic development in our home states. However, efforts to play a more active role within the political process have been met with great reservation from powerful circles at home". [32] The involvement of diaspora community in the election campaign attracted attention and is well reflected in the result also.

In addition, "practically every educated or wealthy family in India has one or more members resident in America with vested interests in good relations with that country". It is estimated that 25 percent of the Indian elites have relatives living in the United States. With 74,603 Indians studying in the United States, India is the largest source of foreign students in the country. Sixty percent of retired Indian generals have children studying abroad—half of them in the United States. [33] Hundreds of thousands of Indians have worked in the United States on H-1B visas. Thousands have returned home, many who are employed in businesses engaged in the outsourcing of services. While an education in the United States does not guarantee support for Washington's policies, it does impart an understanding and transmission of American values and culture. Once back in India they have become an important lobby for better relations with the United States.

Conclusion

The Indian immigrants being well educated and boasting of a large numbers of professionals—doctors, scientists, engineers, entrepreneurs, and computer and software specialists—the community had become increasingly affluent in the last couple of decades. It is better organized, more politically active and has devoted more attention to making its views known on Capitol Hill. Being a multicultural society, having tolerance to ethnic politics, the Unites States is said to be permissive of such activities of a diaspora as long as those pursuits are not prejudicial or detrimental to its national interests. They have achieved remarkable success, supplementing the hard work of many in the government in both the countries. Here, the role of Indian diaspora associations in United States, diaspora literature, newspapers etc. are all significant. In spite of the organized efforts, individual oriented activities have also attracted greater attention.

The new Indian elite that have emerged in both countries have had a significant impact on Indo-American relations. Along with the diaspora efforts, the centres of India Studies in various American Universities are already working on closer relationships between India and the United States. It appears that the Indian immigrants, in general, are positive in their outlook about the future of Indo-American relations. Interestingly, there are think thanks, NGOs and universities in India and the United States, who are promoting Indo-US cooperation through cultural exchange programmes, seminars and conferences.

Notes and References

1. http://www.usinpac.com.
2. For details, see Myron Weiner (1990), "The Indian Presence in America: What Difference Will it Make?", in Sulochana Raghavan Glazer and Nathan Glazer (ed.), Conflicting Images: India and the United States, Riverdale, Glenn Dale, MD.
3. Arthur G. Rubinoff (2005), "Indian Diaspora as a Factor in Indo-US Relations", *Asian Affairs*, Volume 32, No. 3, p. 169.
4. Robert M. Hathaway (2001), "Unfinished Passage: India, Indian Americans, and the U.S. Congress", *The Washington Quarterly*, 24:2, 21-34, p. 23.
5. Philip Oldenburg and Alyssa Ayres (2002), "Quickening the

Pace of Change", India Briefing Series 9, M.E. Sharpe, New York, p. 15.

6. Pieree Gottschlich (2008), "The Indian Diaspora in the United States of America: An Emerging Political Force?", in Parvati Raghuram, Ajaya Kumar Sahoo, Brij Maharaj and Dave Sangha (eds.), Tracing an Indian Diaspora Contexts, Memories, Representations, Sage Publications, New Delhi, p. 160.

7. Ibid., p. 161.

8. Christopher Jaffrelot (2005), "India, the United States' New Ally in Asia", available at:
http://www.ceri-sciences-po.org accessed on 12-02-2010.

9. Mukesh Bagoria (2004), "Indian Diaspora in American Politics in the 1990s", Ph.D. thesis, American Studies Division, Centre for American and West European Studies, School of International Studies, J.N.U., p. 157.

10. Arther G. Rubinoff (2002), "Legislative Perceptions of Indo-American Relations", in Kapur, Ashok et al. (eds.), India and the United States in a Changing World, Sage Publications, New Delhi, p. 447.

11. Mahendra Gaur and Sailendra Sengara (2009), "Foreign Policy Annual, 2001-2009", Kalpaz Publications, New Delhi, p. 254.

12. Ibid.

13. Pieree Gottschlich (2008), op. cit., p. 166.

14. Baidya Bikash Basu (1999), "US Sanctions and India", *Strategic Analysis*, Volume 22, No. 10, p. 1630.

15. Ibid., pp. 1630-1631.

16. Pieree Gottschlich (2008), op. cit., p. 166.

17. Report of High Level Committee on Indian Diaspora (2001), Government of India, pp. xx-xxi.

18. Vinod J. (2007), "India's Policy Towards the NRI Community in the US Since 1998", Ph.D. thesis, Centre for South, Central, Aouth East Asian and South West Pacific Studies, School of International Studies, J.N.U., p. 88.

19. Robert M. Hathaway (2001), op. cit., Volume 24, No. 2, p. 29.

20. http://www.iafpe.org.

21. Anjali Sahay (2009), "Indian Diaspora in the United States: Brain Drain or Gain?", Lexington Books, USA, p. 178.

22. Pieree Gottschlich (2008), op. cit., pp. 166-167.

23. http://pakobserver.net/detailnews.asp?id=97876; accessed on 26-11-2012.

24. Ibid.
25. Jason A. Kirk (2008), "Indian-Americans and the U.S.-India Nuclear Agreement: Consolidation of an Ethnic Lobby?", *Foreign Policy Analysis,* 4, pp. 275-300.
26. Ibid.
27. Ibid., p. 295.
28. Jason A. Kirk (2008), op. cit., p. 276.
29. Jason A. Kirk (2008), op. cit., p. 294.
30. Aziz Haniffa (2004), "Young MPs Wow Capitol Hill", *India Abroad.*
31. The INOC was created as a link between the Indian National Congress and the diaspora in United States. It started out as a 'Malayalee' organization, inaugurated by then opposition leader Oommen Chandy in 1998. It later expanded to include people from all regions in India, Smt. Sonia Gandhi went on to inaugurate the expanded organization in 2003 at a function in New York. The goals of the organization are to function as a forum for NRIs residing in USA, desiring to promote the ideals of democracy, secularism and fraternity so that justice, liberty and equality may be secured for all. The INOC also works towards improving bilateral relations between the two countries. It also engages in dialogue with the Congress Party's leadership on issue that concern the Indian diaspora. Source: T.P. Sreinivasan (2011), "Mattering to India: The Shashi Tharoor Campaign", Pearson, New Delhi, p. 124.
32. Ibid., p. 125.
33. Arthur G. Rubinoff, (2005), op. cit., pp. 177-178.

13

Some Realities of the 21st Century

Sanjal Shastri

The second half of the twentieth century has been regarded by many as a phase of the triumph of democracy. Many newly independent nations decided to embark on the process of democratization and establish democratic processes with varying degrees of success. The disintegration of the Soviet Union and the collapse of Communist regimes in Eastern Europe was also considered a signal of the victory of liberal democracy and reassertion of the success of market economies and capitalism. For writers like Francis Fukuyama, it was a symbol of the ultimate victory of capitalism and liberal democracy (Fukuyama, 1992).

Francis Fukuyama in "End of History and the Last Man" underscored the point that in the 20th century, the two greatest challenges posed to liberal democracy were from fascism and communism. The fall of the Nazis in 1945 and later on the death of Franco and ousting of the Portuguese dictator Caetano marked the defeat of the right-wing fascist regimes. The events in Berlin in 1989 marked the defeat of communism. According to Fukuyama, this meant that capitalism and liberal democracy had ultimately won.

Samuel P. Huntington offers an opposing thesis to that of Fukuyama. According to Huntington, the post-1990s world is going to see a 'clash of civilizations' in what he calls a divide between the liberal west and the conservative east. Huntington does not claim that capitalism and liberal democracy have won an outright victory. Both theories have come under severe scrutiny but at the end of the day it is a given fact that post-1990s, there has been a marked rise in the number of democratic states. Most of the satellite states of the USSR came to embrace democracy. So with some degree of confidence, we can say that liberal democracy has been left with few challengers post-1991.

The disintegration of the Soviet Union and the fall of the Berlin wall had wider implications for global developments and the establishment of a new world order. Between 1945 and 1989, the world was characterized by a bi-polar system. We had the United State of America on one side leading an ideological framework presented by western liberal democracy and capitalism. The Soviet Union led the opposing ideological strand that espoused the advantages of communism. International relations and the world order was built around the reality of a bi-polar world. However, the developments of the late 1980s and early 1990s marked an end to this bi-polar global system. What emerged in its place has been a subject of animated debate.

One of the popular beliefs going around since the 1990s has been that the 21st century will see a uni-polar international system. [1] This school of thought echoes the belief that the United States of America will be the world's single largest superpower wielding un-challenged and un-paralleled authority across the world. However, if the events since the 1970s are anything to go by, then a different picture emerges. There are clear signs that the United States is a superpower in a slow but sure decline. Experts would say that the United State's misadventure in Vietnam was a beginning of this slide. Vietnam for many, is a crucial global turning point as the so called 'world's greatest power' was defeated by a communist guerrilla force: the Vietminh. Besides this, the developments in Vietnam were accompanied by massive internal political upheavals in the United States, a high point of which was the Watergate scandal. The decline of the United States is also to be seen in the backdrop of the rise of China as an economic power.

With the death of Mao in 1976 and Deng Xiaoping's

economic liberalization program, within a span of 20 years China has emerged as an important global player. As of 2014, it is the world's second largest economy and has the potential to overtake the United States within the next 30 years.

The 1990s was also a crucial period in the history of other important powers like India and South Africa. It was in 1991 that Indian Prime Minister P. Narsimha Rao initiated the process of economic liberalization. In South Africa, the 1990s marked the end of the apartheid rule. 1994 saw South Africa hold her first free and fair elections with Nelson Mandela taking over as the President. India and South Africa have since then emerged as important global powers with the capacity to emerge as super powers in the next two decades. The rising presence of associations like the IBSA (India, Brazil and South Africa) and the BRICS (Brazil, India, Russia, China and South Korea) are possible indications of the emergence of a multi-polar world.

It is in this context that this paper attempts to dialogue on the democratization process in South Asia and its implications for an India-United States dialogue.

Changing South Asia in 21st Century
The previous section clearly highlighted three very important realities of the 21st century: the 'victory' of democracy, the emergence of a multi-polar world and increasing challenge to the pre-eminent position of the United States. The impacts of these developments are being seen in the South Asia region. Democracy has been an integral part of the South Asia experience, though not in a western liberal sense. Traces of democratic ideals can be found in the Ancient histories of this region. South Asian history is rich and overflowing with examples of ancient republics and the presence of monarchs who derived their legitimacy from the support that they enjoyed from the people. The western notion and model of democracy came to South Asia during the colonial era. South Asian societies are faced with a very

unique situation. The State of Democracy in South Asia Report, clearly stresses that in this region, "The people's orientation of democracy is shaped principally by political experience rather than by a few inherited identities...The strength of the practice of democracy in South Asia lies in its capacity to move away from the received model of democracy" (SDSA). There are also important differences in the experience of democracy in the different countries of this region. [2]

The drive towards democratic governments gaining firm roots was witnessed in many countries of the region in the last two decades, more visibly at the turn of the century. It is not a coincidence that this comes at a time when ideologies like communism and fascism seem to be in retreat. This transition towards a more democratic rule in South Asia can be seen as a part of a larger global trend. However, the transition to democracy in South Asia cannot be equated with similar transitions in other parts of the world. While some nations in the region (India and Sri Lanka) have seen relatively stable democratic governments, the same is not true for the entire region. Further, even India and Sri Lanka have faced serious internal challenges.

A view across the region indicates the presence of complex challenges. Afghanistan is struggling to stand on its own feet after the United States 'war on terror' was fought from its soil. Now that the US is planning to withdraw its troops, the Taliban still poses an enormous challenge to democracy. The concern for everyone is how the country will be able to manage after the US pull out in the course of 2014. Is the Afghan Army strong enough to deal with the Taliban challenge? Pakistan has had brief periods of democratic rule but these have generally been sandwiched between long periods of military dictatorships. As a matter of fact, the 2013 elections is the first time that there has been a successful transfer of power from one party to another following a democratic election. Like Afghanistan, Pakistan is also facing challenges from the Pakistani wing of the Taliban.

Over the last five years, Pakistan has been a victim of several Taliban attacks and in 2011 they even posed a threat of marching into Islamabad. Democracy in Nepal is in its very early days. For a long part of its history, Nepal has been a monarchy. It is only over the past decade that the royal family has been ousted from power. The source of Nepal's instability is the violent nature of the transition. In the Royal Massacre of 2001, the entire Royal family was eliminated. The memories of that are still very fresh in the minds of the Nepalese people. Another great source of instability in Nepal has been the presence of the Maoists and the violent tactics that they had employed against the government.

Now that they have joined the mainstream government, the threat of Maoist related violence has subsided. While Bangladesh has seen a return to democracy after several phases of military rule, the stability of democratic institutions and processes remains a question mark especially after the recent boycott of elections by the leading opposition party. Bangladesh over the past year or so has faced one of the greatest challenges to her democracy. The war crime trails has deeply divided the country sending it into an internal crisis. Experts say that over the next year the people of Bangladesh have to decide what ideal they want to build their nation on; the linguistic Bengali nationalism on which the nation was built in 1971 or on the basis of their Islamic identity. Maldives' democracy has come under the scanner after the ouster of the former president Nasheed. Apart from this, the country has been relatively stable. Bhutan got a constitution for the first time in 2008. One fact is clear from the above discussion that most of the South Asian nations (apart from Bhutan and some would say India) are suffering from political instability and violence.

The State of Democracy in South Asia report published by the Centre for Study of Developing Societies (CSDS), highlights some very interesting facts about the average South

Asia's perspective of democracy. The Report clearly shows that the people of South Asia believe democracy is the only way forward. The Report highlights the fact that democracy is especially popular amongst the youth. An interesting fact that comes out of the report is that the South Asian brand of democracy is different from the western brand. Generally, the western system places importance on the ideals of freedom, right to vote and free speech. However, in South Asia people hold the view that democracy really implies providing everyone with equal opportunities. So, unlike in the west, at the heart of South Asian democracy is the idea of equality of opportunity. This is yet another reason why the South Asian experiment with democracy is not the same as what was taking place elsewhere (CSDS).

The unique nature of South Asia's democracy and the internal instability in South Asian nations means that the transition to democracy in many of these countries is fraught with contradictions and complications. The coming decade is going to be of utmost importance and is a very interesting period in South Asian history. If these transitions have to be a success there are combinations of factors that will have to work together. Firstly, the idea of democracy cannot be something that is confined to the visions of a group of elite. Unlike what has happened with political power in South Asia, the entire population ranging from the elite to the marginalized have to be taken into confidence. The SDSA report clearly points out to the importance of popular participation in the transition process. Secondly, this phase will have to be coupled with advancements in development in terms of infrastructure, health and education.

The setting up of good infrastructure and a good system of education will ensure that there is lasting stability. It is in the third factor that India and the US come into picture. It is important that the countries of South Asia get the right kind of international support. The next section of the paper is going to look at how India and the US can support this transition.

South Asia's Tryst with Democracy

An India-United States dialogue over South Asia's march towards establishing more stable democratic processes needs to be analyzed in the context of the current equations in the region. Being an important player in South Asia, India has always had a stake in events and developments in the region. As far as the United States of America is concerned, their interest in the region dates back to the 1950s and 1960s when they established close ties with Pakistan. In the 1971 Bangladesh Liberation War, South Asia became one of the flash points of the Cold War, with the United States threatening to deploy the Seventh Fleet. However, the American interests in South Asia appear to have dramatically altered in the 21st century. This is mainly on account of two developments. First, 9/11 and the subsequent 'war on terror' made South Asia an important region in this context. The United States realized that support and cooperation of South Asian nations, principally India and Pakistan was critical to win the 'war on terror'.

Another important reason has been the emergence of China as a major player in this region. China's rapid rise since the early 1980s means that in 2014 it being the world's second largest economy is all set to overtake the US in the next two to three decades. After Pakistan, China was the largest arms supplier to the Sri Lankan army during the civil war. China has interests to set up naval bases in Sri Lanka, Pakistan and Bangladesh. This is the second and possibly the more important reason why the US has changed its approach to the region. The US's 'Asia Rebalancing Policy' has been framed with India as the 'pivot' keeping the Chinese factor in mind.

As far as India is concerned, her relations with her neighbours in the region have had important challenges. India is by far the largest power in terms of population, land area, size, military power and influence in the region. Naturally, this has led to the emergence of a trust deficit between India and her neighbours. Rajiv Sikri has captured this sentiment succinctly when he says, "India's neighbours, fearful of its overwhelmingly larger size, power and hence influence over individual countries as well as the region as a whole, are both envious and suspicious of India and do not fully co-operate with it on its political and security concerns" (Sikri, 2008).

India on her part has made efforts to try and bridge this deficit. India had wholeheartedly supported the creation of the SAARC in 1985 hoping that it could try and bring the regional players closer together. The pillars of the Gujral Doctrine have been the basis of stitching closer relations with the neighbours. India's concern over her neighbourhood has also been impacted by the Chinese factor. Over the last decade, there has been a rapid expansion of Chinese influence in South Asia. India has always been very watchful of the growing Chinese influence. Forging closer ties with its neighbours seems to be the most appropriate step for India to protect its interests in the region.

The interests of both India and the United States converge on closer ties with South Asia. Both see the rising presence of China as a source of challenge. At a time when India-US cooperation is expanding, both nations can play a decisive role in the region. However, the question arises as to what kind of support does India and the United States offer to the region to aid the transition. India and the US could help create the right ambience in the region that would help each of the nations in the region to stabilize and consolidate their democratic processes.

As highlighted earlier, international relations in South Asia has been characterized by mistrust and suspicion. It has to be said that an international atmosphere of trust and cooperation must be in place for any democracy to succeed. Hence, it is critical to promote an atmosphere of dialogue in South Asia. This is where India and the US will have to take the initiative. South Asia can take heart from the fact that there already exists an organization in the form of the SAARC that can help promote this dialogue. India and the seven other South Asian nations are members of the SAARC. The US will also have an important role to play as it is currently holding an observer status in the SAARC. The problem with the SAARC has been that it has been held hostage to bilateral tensions between India and Pakistan on the one hand and frequent differences between India and some of the other nations in the region on the other (principally on the Tamil issue with Sri Lanka, river waters dispute with Bangladesh and the trade relations with Nepal).

It is clear that for SAARC not to fall a victim to bilateral tensions it needs to reorder its priorities. Such a sentiment was echoed in the 35th Session of the SAARC Council of Ministers held at Maldives in February 2014 (Economic Times, 2014). On the occasion, Indian foreign minister Salman Khursheed emphasized on the need for "Institutional Changes" in SAARC. Khursheed's call for reforms is also a reflection of the popular belief on India's role in the reformation process. There is a growing voice not only in India but also in other South Asian nations calling on India to take a lead role in setting the agenda for the reform of SAARC. This belief is quite justified keeping in mind India's position in the region. India is the only country in the region that shares a common border with all the SAARC members (with the exceptions of Afghanistan, Maldives and Sri Lanka). Politically, it is the most stable and economically most powerful nation in the region.

A strong and functioning SAARC will greatly facilitate the process of democratization in South Asia. However, India will also need to tread with caution as the other nations of SAARC should not get the impression that India is seeking to dominate the region by defining and deciding the reform agenda. The process of carrying forward the reforms would need to develop through a consensus and dialogue among the nations of the region.

'Democratization of International Relations' is going to be crucial but at the same time no democracy can become a success if it is not accompanied by economic growth and progress. For the transition to democracy to be a smooth process, economic development does hold the key. The current signs in the region in relation to economic development are not very encouraging. In Nepal, there is a belief among the people that ever since the Royal Killing of 2001, the country has regressed. This period also coincides with the efforts to establish and strengthen democratic processes. Nepal today is still one of the poorest countries in the world. A similar situation exists in Pakistan and Bangladesh. Classified as a 'failed state' by the Fund for Peace in 2013, Afghanistan is struggling to come to terms with the chain of wars that has been fought on her soil. India, Sri Lanka and Bhutan are notable exceptions from this group as they have enjoyed reasonable economic progress.

For the benefit of development to be distributed across South Asia, the application of growth-oriented policies by the respective government is crucial. Another crucial aspect that helps development is trade and aid. Aid, trade and security are seen as the three pillars of co-operation that have been recognized by the Millennium Development Goals. It is in the field of aid and trade that India and the US can play an important role. A good example of this is Afghanistan. There is a great deal of co-operation between India and the US with regards to Afghanistan. "India had enthusiastically supported the US role in Afghanistan and had invested US$ 2 billion in infrastructure projects" (Frontline, 2014). India providing developmental aid to Afghanistan is nothing new. India had backed the Soviet supported government of Afghanistan in 1989 providing the government with humanitarian aid (New York Times, 1989). The 2008 bombings of the Indian Mission in Afghanistan, many say was retaliation against growing India-Afghan co-operation (Hindustan Times, 2008).

India needs to extend the aid she is currently giving to Afghanistan to other South Asian nations. Indian support to Bangladesh, Maldives and Nepal is almost nothing when compared to what it is spending in Afghanistan. India's hands have been tied when it comes to the question of Sri Lanka. Pressure from Tamil political parties means that the central government has found it tough to formulate a clear policy towards Sri Lanka. However, it should be kept in mind that for the post-War reconciliation process in Sri Lanka to be a success, India's support is going to be very crucial. At the same time, the success of the reconciliation process is going to have an impact on the success of Sri Lankan democracy. India will need to provide support to Sri Lanka to help deal with the development of the Northern regions.

Aid is one way of ensuring that the benefits of economic development will be distributed evenly across South Asia. Like how India has done in Afghanistan, developmental aid will prove to be very important for the transition to democracy to be a success.

For any democracy to be a success, the growth and presence of a vibrant civil society is going to be very important. A review of any of the world's successful democracies will show that they are blessed with a strong civil society. India's civil society has played an important role in the anti-corruption movement. The passage of the RTI and the Anna Hazare led India against Corruption crusade, are clear indicators of the role of civil society groups. In rest of South Asia, civil society has played a very important role both in the colonial and the post-colonial phase. "Civil society has continued to play a very important role in these post-colonial societies and can be given significant credit for deepening and strengthening democracy in the region. The level of influence and success of civil society in deepening democracy and the movement for social justice varies from country to country and depends on the level of democratization of polity and the state in each country" (Behar, 2009). What is important to note from Behar's statement is the role that civil society plays in strengthening of democracy.

The maturity of a civil society depends on the structure of the polity of the country in question. What Behar points out in his article is that the civil society groups in South Asia need to evolve and adapt to the changing times. As mentioned earlier in the essay, over the past two decades, South Asia has witnessed a wind of change with the growth of democratic values and principles. However, for any strong democracy, an active civil society is important and nurturing the same is crucial.

An important part of this adaptation process is dialogue with civil society groups across countries of the region. After the 1950s, we have seen an expansion in the role played by non-governmental organizations (NGOs) and inter-governmental organizations (IGOs) in international relations (Ghosh, 2011). The United Nations has granted observer status to certain international NGOs. The growing role of NGOs in international relations further underscores the importance of cooperation between civil society groups in South Asia.

There is without any doubt, tremendous scope for India-United States dialogue over the process of democratization in South Asia. It is imperative to note that whatever role that India and the US play it will be the role of mere facilitators. The leadership of both India and the US need to keep in mind that the ultimate control of the transition process will be in the hands of the respective governments.

Therefore, be it in democratizing international relations, promoting dialogue, providing aid, improving trade and co-ordination between civil society groups, India and the US will be mere facilitators to the change and not agents of the change. The agents of the change have to be the people and the government of each nation in South Asia.

Conclusion

Though there is a great deal of scope for India-United States dialogue over the issue of democratization in South Asia, there are certain hurdles that are bound to come up. The challenges will clearly emerge on account of the contrasting traditions in Indian and American international relations. The foundations of Indian foreign policy were laid down by its first Prime Minister Jawaharlal Nehru. The key features of the Nehruvian school of thought were strategic independence, non-alignment and non-intervention. The American conduct of international relations is in some contrast to this Indian tradition. The American style of intervention is characterized by the demand for a regime change and it generally does not shy away from using its military force to bring about this change. The uses of such strategies by the US have been seen in Vietnam, Iraq, Korea, and Nicaragua and now in Afghanistan. India's foreign policy principles do not permit her to make use of such tactics. So can these two nations with contrasting foreign policy principles engage in a dialogue on such an issue?

Indian foreign policy has always been crafted in a way that preserves India's strategic autonomy. We are today in a multi-polar world and India hopes to be "one of the poles" (Sikri, 2009) in this new global order. The question arises if India and the United States jointly try to facilitate the transitions in the region then India might have to play the second fiddle to the US. Can India create its own distinct space when working with the United States in such a manner that it preserves its strategic autonomy? If not, the case then is whether India is ready to play second fiddle to the United States?

The answer to all these questions lies in the fact that both India and the United States have a common interest in the region. Both are concerned of the visible possibility of China enhancing its influence over the region. Over the past two decades, one has seen that China has been rapidly extending its network in South Asia. They were the second largest arms supplier to the Sri Lankan Army during the Civil War. After the war, the Chinese government has funded several development projects in the Island. Though Nepal has traditionally had close ties with India, it is slowly seeing an increasing Chinese presence and influence.

As in Sri Lanka, the Chinese have started to fund

infrastructure projects in Nepal. Pakistan and China are historic allies. Pakistan is open to the idea of the Chinese opening a naval base on its soil. What these countries have increasingly realized is that China is an important counter weight to India in this region. They tend to use India's strained ties with China as a strategic tool to bring to the table their agenda in any dialogue with India. For the Indians, a Chinese presence in the region has the potential to prove a serious threat to its national security. Therefore, India will need to effectively strategize to neutralize the increasing Chinese influence and presence in the region. Strong democratic traditions and processes in the nations in the region have the potential to facilitate this process.

At the same time, the United States also shares a similar fear of China's growing influence. At the current rate, the Chinese economy will overtake the US in the next two decades. This has put the US on alert. The main purpose of the Asia Rebalancing policy is to place a check on the rising Chinese influence in the region. The fact that it is looking at India as the 'pivot' in this Asia rebalancing plan means that it too is giving special importance to South Asia. This convergence of interests of the two nations means that both will be looking to each other when it comes to the region. The United States after seeing its position in Syria and Iran appears unlikely to push for its aggressive regime change strategy in South Asia. The socio-political dynamics of South Asia is such that such a policy will only push South Asia closer to the Chinese. Hence, such a policy would be counterproductive. These perceived hurdles will not prove to be a spoiler in India-United States dialogue on the democratization of South Asia.

South Asia's march towards democracy is a part of the larger global trend of the popularization of liberal democracy in the post-Cold War years. However, in South Asia the nature and structure of the strengthening of democratic processes has its own distinct trajectory. South Asia is a strategically very important region in the emerging multi-polar world. It holds a very important place in the United States' 'war on terror'. Additionally, the South Asia 'brand of democracy' revolves around the ideas of equality of opportunity, welfare and development. While freedom and liberty are recognized as important dimensions of democracy, the citizens clearly privilege welfare and justice. Thus, the focus of democracy and democratization in the region has its own unique flavour. An India-United States dialogue and cooperation need to acknowledge and recognize this distinctiveness. Therefore, there is a need for international efforts to help facilitate this crucial phase of democratic transition in this region. India by the virtue of being the world's largest democracy and the United States with its status as a pre-eminent power and upholder of democratic traditions and values will need to co-operate to facilitate this transition.

Endnotes

1. For many, this term itself is self contradictory as polar implies the presence of opposites and `uni` assumes the presence of only one.
2. While speaking of South Asia, this paper includes the following countries of the region: Bangladesh, India, Nepal, Pakistan, Sri Lanka, Afghanistan and Bhutan.

References

Behar, Amitabh (2009), "Re-imagining Civil Society", *Infochange India*, November, March 1, available at: http://infochangeindia.org/agenda/role-of-civil-society/re-imagining-civil-society.html.

Behera, Navnita Chanda (ed.) (2013), "India Engages the World", Oxford University Press, New Delhi.

Chand, Gurnam (2010), "India and Sri Lanka: Changing Political Relationship Post-1990s Phase", *Mainstream Journal*, Volume XLVIII, No. 25.

Chaudhury, Anasua Basu Ray (2006), "SAARC at Crossroads: The Fate of Regional Co-operation in South Asia", Samskriti, New Delhi.

Cherian, John (2014), "Talking Tough", The Frontline Archives, January 10, available at:

http://www.frontline.in/world-affairs/talking-tough/article5492494.ece.

Cherain, John (2002), "Counselling Caution", May 11-24, *Frontline*, Volume 9, Issue 10.

Crossette, Barbara (1989), "India to Provide Aid to Afghanistan", The New York Times Archives, March 7, available at: http://www.nytimes.com/1989/03/07/world/india-to-provide-aid-to-government-in-afghanistan.html.

CSDS (2008), "State of Democracy in South Asia", Oxford University Press, New Delhi.

"Declarations of SAARC Summits 1985-2008", SAARC Secretariat, Kathmandu, Nepal.

De Silva, Chandra Richard (1987), "Sri Lanka: A History", Vikas Publishing House Pvt. Ltd., New Delhi.

Fukuyama, Francis (1992), "The End of History and the Last Man", Free Press, New York, US.

Huntington, Samuel (1996), "The Clash of Civilizations and The Remaking of World Order", Penguin Publications, New Delhi.

Huq, Muhammad Shamsul (1993), "Bangladesh in International Politics: The Dilemmas of Weak States", University Press Limited, Dhaka, Bangladesh.

Kharat, Rajesh S. (2005), "Foreign Policy of Bhutan", Manak Publications Pvt. Ltd., New Delhi.

Kulandaswamy, M.S. (2000), "Sri Lankan Crisis: Anatomy of Ethnicity, Peace and Security", Authors Press, New Delhi.

Mehrotra, L.L., H.S. Chopra and Gert W. Kueck (eds.) (1995), "SAARC 2000 and Beyond", Omega Scientific Publishers, New Delhi.

Narain, Virendra and B.C. Uperti (1991), "SAARC: A Study of Perception and Policies", South Asian Publishers Private Limited, New Delhi.

Noorini, A.G. (1978), "Aspects of India's Foreign Policy", Jaico Books, New Delhi.

PTI (2014), "India for Institutional Reforms within the SAARC", Salman Khurshid, *The Economics Times*, February 20, available at: <http://articles.economictimes.indiatimes.com/2014-02-20/news/47527225_1_saarc-secretariat-observer-status-institutional-reform.

PTI (2010), "Intel Had Warned of Attack on Indian Embassy in

Kabul", Wikileaks, *The Hindustan Times*, July 26, available at: http://www.hindustantimes.com/world-news/intel-had-warned-of-attack-on-indian-embassy-in-kabul-wikileaks/article1-577772.aspx.

Reddy, K.C. and T. Nirmala Devi (2002), "Regional Co-operation in South Asia: New Dimensions", Kanishka Pubishers, New Delhi.

Sikri, Rajiv (2009), "Challenge and Strategy: Rethinking India's Foreign Policy", Sage Publications, New Delhi.

"Sri Lanka Foreign Affairs". (1998), Ministry of Foreign Affairs, Sri Lanka, Colombo, Sri Lanka.

Index

Index